Two Minute Noodle

A Backpacker's tale
by

Howie Cobb

www.twominutenoodle.com

Copyright © 2013 Howie Cobb
Lemongrass Publishing
All rights reserved.

ISBN:ISBN-13:978 1481111317

For my wife – Paula,
and my sons – Hai and Bao.
Thank you.

A percentage of the proceeds from this book will be donated to...

Saigon Children's Charity was founded in 1992 for a specific purpose: to help disadvantaged Vietnamese children to get an education and a fairer start in life. Their programmes aim to help the most disadvantaged children of Vietnam to escape from poverty through education and training.
They operate in the south of Vietnam, around Ho Chi Minh City, extending to the Cambodian border and down into the Mekong Delta.
www.saigonchildren.com

I would also like to recognise the amazing work, carried out by The Vietnam Volunteer Network, for disadvantaged, handicapped and orphaned children. They can offer you a rewarding and life-changing experience as a volunteer.
www.vietnamvolunteernetwork.com

TWO MINUTE NOODLE

I held Chantal close, kissed her one more time - before she was obscured by the smoked glass windows of the minibus. I was standing in the middle of the Khao San Road waving as the bus disappeared round the corner, and it wobbled slightly through my unshed tears. I wasn't to know then, but I would never see her again; nor would her family or friends at home.

This book is also dedicated to the memory of

Chantal Geets,
Neerweg, Belgium
(11/3/68 - 31/3/95)

with whom I had the privilege of travelling through Thailand and falling in love. Returning home after backpacking for a year, her flight from Bangkok crashed in Romania; two hours from home.

CONTENTS

Prologue: THAT WAS THEN
CHUNGKING MANSIONS, HONG KONG......................7
CANTON (GUANGZHOU)..16
HOLIDAY INN, YANGSHUO..23

BI-BI HOSTEL, OLD QUARTER, HANOI......................37
MINX, HIGHWAY ONE..53
SAM SONG BEACHES..63
THE RAILWAY HOTEL, VINH.......................................70
98 TRAN PHU, HOI AN...75
NHA TRANG – THE NIGHT TRAIN..............................85
HOANG TU HOTEL, SAIGON..89
KIM & SINH CAFÉ..91

KHAO SAN ROAD, BANGKOK......................................95
RHANEE'S GUEST HOUSE, BANGKOK......................96
LEK HOUSE, CHIANG MAI...102
RAK'S TREK..110
SUMPRASONG GUEST HOUSE, SUKOTHAI............115

KUTA BEACH, BALI...116
MERTHA HOUSE, FOOTBALL FIELD, UBUD...........125
LITTLE BEACH, PADANGBAI....................................133
AMPENAM POST OFFICE, LOMBOK........................137
GILI TREWANGAN...142

CAPTAIN COOK'S, CAIRNS, QUEENSLAND............149
THE EAST COAST TRAIL..161
GLEBE VILLAGE HOSTEL, SYDNEY........................174
MELBOURNE..189
HOPKINS HILL, VICTORIA...191
THE PARK ROYAL HOTEL, MELBOURNE...............198

AUCKLAND, NEW ZEALAND.....................................203
WEST COAST EXPRESS..212
DARGAVILLE 215

USA...223
HOME..226

Epilogue: THIS IS NOW
THE HOMECOMING...229
TRAVELLING - BACKPACKING.................................232
VIETNAM...234
VAN HAI...238
QUOC BAO...242

THAT WAS THEN

The British Midlands Tri-star broke free from the clouds above the coast of Spain and headed north on the short hop to Gatwick.

The No-Smoking light above me, went out, accompanied by the symphony of a hundred lighters and matches putting flame to cigarettes. The resulting smog rolled along the aisle and under seats to mingle with the non-smokers, and the aroma of beef, mashed potato and Yorkshire pudding with gravy, drifting from the galley.

We'd had ten days in Lloret-de-Mar; ten days of drunken Brits, full English breakfast, tower block hotels, Red Lion pub, Black Cat disco, chips, horse riding with Brits, sunburn, brown ale. Three teenagers - abroad for the first time; it's what us working class boys did you see.

At my posh Grammar School, my long-haired peers (we called them Gimps or Hairies) walked around carrying albums by Led Zeppelin, Pink Floyd and Genesis. Their elder siblings were tripping along the Hippy Trail - following the exotic spice route through India, Iraq and Afghanistan whilst enjoying a gap year or ten – they could afford it. The gimps would be joining them soon; after 'A' levels.

Me and *my* mates had Prince Buster, James Brown and Stevie Wonder on our turntables and our Mecca was the Hammersmith Palais. Our holidays were for working; earning enough money for that scooter, first car – sharp clothes, but we'd managed to save enough for a trip away and I guess we must have enjoyed the Costa Blanca, albeit completely lacking in local culture or interest, as we were away from our parents and misbehaving.

But, as I saw the Fasten Seatbelt sign light up for the descent to London, a wave of disappointment washed over me. My mum and dad had managed to take us to Australia for 2 years when we were kids – stopping off in Africa, Egypt and Ceylon; surely I should be aspiring to something more like that? I *did* want to go back to Sydney one day to revisit my childhood; perhaps I could visit some more exotic places on the way out or back. The question was – when and how?

I stubbed out my cigarette; clicked the seatbelt into place.

CHUNGKING MANSIONS, HONG KONG

The British Airways 747 banked right, hard, its wingtip almost tearing a Guns & Roses T shirt from a washing line hung across Jardine Street, then jiggled down amongst the buildings to bellyflop into Hong Kong airport.

As the sliding doors of the air terminal opened, the heat wrapped round me like a poultice and dragged me silently screaming towards hundreds of Asian faces; none of which were waiting for me.

The rivulets of sweat from my face gathered momentum, joining the streams from my armpits, and raced to the pool at my feet. Splashing onward, I found the bus terminal, the correct fare and destination, and my first hostel tout. I feigned indifference as I slipped my backpack to the ground and affected a thousand yard stare.

'You wan' hostel?'

'No.' I said feeling slightly guilty, as I lied to the first Asian I'd met. While he tackled a fellow backpacker, I tried to slip past him onto the bus.

'How much you pay?' he rounded on me.

'Single room with a bath?' I asked, destroying my alibi.

'200 dollar!' he snapped. Virgin backpacker I was, but not that stupid.

'100 dollar.' I replied in his general direction, my glasses steamed up.

'Dormitory!' he spat at me, 'only dormitory for 100 dollar'.

I sneered as he turned back to his other 'kill' to help him on the bus. As we headed towards Tsimsatsui, I stared out of the window past his Beatle style haircut. He turned, and with a tobacco-stained finger wrote like a whisper on his veiled hand - '150'. I didn't want to lose my first barter, so I replied '120' - as quiet as Tom Jones singing 'Delilah'. He winced, put a finger to his lips and signalled OK.

'Keep quiet! I charge *him* 180 dollars.' Yesss! I'd done it.

We tumbled from the bus onto Nathan Road, and under the sort of deluge that flattens crops and whole acres of Bangladeshis. Gargantuan signs snarled and spat neon across at each other, using the wet roads as a palette. Raindrops the size of grapes hurtled down, bouncing back up to knee height. Like eggs carried by unseen ants, umbrellas scurried up and down to find their nest. The tout disappeared into the storm with his victim, shouting back...

"You go with her!"

Looking round I could see no *her*, but I noticed that near my feet, my backpack was crawling onto the hump of a woman the height of cricket stumps. I followed it as she scurried like a tortoise on speed, into a building; pushing through the melee, bowling aside two huge Africans and nestling in the corner of the lift. The illuminated numbers above me climbed slowly to fourteen.

The accommodation in Hong Kong is multi-layered. At the top end, the four-star hotels sit smugly on Hong Kong Island. Some quality hotels flirt around Kowloon, which also contains the majority of the travellers' hostels. The epicentre of this phenomenon is at Tsimsatsui, and the Nathan Road; a six-lane, neon disaster, with a weather system of its own making.

When dodging along the pavement, the condensed waste from thousands of air-con units descends like a summer shower. Even at 95 degrees the refreshment value is diminished by the possibility of Legionnaires Disease. Midway along this lunatic thoroughfare, under its very own brown cloud, smouldered Chunking Mansions - sixteen stories of fire hazard and filth that housed the escapees of Europe, Australasia and Africa in every nook and cranny left between the sweat shops, Indian messes and knocking shops.

Room prices lower as the floors rise, due to the lift queues and reduced chance of escaping a fire whilst racing the rats to the ground floor. So it was with some trepidation that I followed my backpack into a cupboard on the fourteenth floor. The room was the size of a single bed and included a single bed, but also a bathroom. The ceiling fan threatened to scalp me if I stood on tiptoe and the shower and basin were above the toilet, allowing the possibility of having a snooze, a shit, a shower and a shave, without moving from the same spot. It was a haven though; it was privacy; and although I knew I would have to move to cheaper dormitory rooms the next day, I was going to sleep well this night.

So, lying prone beneath a ceiling fan that whirled chuck-a-chuck-a chuck, pressing me into the mattress, I looked back over my first day and wondered at my own audacity.
  I was ill-equipped for such an adventure. Well above the average age for backpackers, I was carrying with me the mental scars of divorce, bankruptcy and a parcel of broken hearts in a spotty hanky on a stick. I had no idea of how backpacking worked, what hostels were like, or how to get around, and I was going to try to do it on my own!

A fresh film of sweat washed over me at the thought of it. But then the reason I left came back to me. Things could only get better - couldn't they? And I wasn't running away, I was running *to* something - I just didn't know what it was yet. I turned onto my right side to sleep.
I turned to the left, to the right, face down, onto my back, sat up and stared into the dark. Thoughts of home had crept back into my head like Pol Pot re-entering Cambodia. I wanted to pretend they weren't there but they were, and some were good - so good they hurt. Lying back down, it wasn't the salt from the sweat that stung my eyes.

The next morning, refreshed, I apologised to the owner for being unable to carry on accepting his luxurious hospitality, loaded up my backpack, and with glasses steamed up, trudged one block north through the shower of Legionnaire's disease to Mirador Mansions, which looked like the ugly twin of Chungking Mansions; another sixteen stories of fire hazard and filth, but this time I was only on the third floor. I was going down in the world.

It was here that I made my first breakthrough. Mirroring my thinking, Phil had spent his first night in a shoebox in Chungking, whilst I was in my cupboard, and he was now moving to the dorms. As I arrived at the reception a myopic Indian was processing Phil, who looked the epitome of calm. I slipped my backpack to the floor with ease due to gravity and sweat. Mohammod's eyes seemed fixed on the cockroach on the wall to the left of the shower, or an insect stuck behind his glasses - I couldn't tell which.

He dismissed Phil with a grunt and a key, and I stepped up to sign in. His eyes didn't move from their target, although he was somehow still processing my details. I bartered the price down by absolutely nothing, signed in, and pulled out my wallet with hands fit to turn milk into butter, chaotically spraying the reception with small change. A coin with a crinkly edge like a mince pie rolled across the room and jumped the threshold of the shower room, indicating the target of Mohammod's long hard stare.

There, peeking out from below a towel, whilst its Swedish owner bent forward clipping her nails, was a freshly laundered front-bottom, puffy and fluffy from its shower. Mohammod wasn't as short-sighted as I had thought – just focused..

Whilst their attention was diverted, I gathered the widespread coinage, shoving it willy-nilly into my new, but now sweat-soaked Black's

Outdoor Clothing Range safari shorts. I left the crinkly coin in the shower room.

Almost bigger than my en-suite room at the previous Garden Hostel, this room had no toilet and four bunks, not so you could shower sitting or shit standing - but change clothes simultaneously if more than two people left their bed at the same time and stepped into the communal area. Phil, shuffling as far as possible into the room, looked relieved to have another new boy in the camp and climbed onto the top left bunk to leave me room to move in. Beneath him sat a sparsely thatched man, collars up around his chin, struggling to tie a knot. The white shirt was translucent with sweat by the time his black patent shoes were laced, and he cloaked his misery from the public eye with a thick dark suit.
  He jumped up and exclaimed 'How do I look?'
  Swinging his gaze from Phil to me and back, taking in our puzzled looks, he explained...
  'Film extra tonight... must dash chaps... Giles is the name... ta-ta.'
  Squeezing his sizeable head back round the door, he pointed at the last vacant bed and announced - 'the other bod's name is Keith.'

Keith wasn't actually present in the other lower bunk, but like a murder victim's chalk outline, his body area was marked with clothes, yellowing newspapers, old takeaway menus, educational aids, sex aids and probably - Aids. I saw later that Keith did indeed fit very snugly into the mould he'd created. It was one of the very rare occasions that his activities coincided with the rest of the world's time frame. Keith slept all day, and at ten to four, ten minutes before his alarm rang, would rise from his pit, fully-clothed, clean his teeth and leave to teach English to Chinese kids; leaving us to turn off his alarm. After work he would go onto night school to teach English to adult Chinese, and then to the cinema complex at 1am to watch two films: onto a couple of bars and back to his hole by about 8am. What amused Phil and I more than his routine, was his choice of teaching material. There, piled amongst the cinema tickets, bar receipts and food wrappers, were photocopied pages from Viz magazine, starring Buster Gonad and his Unfeasibly Large Testicles and The Fat Slags - each copy with the pupil's name at the head of the page. I would have liked to ask him about it, but we were never awake at the same time.

I took the remaining bunk next to the window. Was this good? Why hadn't Phil taken the window bed? Why was I here? Already my life decisions were becoming simple - yet confusing. I hiked my brand new backpack up onto the bed. (I had cunningly dragged it around the garden before leaving home, to indicate how experienced a traveller I was; it looked like a new backpack that had been dragged around a garden.) The mattress was the thickness of a biscuit and soaked up sweat and body tissue incredibly well. This was ineffectively masked by the thousand micron sheet, which stuck to your body and aroused the mattress into life like a desert orchid blooming after an unexpected shower. Four of such outputs created a cloud that hovered in the centre of the room. Thankfully at high altitude, and next to the window, I could escape this smog, until either a fart or movement from a body below, elevated it level with my nostrils. Sleep would not be arriving very soon in these circumstances, so, having formed a deep dislike of my bed, and needing food, beer and experience, I decided to go out.

Pausing a while in the common room, a very beat room with a motley collection of vinyl chairs gathered round an old TV, a girl leant over my shoulder and exclaimed, laughing from the depths of Adelaide...

'Jeesus mate, yer wife's a bit of a mongrel!'

I'd been advised by more experienced travellers to carry photos of home with me, to show to villagers, locals and other travellers. So, packed fondly into my wallet were my family, my Volkswagen Camper; and foremost on my mind and in the clear window at the front, Bumble - my border collie dog. As handsome as any star of 'One Man & His Dog', with a lopsided smile on his face, I would soon realise how appealing he was to others, and eventually came to regard him as my second passport. At home, Bumble was normally 18 inches from my legs on an invisible wire, or lying with his head on my feet, so at the end of every check - backpack, passport, tickets, wallet, cameras, I would halt. God, what have I forgotten? I know - it's Bumble, he's not here. Which was why I'd been staring into the wallet, missing the wee boy more than a tad.

'Aagh jeez, that's a choice dog mayt! What yer doin'?.. m'name's Catherine, not Cathy. I'm going t'work, coming? get yer a cupple a beers free, I'll introduce ya to the girls, c'mon then move yer arse!' Well you would, wouldn't you? We hoofed it along, Catherine shouldering the tailors' touts aside.

'Yer bin travellin long? - one day? shit yer a virgin. Bet yer not a real one - yer look like you've been around, get yer leaflet out of m'face mayt!' We hopped on a number something bus.

'I hate bloody Hong Kong business men with their bloody mobile phones,' she said with venom '...look at this drongo here with two!'

The Armani-suited trendy had a mobile slung on each hip like a gunslinger, and as I looked he reached for one, tapped bip, bip, bip, beep, bip, beep, and put it to his ear. At this moment the other rang, still

in its holster, and he looked at the two of them in turn. Catherine was off. Pushing her face to within inches of his she bellowed...
'You've rung yerself yer dumb fuck!'
When I left the bar, many hours and free beers later, I needed food; I'd needed food for hours. I wasn't going to succumb to the universally bland Big Mac that was on offer - I picked a Chinese cafe, menu in Chinese, full of Chinese, and sat at the round table in the centre of the room, alone. The menu had subtitles, the tea was free and bottomless and I sucked, slurped and chop-sticked with the best of them. My old friend - beer, had taken me by the hand and led me through the streets of Hong Kong, depositing me in probably one of the best eateries around. Returning to the hostel common room, the other inmates were gathered round the TV noshing McDonalds from styrofoam trays and two-minute noodles from mugs.

Phil, awake but groggy, asked... 'Where did you eat Howie?'
'I went to a Chinese restaurant on Cameron Rd; I was the only Westerner in there - the food was fantastic and it only cost fifteen dollars – less than a quid.' I replied.
Several pairs of eyes looked into their soggy, tasteless meals and back at me. Someone muttered... 'I can't eat that foreign shit, you don't know what you're eating.' and others just kept staring at the TV.
'Well, I'm off to bed,' I said, with a slightly smug smile...'I've got a busy day tomorrow.' If I had been a virgin - I'd just lost my cherry. I know it was only Hong Kong, but perhaps I could do this thing yet.

❖

It was a bull-terrier of a day, with a hot, steamy wind buffeting the harbour, causing the khaki waves to snap at the ferries and sampans. Victoria peak, above and unseen, was being strangled by mist.

A quick call home to confirm I'd arrived brought bad news. No, all was not well; Bumble hadn't eaten for days and was very sick. My parents had taken him from the friends who were dog sitting, to look after him. I panicked, and then thought - well, I've got a whole year, I might as well hang around here a few more days, and if I have to, I could fly home. But a little voice in my head whispered - 'You're using the dog as an excuse to bottle out – to head home to safety.' I had a word with myself and realised the voice had been right.

Phil and I were out sightseeing, and seeing more than we'd bargained for. Before we'd even left Nathan Road, we realised that, scattered like jewels on a stable floor, there were dozens of flawless Chinese girls with skin of honeyed porcelain and clothes that revealed nothing - but shouted of the beauty below. The fashion was a skin-tight black skirt that ended just two inches below the plimsoll-line, and black stockings that failed to meet it by three inches. The resulting area of bare flesh had two effects; one... to produce a new layer of sweat, due to increased metabolism, and two... a tendency to bump into lamp posts, small Chinese or any other sights we should have been looking out for.

But these were 'bought' girls, with bought apartments, bought clothes, bought with big money, and the pitiful amount in my pocket would never have caught their eye. The two most beautiful that I'd seen yet sprang from an ice-cold store that screamed - 'Gold cards only' then sashayed down Nathan, seemingly a few inches above the ground. I followed slowly for a couple of hundred yards, feasting my eyes, then before I got too greedy, speeded up to come abreast of them; steady. As I edged up to them, the nearest beauty let loose... 'It's not my forlt ees got the fuckin 'ump, ees bin like it orl day, wot am I meant ter do ay?'

I'd cleverly arrived on the Friday of a holiday weekend, so I had to wait until Tuesday to pick up my Chinese visa. But it gave me time to acclimatise to the noise, the heat, the humidity; to being away. Phil and I spent the weekend wandering the island, on foot, bus and tram, funicular up the mountain and ferries around the harbour. And though the water lapped lazily, invitingly, onto some half decent beaches, the pollution warning boards showed 'high', so we stayed dry.

Leaving the cross-harbour ferry heading north, a strange sound grew – a twittering. Turning a corner the sound became a noise, a clamour. As we entered the square it was a deafening screeching, like a huge aviary in panic.

The square and surrounding streets were barely visible under a vast host of women, sat in circles, groups and clusters, all picnicking. As we wove our way through, they flirted with us, shouted things that made their friends giggle, invited us to sit with them and eat. We stopped several times to talk and took small mouthfuls out of politeness. They were each and every one - a Fillipino maid. Apart from their Sunday afternoon off, they worked constantly, living in at their employers' homes - alone. Every penny that these ladies earned was sent back home to their family, to the children and husbands they may not have seen for years. So this one afternoon belonged to them, their chance to talk of home, enjoy each other's company; and despite the lively chatter and the trilling of laughter, I found that gathering incredibly sad.

Taking a water taxi, we checked out the new airport site, where Phil would be starting work the very next day – his first Monday morning at work. I felt privileged to be swanning off around China, whilst he was strapping his tools on; and more than a bit guilty.

But later, at the arse end of yet another fine Chinese meal and many Linquan beers, we toasted each other.
'Good luck in your new job and your new life here Phil' I said.
'Hope you have a great trip old mate!' he replied. And it seemed that we *were* old mates, after just a few days, and I realised that travelling had already given me a small gift, and maybe a new talent.

I lay, hands behind head, pondering the useless air/con unit above, happy with the news that at home, Bumble was finally eating. I could pick up my visa to China the next morning; time to put the next foot forward.
'Do you have to pay to get it working?' I asked nobody in particular.
'No,' replied Giles, seeing the object of my gaze... 'I think it's just knackered.' Whilst I twiddled the knobs in vain, Phil hit the switch by the door that wasn't for the light, the fan or room service, and the unit 'vrroooomed' into life.
'Bugger me!' said Giles; he'd been in this sweatbox a month, 'Keith told me it didn't work!' Keith had been in this sweatbox three months.

Giles resembled Mister Potato-Head, a toy I loved and often found in my Christmas stocking as a child. At birth, the mid-wife had stuck the oversize ears haphazardly on his head, selected the larger of the two noses from the box, and put it roughly central between his eyes, leaving hair to sprout at a later date. Fortunately for Giles, the mid-wife had lacked a sense of humour, and had refrained from adding the Groucho Marx glasses and moustache. As with all potato men, the whole head ensemble over-shadowed the body and hunched forward. To balance this caricature though, Giles had been blessed with intelligence, a bubbly sense of humour, honesty and an infectious grin. If they had used a giant parsnip or water melon instead of a potato, I would still have liked him very much indeed. Which is why, when Giles asked me to help - I jumped at the chance.
'Howie, didn't you say that you worked in advertising?'
'Yes... in my old life I had my owned agency.'
'Well I can't just go on being a film extra, I need a proper job. When we were on set last night, two priests grabbed a woman thief, who was being chased, and beat her up. One had her in a headlock between his legs while the other punched her.'

'Was this a martial arts film or something?' I asked, puzzled.
'Good God no!' laughed Giles, 'these were just spectators! I've applied for a marketing job and you've got to help me get it; help me to rewrite my CV - give me some of those whatsits, you know, thingamee phrases.'
'You mean...' 'Exactly old chap - you spout them and I'll write them down, chuck a few around at the interview eh! - pretend I know what I'm going on about.'
Giles scribbled like a maniac, almost dribbling with delight and exclaiming to each new one that I dragged from my past.
'OPTs - Opportunities to see'... 'Excellent'
'Publication frequency'... 'Brilliant!'
'Bullet points"... 'Oh yes!!!'
'Demographic distribution... 'Bloody marvellous!!!!'
And then I finished him off with 'Full page, full-colour bleed, first right hand page opposite letters'... and I swear he almost swooned.
'Now, what do they all mean old chap?'
We reshaped and rewrote his CV, bought a printout from a girl in a hostel one floor up who had use of a computer, then Giles rushed out to present it by hand to the company he was hoping to join. Returning, breathless and sweaty, he asked...
'Thanks a million old chap, how can I ever return the favour?'
'You can give some advice. You've been up to Yangshuo before, have you any tips or recommendations?'
'Oh yes!' said Giles, 'I certainly have.' and fell silent.
'Well?' I asked after a long pause.
'Avoid Canton station by any means possible.'

CANTON (GUANGZHUO)

Phil started work that morning, labouring at the new airport site. I'd enjoyed my time in Hong Kong, but it was my day to leave. Scattering the cockroaches to the four corners of the shitty room, I slipped a cold beer into Phil's plastic bag, which huddled noisily amongst the others in the smelly fridge. I knew how welcome it would be when he returned to the hostel in the evening. A defiant roach stood its ground in a puddle, lit by the glow from the open fridge door, and I asked myself - would I ever see Phil again, my first travel companion? I shut the fridge door, leaving the roach in the dark.

I'd worked out that two easy trains, a boat ride and a long bus journey would get me to Yangshuo; to the peace and quiet of rural China. This was never meant to be intrepid exploration, and I had no intention of hacking all the way around one of the largest countries in the world. I might drift further on to Dali, or even Lijiang if time permitted, but I thought... 'let me just see what I can accomplish in getting to Yangshuo - and what I can learn on the way.'

❖

The morning was as blunt as lead, greyer, heavier, as I stood with my back to Chungking Mansions. My journey started twenty yards across the Nathan Road on the subway, and went downhill from there. Down on the platform, there was a tidy queue of roughly ten people at every ten feet along the platform, their feet each side of a yellow line, noses pressed against the back of the person in front. I joined one - curious, and when the train arrived I saw that this was where the doors opened; simple. It was the last bit of order I was to see for a long time. Arriving at Shenzhen, to change stations and trains, I walked from the building and into a storm of humanity. I stepped aside from the throng to try and make sure they were going in the right direction for me. It was then I realised that everything was written in Chinese, the characters like exploded boxes, the people all Chinese, and I was in China. People were talking at me; I didn't know why. The language was full of spitting and gulping and galumphing, as if the words were being broken in the teeth. My self-esteem collapsed like a biscuit in hot tea. I held off a panic attack by lighting a cigarette and sucking down the smoke; I could do this. I couldn't. Spotting a blond head in the crowd, I rushed after, not caring if it was German, Swedish, or Danish, as long as it wasn't a Chinese person in a wig.

'Can you speak English?' I asked desperately. Yes she could - but didn't know where the train departed from; but she knew a man that did. She was being met by a courier who shook my hand, and they went with me halfway. Taking my pack off for a rest, I didn't notice my watch come off, but on setting off with the masses - it wasn't there. I expected to see it on turning, having only lost it for a few seconds, but no, it was gone. I noticed a young Chinese man at the edge of the road, and had the feeling he'd seen something. Tapping my wrist I asked...

'Did you see my watch?' He discreetly nodded at a man standing in a group nearby, with his back to me.

'He has my watch?' He shrugged his shoulders and looked the other way. I marched over to the huddle, in the middle of which was my watch. Now this was not a Rolex, merely a five pound Casio from a garage, but it was useful. Breaking through the people, I pointed to the white mark on my wrist, and snatched the watch from an outstretched hand, which stayed hovering in the air like a swan with its beak open. They looked at me - mouths agape, as I said 'thank you.' and walked away smiling. Should I have given it to him – it may have fed his family for a week, but I needed a watch didn't I?

All the signs at the ticket office were in Cantonese, but after studying the Lonely Planet, and seeing that every booth had the same characters (Guangzhou-Canton), deduced that I couldn't buy a wrong ticket if I tried. Clutching this gem of knowledge I joined a queue, and spotted two backpacks ahead; they had also spotted me. It was love at first sight, as I needed them and they needed me. They were Doron and Sharon - an Israeli couple. We chatted throughout the train journey to Canton, and enjoying our mutual support, left the station building with renewed confidence, me to catch a sleeper bus to Yangshuo - they to stay in a hostel in the city.

We entered the gates of hell and damnation came down upon us. It was like being a lone Celtic fan at a Rangers match, a ping-pong ball in raging rapids; a piece of meat. They hassled and pushed, pulled and poked, whilst we tried to watch each other's backs. Hands were pulling at our straps, our arms, and Sharon's blond hair. They seemed to know we were virgins. Doron and I put Sharon between us and pushed and slapped back until a space formed; there was no refuge in sight and I realised that the safest thing to do was to get out of the station. Dodgy geezers were thrusting Chinese characters in our faces. We bartered a taxi driver down from a terrible price to a bad one, and were being led away; a crowd following us like gulls about a trawler, shrieking and laughing. To our horror, they led us to a dark, dank corner at the back of the station, to a car without a taxi sign. We were completely surrounded and things were looking nasty - as the driver now insisted we put our packs in the boot, which we knew was when they often got stolen. We refused, and putting them inside, got in and locked the doors. We urged the driver to go, but he kept getting out of the car. Sharon had real fear on her face now, and the car resembled a pop group arriving at an awards ceremony, people beating on the roof, shouting faces against the windows.

'Go, go, go!' Doron shouted, two inches from the driver's face. I joined in shouting, and then grabbed the handle that the driver was reaching for, trying to get out and away from us. He seemed to make a rapid decision and, turning the key, the car fired into life with a 'bang' - like a circus car.

As we rattled off through the crowd, Sharon crying in the back, I noticed that most of the crowd were laughing. In hindsight, away from the panic, I thought that the reality of the situation was probably more mundane - more amusing.

> *'If you want to go to this hotel, it will cost you $20.'*
> *'You can't charge them that Li!'*
> *'I can try.'*
> *'No, see, they are very angry at your audacity.'*
> *'Did the big nose with glasses just offer $15?'*
> *'Yes! Jesus - he sweats so much he has a puddle at his feet.'*
> *'Take them Li, quick, before they change their mind.'*
> *'This couple sound like they're clearing their throat when they talk, but don't spit it out like we do.'*
> *'Hey, look everybody! The big noses are paying $15 to ride in Li's car, what a laugh, let's go and watch.'*
> *'They're looking very worried.'*
> *'So they should be, getting in that heap of shit.'*
> *'One of them was shouting 'Go, go, before the wheels fall off!'*

The hotel that the Israelis had been recommended - The White Swan, turned out to be one of the plushest in Canton, and a room for the night would have kept me in Chungking Mansions for a month. We trudged over to the youth hostel and booked in, although it was three times the price quoted in the Lonely Planet. The place was luxury; sanctuary. It had other travellers who spoke English, bucket-loads of English, albeit tinged with Israeli, French and South African. After introductions, we were told that we'd have been wasting our time trying to get any tickets; the Wouzhou region through which we had to travel, was in the midst of its biggest flood for a hundred years; many people had died. There were no buses or boats to be had that day, but 'There may be tomorrow.'

I took a walk away from the island, to the infamous market, where I'd heard that dogs hung - skinned, from hooks. I didn't really want to see this, but thought that I needed to look at a western taboo through another culture's eyes. At first I walked through mounds of fruits, foodstuffs, silks, porcelain and a host of other commodities. The air was heavy with the pungent reek of salted fish and spices, and then I saw it, like something from a horror movie, unmistakably a dog - its muscles, sinews and ligaments exposed to the world, shining scarlet, a cruel hook impaling its eye.

The floor was slippery with blood and guts, claws, eyes, hearts and livers, and all things that crawl or hop or slither were here to be dispatched and eaten. A litter of kittens, their necks tied together like a posy of summer daisies, 'meowed' and cried. Two fish, each the size of a small boy, wriggled in an inch of water - their tails flapping faster than the tongues of the locals. Selected by a shopper, one was laid on the slab. The cleaver sliced into its side just behind the gills, and holding the blade flat, she ran it up the fish, then took the steak and wrapped it in newspaper. As she dropped the coins in her pocket, she hung the fish by a hook to the roof, where the still steaming organs, yellow and purple, carried on beating and throbbing - open to the air.

Each time I stopped, a crowd would gather like flies round a fresh turd, then call over other flies they didn't even know to take a look at me. And when I moved away, some would follow, hoping I would stop again. Writing this, I had a spectator across the table, the hostel guard, in uniform. He was genuinely fascinated at the marks and squiggles coming from my pen. With a big smile he accepted a cigarette, and when other Cantonese moved to occupy the spare seat next to me, he shooed them away. An Australian girl walked into the lobby, the majority of an ample breast clearly visible through the armholes of her vest. He was embarrassed and looked to me for help. I shook my head with disgust.

A girl was asleep in the bed by the window when I moved into my room; a Kiwi - I presumed her boyfriend, between us. I felt a bit of a gooseberry sharing their room, but meeting her later in the lobby and finding she was Israeli, introduced her to Doron and Sharon. They immediately fell to jibber jabber and talk of home, but were kind enough to include me every now and then. Keren already had a ticket to

Guilin for the next day, so we agreed we would meet her there. I asked where her boyfriend was, but she told me that she didn't know the Kiwi, hadn't actually spoken to him yet. It was my first mixed room you see, I was still learning.

We re-entered the maelstrom of Guangzhou station the next day, and with the time running out before the 5.30 train, tried to buy some tickets. We were tossed around like straw dolls in a whirlwind; sent from black marketer to crook; crook to beggar. Tickets were offered, but were they real? What was their destination and time? We held hands to try and stay together, but eventually, whilst chasing after a man who had spoken some English, Keren was swept off into the swirling crowd.
 A baby-faced man whispered 'I can get you tickets to Guilin.' and led us off into a shopping arcade. Here, an aisle was blocked off by two men at each end; Doron and I stood back-to-back watching them, whilst Sharon exchanged the money. The man only had two tickets so the couple came first of course; they went. Keren had already gone. I was alone again.

Heading back to the safety of the hostel, a realisation glowed dimly that I would very much like to see Keren again - Doron and Sharon likewise, but in a different way.
 Their tickets, I found out later, had turned out to be counterfeit, and they'd been taken off the train at some god-awful station, Sharon crying, Doron threatening violence, and made to pay again; the full tourist price. I was going have to catch up with them in my own fashion.

Back on the island, I went with an Australian South-African Pole to a ticket agency, as he claimed he knew how to get proper tickets for a great price. Trevor's accent made it impossible for him to pronounce Chinese names, they were far too soft for him. Despite endless different phonetic variations, Xho, Chu, Shuo, Ju, Tsu, Trevor reduced them all to 'shoe', so as we sat in front of the agent he barked:
 'Ken you git us a tren tickit to Yangshoe?'... 'No.'
 'How about a bus tickit to Xangshoe?'... 'No.'
 'Boat to Woushoe?'... 'No.'
 'Any tickit to Goushoe... or Gangshoe?'... 'No.'
 'Any bluddy tickit man?'
 I realised I was going nowhere with Trevor's help, but it was fun.
 'Do you have something in a brown walking shoe?' I asked.
 'Ah you want shoe, my brother make shoe – come!' replied the agent.

I finally got a sleeper bus ticket to Yangshuo for the next day. I stood with a German woman, at the place we were told the bus would pick us up; an Irish couple catching it too. A bus pulled to a halt fifty yards further up the road and quickly filled with Chinese. We had the feeling it was ours, and rushed up the road so as not to miss it. The doorman looked at my ticket blankly, as though I'd tried to board a 747 to Los Angeles with a Blackpool tram ticket.

'Guilin? Guilin? Yangshuo? I asked. The passengers near the door were nodding, the doorman pointing down the road. The bus was pulling away, doors closing on the German girl behind me, the Irish outside fighting to get on. The bus stopped, and I wrenched the doors open and pulled them in; we were in this together. We roared off, being shouted at to sit down. We sped off, a hundred yards to a bus depot, and parked. We stayed parked. The 4.30 was now the 5.30. At 6.00 we moved - forward into the next parking space. After a furious row with a passenger which lasted fifteen minutes, the driver reversed into a sort of garage. 6.20, 6.40, 7.00, and then at last we were off.

The seats were quite comfortable; half-length bunk beds with a tilting back, lined up in three rows along the bus, so we looked like a busload of pensioners in bath chairs, watching a Gloria Swanson movie ahead.

We drove into the deepening night, and further up the route reached the flood area. The rain had caused landslides that had all but closed the roads. At these obstacles, dozens of buses and a mass of trucks battled to get through, amongst the diggers and bulldozers trying to clear the road. I stayed awake watching the confrontations, and several times saw labourers leaping for their lives from the path of our bus; the driver, trumpeting his cigarette, seeming to ignore their very existence. At one narrow point, the left side of the road was a solid line of trucks; the right - a rat run for those chancing their arm. At a dip where the road was just slurry, the edge dropped forty foot into a flooded paddy. Our driver didn't even break wind. He bowled some watchers aside and flew into the dip, the bus sliding sideways. We straightened up, slid, straightened up, and then I felt the rear end going over the side, my heart skipped several beats. I reached for a handhold and heard people the length of the bus, scream in many languages. He gunned the engine at the front and the rear followed on behind; up the hill and onto firm ground. Where the road wasn't a sea of mud it was potholes, and when not potholes... crevasses, and we drove across them all whompity-whompity, bang into China. Whilst the rest of the bus slept, I saw things; I heard things; I'm telling.

I saw glow-worms twinkling beside the road; a wobbly moon jitterbugging on a flooded plain - brighter than its twin in the sky, as though it was fed by the water. Old men and children rode on bicycles with no lights, like ghosts on two wheels, with wicker baskets in which to carry their troubles; two young lovers pootled past on a scooter, the girl riding side-saddle, flimsy dress flapping; late home.

❖

I saw a meteorite blaze an arc across a black sky like a sparkler tied to a cat's tail, and then disappear behind even blacker hills. And to this I could only say... 'Wow!' But nobody heard me.

❖

I heard the bus engine straining and spluttering, wheezing and gasping, but like a racehorse – it was determined to run to the last for its rider. Great creaks and groans came from the coach, as the driver coaxed it over humps, through trenches and ravines, thrashing the engine and murdering the clutch. Then a landslide brought the convoy to a halt; a dead stop; engines off.

All was dark, but I could hear frogs croaking and barking, and insects whispering sweet nothings. The sounds illuminated the night, competing against the noise of the passengers. They snoozed and snored, sometimes talking to worlds unknown. Whistles were interspersed with coughs, galloops and farts; some arriving wrapped with ribbon. I chuckled to myself as the bus moved off to new trials – bubbling and backfiring into the dark, over the corrugated road.

❖

THE HOLIDAY INN, YANGSHUO

Then it was morning, and in the weak light - trees, mountains and bullocks were waking, brushing themselves down and listing their chores for the day. The mountains were strange, un-joined, like a giant's discarded toys or a fleet of sailing ships, and the morning wore on as we tacked through the peaks. I'd been on the bus eighteen hours by the time we entered Yangshuo, a harbour amongst huge limestone schooners and frigates, and further out, cutting through an emerald sea of rice and vegetables, men-of-war sailed south to pillage Hong-Kong.

❖

Yangshuo was a small and ancient town set on the banks of the Li river, which had the serenity of a silkworm, but could grow into a roaring dragon with heavy rain, submerging the island in the middle under thirty feet of water, washing the stilts away from villages that had been built too near the bank. The mountain that rose up almost from the back of my hostel, was called 'Telegraph Hill', the least romantically named of the peaks that wrapped around the town. 'Man Hill' bowed to 'Lady Hill', 'Swan and Crab Hill' swam below 'Dragon Peak'; there was even one called 'Green Frog watching the Moon dance.' They were all there to be gawped at and then climbed, stopping at altars, and galleries bedecked with pagodas, for a rest and sip of warm water.

The second morning, with the night still wearing its silk pyjamas, I slipped out of the hostel and walked over to the public park. Here, at sunrise, the locals came, and as the light shafted through the trees at angles, and shuffled through the leaves, they mirrored it with their Tai Chi. The old people's bodies looked as supple as saplings, as they swayed and stretched. I watched until the heat grew, sending them scuffling and pedalling off to work, leaving me alone with the butterflies that crashed through the sunrays; silently.

Yangshuo was certainly geared for backpackers, which suited me fine for this stage of my journey. It meant people to meet and talk to, balmy evenings, minor difficulties. At the same time it took very little effort to take a bike and ride off into the countryside to see things the way they had always been.

I took a boat trip up river to Xing Ping, still unspoilt, and on another day - down river to Fuli. I walked straight out of the town on any old path that came my way, stumbling upon and into villages, circling lakes with their own pet mountains reflected on their shiny faces. I followed the opposite bank of the river and conversed in sign language with swimming children, too bashful to come out of the water and show their nakedness. I found my own Banyan tree, not the tourist one where Mao was meant to have spoken, but in a clearing by a rushing waterfall. I sat with my toes in the chill water, as tumbledown women fanned ochre chaff from their threshing, onto the surface of the pond. And in the town itself I could go to the station yard, sit on midget stools and eat with the locals, or stroll through the market at night to savour dubious delicacies, sift through the gee-gaws on tables in front of the flaky shops. I could sit outside the dentist with its open front, and watch a performance of human emotions. Rows of hairdressers shared whole streets, the girls at the door enticing you in. They were prostitutes, all instant charm and lies, but they would also cut your hair. Oh yes; Yangshuo was a fine place to be.

I was helping Huang, who worked in the Green Lotus, with his English.
'Is it safe to swim in the river Huang?'... 'Yes.' he said.
'But why don't I see anybody in it?'... 'Many people.' he said.
'No Huang, I've never seen anybody in the river.'
'Many people - 7.00 o'clock.'

I went to the river at 7.00; dubious. A full moon hung from the sky, brightly smiling, dipping its wick into the river to draw up more light. The Chinese, hordes of them, for as far as I could see from left to right, stood up to their waists in the normally empty water – moon bathing. For, wherever you stood, the Moon's reflection beat a wobbly path right to your stomach, where it imparted some of its power, and you could reach out, cup a handful and let it slip through your fingers... slivers of light. I joined them, the current tugging at my trousers, and I felt the energy. Well I'd had a few beers.

A crowd was gathering by the station, around a domestic dispute. A young woman was being chastised by her husband under the scrutiny of an old lady stood between them, head swivelling left and right. He raged at the girl, then stepping up pinched her cheeks painfully. Her eyes watered with the pain. He ranted, then - rushing forward, poked her in the eyes with two fingers. The old lady nodded in approval and he carried on his shouting as the girl sobbed quietly. The onlookers were unperturbed, or perhaps it was their duty to watch to ensure she was properly humiliated. I had no idea what she had done to deserve the punishment and no means of finding out, but had to accept that this was the status quo. As he snapped her head back by the hair, viciously, I had to leave; it was too painful to watch and do nothing.

The view from 'Moon Hill' was considered the most beautiful in all of China, and here, whilst taking it in, a band of ladies with swaddled infants and toddlers appeared as from nowhere around the rocks. They held out the babies, pointed at the children, and asked me to take them to England. The mothers explained that they were too poor to feed them, and I could have them for free! And these were the loveliest of poppets, chanting their alphabet in a sing-song that made your heart skip... tra-la-la.

Boats lined up on the river, waiting for darkness, cormorants tied to the front, oil lanterns primed. Their owners were old men with white beards and parchment skin, waiting for the night fishing. Whilst I watched them I attempted to tally up the beauty, spirituality and tradition, the cruelty and the kindness I'd seen. Later, when I recounted my trip to Yangshuo, and people said, 'But Yangshuo is not the real China.' I would reply, 'You need to take off your blinkers.' or words to that effect.

❖

I'd made a very difficult decision before I left home - to travel alone. The opinion on this was split; 'You must be mad - I couldn't do that.' or 'It's the best way - you'll meet more people.' The latter, though more frightening, was proving to be true, and the former only strengthened my resolve. In only two weeks I'd met a menagerie, a pot-pourri of people, and I wondered how long I would remember their faces and places. The everyday conversation of the backpacker revolved round places been, or going to; how to get there, what to do; picking up pieces of information like magpies stealing shiny objects. Though this led to a well-trod path and hardly intrepid, it was still an exciting road with surprises to be had; and it was sociable. The ease with which a conversation could start, still surprised me, and it became second nature to share my living space with complete strangers.

In my little room, I'd seen them come and go like the tide. There was an American boy who was studying Chinese, but excited to be going home. He told me to be glad I couldn't understand what the Chinese were saying about us - it really wasn't pleasant. The incessant babble from a chattering French woman seemed to increase the output from her stinking feet. An Englishman who slept the whole 36 hours he was there, woke briefly while I was reading, looked at his watch and said...

'Oh shit, it's gone twelve. I might as well stay tonight as well.' Then rolled onto his back and within seconds, rattled off snores that could cut down trees.

When the other bed was empty, the room seemed smaller - through lack of talk, as though conversation was necessary - to push out the walls with a cloud of words, all chopped and jumbled by the ceiling fan. It was exciting waiting to see if the next occupant would be a fat, sweaty Turk, or a vision of beauty.

Backpackers could be split into three groups. The hardened ones had a major aim in life - to see as many places as possible by the cheapest means, resulting in perhaps three days sleeping on a spit-carpeted floor, with other people's feet as pillows.

Arriving at their destination, there were things to be done before moving on. If these could be done in the shortest possible time and more information gathered about the next, honour was satisfied and you could go direct to the next place, without passing go or collecting your wits about you. Shell-shocked scarecrows with a self-satisfied smirk, usually induced by dope, were often seen entering town looking for the ultimate low, the weed being necessary to dull the wits and avoid boring each other shitless about how they slept on a piece of toast for a week, used it as an umbrella on the bus that had no roof, and finally ate it for six days, as the fungus growing on it induced a magic mushroom effect. Whilst in a place, there was no need or time to actually look at the countryside, feel its warmth, or drink in its presence.

The locals were obstacles that made it difficult to move around, and always wanted too much money, even though the tiny amount they were trying to extract could save them from giving away their children.

The second category rode in Posses, backpacks slung casually like bandoleers, and their aim was to stay among their own, sing their own songs, breath their own air. The undisputed champions of this were the Israelis, but the Dutch and Swedes could give a good account of themselves. My theory was that it had been instilled by compulsory national service, and that they rang home at night to receive orders for the next day.

One advantage of their technique was that they could sweep through streets and stations in a wedge, parting beggars, hawkers and whole dynasties, like a combine-harvester in a field of wheat. Another was that you could absolutely perfect your Israeli, Dutch or Swedish with each other over a long trip, as long as you didn't tag onto the wrong squad in a station melee. The English could never be in this category, as in any number over three they would fight amongst themselves, or would want to fight another posse.

And then there was the sector to which I think I belonged. I liked to call us the Romantics; or the Fools. We could be seen wandering around, normally alone, eyes wide in wonderment and confusion, completely ill-equipped, bumping into situations and lamp-posts. Though alone, we craved company and had no qualms about approaching another traveller, not due to a sudden increase in confidence since leaving home (or perhaps it was) but a survival instinct; a need to know the answers to the problems gathered along the way.

We could often be seen unsuccessfully talking to locals, to their amusement (and ours at times), paying over-inflated prices knowingly, for peace of mind or a piece of melon. We understood you see, how far the money could go compared to at home, and appreciated it enough not to wring its neck or suck its bones dry.

Regardless of category though, I was proud of them all at the time, proud to be one. Somebody asked me to define the difference between a real traveller and a tourist and I told them:

'The tourist interferes, spoils, whereas the traveller tries to move through the country without disturbing, so that smells and sights and sounds cling to his clothes and hair like dandelion seeds, and drift through his head like a senseless children's rhyme.'

'Pardon?' he exclaimed.

'They're different.' I said.

I lay semi-naked on my bed, the one next to me empty. It was so hot outside, the droning insects were sporting sunhats, water-buffalo were living up to their name, and Chinese eyes were rounding with disbelief. Refuge was my room; cool concrete floor, mosquito-net dancing mambo under the fan. Through my earphones blasted The Cure - Robert Smith crooning interminable woes. Organs ground, trumpets blew, and flute danced merrily round the melancholy. I ventured out for a beer, and as I met the road the heat picked me up and slapped me, daring me to carry on. I made it to the shade of the Green Lotus Cafe on the corner, the best viewing point in town. Little moved but trucks, which thundered through, air-horns blasting, day and night.

'Too hot!' I said to Huang.

'No problem!' he slung back; liar. It was 98 degrees. Through a heat-shimmer above the dusty road, three figures appeared - Doron, Sharon and Keren. It was like the arrival of long lost friends and it had been less than a week since I'd seen them. Whilst Doron and Sharon went for a siesta, Keren and I trotted on down to the market. It ran along a narrow road parallel to the river, stalls each side, stretching for half a mile. On the left-hand side, every stall sold jade eggs, bracelets or figures, all the same colour, all the same. On the right the choice was bountiful. The stalls alternated between selling a fruit like a giant pear and dried ginger. On an English scale this would be a road the length of the M40, with 'Boot's the Chemist' up one side, and pears and ginger down the other. A bit of competition is good for business, but how you were meant to make a choice from them all was beyond me, and at the end of the day they packed it all away, possibly minus a large pear.

A strange species arrived in the market; like cartoon characters. I was starting to consider myself a bit of a traveller now, and the sight of overdressed, overfed Americans wearing coolie hats, sunglasses, brash jewellery and Nikons, jagged a nerve.
'What are they Howie?' asked Keren. I told her they were American tourists.
'What are they doing here? Ask them please... for me.' They were on a package tour. They were doing China in two weeks. It seems that they were shipped by bus from one market full of crap to another similar.
'Do you like it here?' I asked one.
'Do I like it where?' he replied.
'Yangshuo - it's a very beautiful town, don't you think?'
'Hell, I don't know, is this Yangshuo? well we're only here overnight aren't we honey? It's Guilin tomorrow. I hear they've got a great market.' I stared at him the way that the Chinese had been staring at us. I was thousands of miles from home but a million miles apart from this man.

Since I'd introduced them in Canton, the three Israelis had taken to each other like a duck to orange. Keren was their mother, sister, closest friend. Doron was dark, lantern-jawed, with a gaze that still scanned the Golan Heights for danger. He tended for and worshipped Sharon; small and fair, with eyes that cuddled you with honest sympathy.

Keren explained that they were Kibbutzniks, used to sharing their lives, bodies and feelings, and that they were very innocent. Doron, unashamed and unconcerned, greeted the cleaning lady's knock at his door – naked; arms and genitals flailing, as he explained that he was trying to sleep. Unable to look down below waist level, the maid ran off shouting, leaving Doron confused in the corridor.
The Kibbutzniks didn't agree with national service and resented meeting so many Israelis when they were trying to get away from home. Sadly for them, Keren had been an instructor in the army, and

we were constantly approached by her past recruits, who spoke only to her and watched me - strangely. I would find out why later.

'Howie,' Doron would say, nodding at an approaching squad, 'look what's coming into town.' 'Israelis.' I would reply.
'Yes...' he'd say, eyebrows knitting, 'more bloody Israelis!'

The heat broke the sky that evening, and the four of us sat as the rain sheeted and sluiced through the cafe and under the tables. The fish that normally lived in the red bowl on the toilet floor, swam past in a bid for freedom, Huang in close pursuit - trousers rolled up to his knees. The sultry air had forced a group from Hong Kong, behind me, to shed their shirts. Doron's gaze was fixed on them.
'Don't stare - it's rude Doron.' chided Sharon.
After a long silence he remarked... 'When you see something so ugly, it's hard not to stare.' And as I turned, I saw what appeared to be a sealion, with thick black glasses and sagging breasts, shovelling rice into his mouth, some of it falling back out. His friend looked like he'd been eating cushions. He slicked back his oily hair with his hand, then wiped his mouth with the back of it.
'I'm sorry Sharon,' I said ... 'I have to agree.' Doron winked.

The next day, the sky a washed-out blue, we cycled and walked in the park; talked and talked. We stood atop Moon Hill, in a film of sweat from the hard climb, and below us lay what looked like a patchwork quilt, spread with precious stones, with silk ribbons winding between them as rivers. It was as beautiful as the Chinese proclaimed. It was then I realised I'd also been studying Keren. Slight, with soft brown hair, her glasses failed to hide her smiling doe eyes. She shone. We left the other two and cycled out of town. And despite slaloming between other cycles, people and bullocks, and being beat by the air-horns, we managed to tune in to each other. She was attracting me more by the minute. I shook myself, knowing that, given the chance, I could easily fall in love with her - I was alone and far from home.

Several golden days later I am sitting, writing, with the usual Chinese observer looking on. A worn old woman walks by, basket in one gnarled hand, a squawking duck in the other twisted fist. Behind in ragged formation, six ducklings race to keep up with their doomed mother; and such is the value of a duck in China, a gargantuan lorry screeches to a halt when one of the brood skips into the road.
My tablemate watches and talks whenever she thinks fit. She is a kitchen-girl, and a new word, picked up like a scrap from the table, is

stored for the future like a precious coin - as in most of China, the riotous life of colour juxtaposes with grinding poverty and filth. The western style cafes are a stage set, a window dressing.
  The 'Minnie Mao Café' presents a smiley face to the world in the daytime. On a late-night stumble to the toilet, from the front of the stage, you cut across the kitchen, where food prep is done on the piss-stinking floor, cockroaches whirring around like clockwork toys. You tiptoe around the iron bed, where three girls are sleeping, into the toilet with no door, and try to relieve your bladder of a full load which, minutes earlier, was bursting to get out. It's not possible now, as the three girls - their raven hair faded to grey by the mosquito net, are barely two feet from your dick; and a pair of almond shaped eyes, are flickering open and shut. So you retire to a dark alley for relief, where again, almond eyes stare, but this time at the opposite end of a thick hairy tail.

I met Keren in the park. It was raining hot water. We kissed briefly under the umbrella of a banyan tree, ignoring the statues of good Chinese workers, their arm muscles exaggerated by the teachings of Chairman Mao. We kissed like school children. I knew that if we climbed inside each other's bodies we would break our hearts, as she had a betrothed to go home to. She had to go on alone; I had to go somewhere else. But I did care for her; she was the cat's meeoow.
  I bought her a jade butterfly from amongst a mountain of trinkets, wrapped it in park tickets, hostel cards and receipts - reminders of a fine time, and wrote a farewell letter full of angst. The jade had cost almost a shoe-box full of money. It was my penance for falling for a girl who couldn't be mine, and I paid it gladly. The three amigos had a jade name-stamp made for me, which I packed away into my backpack with much feeling. And then they set off for Dali, and Keren further into China; me to stay and watch room-mates come and go with the moon, and then struggle back to Hong Kong, with fragments of my heart wrapped in a Chinese newspaper.

Having waved goodbye, and returning from the station, I saw a large potato strolling towards me, dressed in conservative shirt, shorts and sandals, waving stick-on hands and waggling its ears. Giles had arrived in town. It seemed that the new CV had worked, and he had a few days grace before starting his new job. He said he was glad to have found me, and thanked me. I was touched. Giles had been relieved of his cassettes on the bus, but not his sense of humour. His gentle and

thoughtful companionship carried me through my gloom, until he also left for his new career.
Then, having just seen three Israelis off at the front door, three more crept in through the back. After a solid knock at my door, I woke, I saw a woolly head appear in the dawn light.
'I must move in here.' it said; with conviction, who was I to disagree.
Issel was short and stocky, and looked ironically very Arabic, like the enemy he despised. Again the room grew with conversation, and sunlight crept up the walls and into the corners. With him - as a package, came Guy. He was handsome, full of games and tricks, mischievous, and charm dripped from his riotous garb. Guy was very careful to dress carelessly. And to complete the trio the inevitable - Shirley, those same brown, doe eyes, fair hair and golden skin.

So I joined them on the Ferris-wheel of life, and it spun oh so fast, lurching over and over for three days, its lights twinkling and dancing. One evening I told them about my previous Israeli connection. Guy and Issel looked at each other delightedly, clapped their hands and said 'You're the one. We heard about you in Kunming - the Englishman that was having an affair with Keren!' They were delighted, as they didn't like the four who'd told them, and slapped my back with glee. I hoped it wouldn't pass down the way, as I wanted her to be happy.

Their intrigue at the photo of Bumble in my wallet, and my explanation of his skills, led to the strangest episode of 'One Man and his Dog' ever seen. Cycling out of town, in a vast area of rice fields and crops, they demanded a demonstration in working a dog. So, telling my invisible dog to stop barking, I whistled him away a few hundred yards to the base of a mountain, then dropped him down.
'What's he doing ?' asked Guy.
'He's lying down.' I was whistling very loud now, as he was so far away, and peasants in the field and on bikes were stopping dead, as though also responding. I sent him slowly, then quickly, across the valley to the west, and the three followed him with their eyes. He swam through paddies, vaulted coolies and tore across the plain like a wonder-dog. They looked at me in unison to see if he'd got there, and I whistled him down.
'Well he did that alright.' I said.

Unaware of the ridiculous situation they'd conjured up, Shirley asked, sweet and hopeful, 'Could you bring him over here now?' as if she was going to be able to stroke his ears and ruffle his chest.

'No,' I said, 'when you weren't looking, he ran off and he's fallen down a well.' They realised what they were doing, and sheepishly grinned.

On a final turn by the river wall on their last evening, Guy said quietly... 'I want to do you a favour Howie.' and held out a small string bag containing the biggest lumps of hash I'd ever seen.

'You can have these for twenty dollars - I can't take them home with me.' I could have sold them for a thousand pounds at home.

'Guy, thank you, but in three days I fly into Vietnam, do you really think I want to take that with me?' He pondered that for a moment and replied...

'No, you're right.' He swung them around above his head and flung them into the Li river, giggling.

'I'll see you at Minnie Mao's - I have a phone call to make.' he said.

Whilst waiting for him at the café, a trio of extremely well-dressed backpackers approached, and in a mid-American drawl asked...

'Could you tell us where there's a hotel with western-style toilets?'

'Not here I'm afraid. That's the most expensive hotel in town...' I replied pointing it out, 'and they don't have them.'

'Really?' he said, shocked. I nodded. 'What are we going to do?' they said in unison and despair.

'You're in the middle of China, I suggest you go back to Hong-Kong.'

They stumbled away just as Guy, Issel and Shirley arrived, a screaming Chinese man chasing behind them, waving his bony arms.

'6 dollar, you owe me 6 dollar!' They sat down with me, ignoring him, as he fluttered and batted around their heads like a ninja moth.

'GO AWAY!!' Guy shouted.

'What the hell's up with him?' I asked.

'He's trying to rip us off for a telephone call. We agreed a price and now he's trying to double it.' A crowd was gathering at a discreet distance. We tried to ignore him and his noise, but he made a grab for Shirley's waist bag. Issel had hold of his wrist before he could blink, his other cocked fist held back by Guy. 'Leave him Issel, sit down, drink.'

'You give me 6 dollar or I bring the police!' he threatened, and made another grab for the bag, now on the table. I got there before him and Issel, who was coming round the table.

'Look, back off!' I said, in a friendly tone, 'or I think you might die.' nodding towards the approaching Israeli. He took the hint and jumped away to his bicycle. 'I get the police!'

'Yes please do - we'll be here waiting.' I said, innocently thinking that the Police would see reason. Guy explained the problem after he had gone, and showed me the piece of paper they'd written the agreed price on. It dawned on me as we spoke, that the spectators were melting away. In their place, the cafe seemed to be acquiring some new customers. Pan-faced men had moved into the bar, and contrary to normal behaviour, wouldn't look at us. From the corner of my eye I saw the seat next to me fill. I looked at my neighbour, whose thigh was touching mine. 'Nice day?' I proffered to the side of his head.

He turned his head, and I saw a strange and frightening thing. I saw nothing in his eyes. No fear, no anger; a cold dark pit.

'I think it might be a good idea to pay the money Guy,' I said, as two more men ferreted into a dim corner, 'he didn't go to get the police.'

'No, fuck him, I'm not paying!' Guy spat, and I realised that they didn't know what was going on. Marcus, a Swiss football fanatic who'd been watching the World Cup in Chinese, night and day, joined us from another table by the exit, but we still weren't enough. The gangsters were still arriving, and then, a policeman on a motorbike. 'At last... the cavalry,' I thought.

'I am the foreign liaison officer,' said the bullet-headed, pig-featured, gendarme, 'pay this man his money!' 'Good liaison' I thought, my heart sinking. Guy explained the problem first, while the phone-man and his friends whispered in the officer's ear and fed him cigarettes.

Shirley also explained it, while he supped free beer. Issel explained that if they didn't stop giving the policeman cigarettes, he would shove them down their throats. They carried on whispering, the officer carried on drinking.

'You pay him his money.' the policeman suddenly shouted.

'We will not pay him.' said Guy quietly and calmly, and I tensed, ready. The policeman went off on one. He ranted, screamed...

'You fucking foreigners come here, everything is wrong, you don't want to pay for anything!!' and flicked his fag butt in Guy's face.

'PAY HIM!!!'

'NO!'

He stomped off to his bike, and I waited for the gun to come out. But no, he shouted something back in Chinese and rode away. There was a deathly silence, in which I quickly worked out what he'd said. Half out of my seat, the adrenalin pumping, I saw the gangsters fidgeting, hands reaching in pockets.

'Guy, pay him the money NOW!'

'Yes, I think that would be a good idea.' added Marcus who, like myself, had probably learned some savvy from the football terraces. Outnumbered by knife-wielding hoods is not the time to get heroic.

'Oh shit! Here is the money that we don't owe you.' Guy spat at the phone-man, peeling off six notes and ramming them in his shirt pocket. 'Now go away!'

He walked away cursing. Looking around, I saw that the hoods had already gone; melted away into the dark, and I wondered if they'd ever been there. The sweat trickling down my face told me that they had. The bar owner appeared sheepishly, and I asked him to tell us what the policeman had said. 'I not frightened of policeman, frightened of men, they not care if they go to jail, kill people. The policeman was scared.' 'He said that he could do nothing and they would have to fight you when he had left.'
'Would they have fought us?' I asked.
'I don't know. They are frightened of Israeli and English, so maybe not, but probably they would - as they had knives.'
'They had knives?' asked Guy. Dumbfuck.
I was starting to weary of Israelis.

Outside the Green Lotus, the truck horns hitting me like a soldier beating his drum, I saw an English couple that I'd met previously, being led by a policeman from the back of a van and into the post office. The girl was crying. I slipped over the road and followed them in. The man was on the telephone, guarded on both sides, the girl leaning against a wall, bottom lip trembling.
'What's going on...who's he phoning?' I asked. She told me.

'John and I were out cycling towards Fuli. We came up to a village and a man stopped us. He said we couldn't come through without paying twenty dollars. John told him that it wasn't a closed village and we didn't have to pay, so we went to cycle on. This bloke smacked John round the ear, so of course John laid him out.' John had now handed the phone to the officer. 'Well,' she carried on, 'this bloke gets up from the floor, pulls out a gun and shows us his police ID. Now we're under arrest and the policeman's demanding compensation, as he reckons he's gone deaf!'
'What's happening John?' she asked.
'I got the Consulate. He's demanded that we're kept out of the jail until a doctor examines the policeman, and then he'll discuss compensation.'
'You're joking John, yeah?'
'No; we're under house arrest at the hotel, and he's demanding five thousand dollars. The Consulate say's we'll probably have to pay it.'
'Look, I've got to go now – sorry' I said, scuttling out the door, as I'd spotted our old friend - the Foreign Liaison Officer, approaching the post office.
'I know it's not much help but - good luck.' I offered. The Officer shoulder-barged me aside as I tried to leave. Returning to the café, I

asked the owner - a ticket broker 'What time does the sleeper bus leave today?... 4 o'clock? ... well I want to be on it.' And I was.
I was starting to weary of China.
I was relieved to be on the bus and on the way back to Hong Kong, but not so happy about my neighbour, one level below; a policeman. To add to my discomfort, he'd removed all of his clothes apart from his boxer shorts. Six hours later the whole bus was sleeping, apart from the two of us; him sitting bolt upright - me watching out of the corner of my eye. Was he going to wait for me to fall asleep and then bugger me? No... he was travel-sick. He rushed to the doors, and with the conductor hanging onto the waistband of his briefs, leant out into the dark to throw up. A long time passed, and I began to wonder if the conductor was just holding a pair of pants in the breeze, but eventually he was swung back in. Almost as soon as he regained the upright position on his seat, the bus slammed to a halt - bags, bottles and bodies flying down the bus. Ahead, a white van had blocked us in a narrow lane, and in the stark headlights I saw what appeared to be the cast of 'Hawaii Five-O' leap from every door; loud shirts, white trousers, barracuda faces. I was in the front seat, street-lit through the windscreen, in full view - as they formed a semicircle round the front of the bus; I knew they weren't about to sing Christmas Carols. I was the only Westerner on the bus. I tried to screw my eyes up in an Asian style, but I was fooling nobody - I *was* the target.
The conductor held the doors shut with his back as the driver spoke to them through his barely open window.
Holding grimly onto my bag, I looked down to the left and straight down the barrel of a Smith and Wesson revolver. The policeman was smiling manically up at me with one finger to his lips... 'sssshhhh!'

Whatever the driver said – worked, as they moved off back to the van; apart from one, who remained dead centre between the windscreen wipers. He stared straight at me, and I stared back - mesmerised like a rabbit in a stoat's gaze. My arse clammed up in fright. He slowly raised a hand and pointed a loaded finger at me – fired an invisible bullet, turned and walked. I looked down at my policeman   he was 'my' policeman now. He buttoned the gun back into his holster, resumed the lotus position and looked over at me with a sickly grin. I knew it had been my lucky day.

At a food stop, in those heinous hours that are neither night nor day, I found that there had been another Westerner on the bus, tucked way down on the bottom tier at the very back. He looked like Jesus of Nazareth, but more ginger, and was 'Aaron of Swansea'. We were both

too weary to brave the circus inside the very beat café, so we sat out in the air. At least I would have some company for the trip back. Attracted by his hair and colour, a toddler stood in front of Aaron, expertly smoking a cigarette and giggling. He was joined by his brother, who could barely walk. A shout from inside pulled the older boy away, but hesitating, he stepped back and gave the cigarette to the little brother to look after. The baby smoked it, and stared at Jesus.
Once again, Guangzhou Station had me in its grasp, and try as hard as we could, we failed to get a train ticket. We took a bus; hard seat. I was already getting used to the category of seat in Asia. 'Hard Seat' meant just that – a bit like a wooden park bench bolted to a bus or train floor. 'Soft Seat' implied a level of comfort, due to some cushioning encased in vinyl. This of course elevated it to a higher price bracket – particularly for a 'foreigner', so these were kept on the budget as luxuries, infrequent splurges. 'Soft Sleeper Air-con' was the top-dog, and only to be dreamt of, which of course couldn't be done whilst travelling hard seat - as sleep was impossible.

The two hour train journey took five hours on the bone-jarring bus. We were sandwiched between Chinese women either spitting on the floor or being sick out of the windows. We were a contributing factor to this apparently, due to our body odour, and at one stage the rest of the bus were triple-seated until two rows from the back, where we both sat in glorious isolation, grinning at our revenge.

The conductor was, however, unwilling to allow us our space, and forced them to sit next to the smelly foreigners by threatening to hit them with a bottle. He pulled unwilling people from the street onto the bus; God knows where they had been hoping to go. He worked up and down the aisle, fleecing the passengers one by one, the bottle raised to any objectors. Each time he came to the back of the bus he spat...
'You foreigners pay double!'
'Fuck off.' we told him. He hadn't endeared himself to us.
'If you don't pay double, there will be men to take care of you at station.'
'Fuck off.' we told him.
I can only think it was our red-rimmed and wild eyes, crappy clothes and apparently - terrible stench, that persuaded him to leave us alone.

He accused a very young and vulnerable college student, sat between us, of not paying. He snatched his satchel bag, emptied it onto the floor, stole some postcards and rifled the boy's pockets for money. Not finding any easily, he raised the bottle and threatened the boy again, but we were both out of our seats and glaring. He sidled back up the aisle, clipping random people round the head.

The boy was gulping air with fright and made to jump out of the window next to me. I grabbed his shirt and told him the driver would see him, and that he should stick with us. The gangsters were there, as the bus rolled to a halt, waiting for the doors to open and then deal with any offenders. We took the boy out with us and put our packs on the ground, waiting for the trouble, hoping it wouldn't be too bad. The conductor however said nothing, and shrugged at us as if to say - 'Well you have to try it on, don't you.'

We had no idea what town we had been dropped in, but went round and around it on buses, looking for the train to Hong Kong. Each time they set us down, they said, 'Yes, station, over there!' It never was.

After producing a flamboyant imitation of Thomas the Tank Engine - arms pumping, choo-choo-ing through a huge crowd that had gathered, we finally got the right directions. By now we were both demented through tiredness and anger, and battled the rest of the way into the city on a couple of trains. We had only Yuan in our pockets, which were useless in Hong Kong, so to finish us off completely, we were forced to beg for Hong Kong dollars outside the underground station. Finally, we took our last ride to Nathan Road, stood outside Chungking mansions, and shook hands. Aaron had five days left until his flight back to the UK, and no money for a hostel. I knew it would impossible for him to get a job for just a few days, so I prised a folded ten pound note from the back of my wallet and asked him to send it to my brother when back in Wales. Kind - or soft in the head? I don't know; but it felt right. He never sent it back.

On the way out of Hong Kong, the 747 neatly pegged the Guns & Roses T shirt back on the line in Jardine Street, next to a pair of Levis, and then climbed into the cloud obscuring the peak; Soft Seat, Air/con.

❖

BI-BI HOSTEL, OLD QUARTER, HANOI

Throughout the flight, I ruminated on the cruelty I had seen, the hardships I had encountered in China, and how relieved I felt to have left it all behind. Then it dawned on me, suddenly enough to make me jump and cry out a small gasp; I was on my way to Vietnam. I would be landing in a country known only as being a war. I'd watched Vietnam in black & white on the goggle-box for years, and the images were only bad.

❖

We planed across a green patchwork quilt and touched down on the runway, after a small leapfrog over a particularly wet patch. There were no bomb craters in sight, and napalm was absent in the morning dew. There were no gunships buzzing around, spitting fire and damnation at peasants and soldiers, only bullocks wading through the paddies - their coolies waterskiing behind, failing to mix together the different shades of green. The family working in the last paddy before the runway had taken advantage, and spread their clothes and cooking pots out on the end of the concrete.

Still stressed from China, the Lonely Planet's warnings of police and customs hassles at Hanoi Airport had me at boiling point. I realised that I'd had no time to even try and imagine what to expect; and now I was there. I'd found my visit to the Vietnamese Consul in London quite odd; but then a small piece of Vietnam tucked away in Kensington, staffed by 'Charlie', is hardly everyday. I was given one piece of paper with my details and photo attached and a replica, both of which I signed. They kept one copy, and I was to present mine on arrival at Hanoi. I assumed it was a version of 'Snap' - if mine matched theirs, I could come in. But that was in London.

I had visions of child-sized men in drab-olive fatigues, pointing machine guns at my chest, locking me in a bamboo cage up to my neck in water, and questioning me about the photo of a dog in my wallet.

Thus began the most trouble-free arrival I'd ever had the privilege to experience. The terminal handled one plane-load of passengers at a time. There was no comment from immigration on my half of the form, no hassle from customs, no waiting for baggage; it was all smiles and politeness and then... 'Here's a seat for you, sit! We find a person to share taxi with you; make cheaper! We can go if you like, but more money; please wait. Want cigarette?'

We waited, but they couldn't find another body, so worryingly I got into an empty 12-seat minibus with two strangers – my Mum would have had a fit. They promised - 'We will take you to as many hotels as you wish until you are satisfied.' They did. I was. It was cheaper than the Lonely Planet had said. True, they did put me into a relative's hostel at the south of the lake, when I'd asked to go to the north, but I didn't find that out until I ventured into the evening.

I walked north, shy but excited, buzzing to be there. Hanoi had a smile hanging over it, moonlike, and grinning through its streets like a Cheshire Cat. Here, the youth sneaked to the lake in the evening and loved each other under dark tree umbrellas, kissing and necking, to fuel their daytime smiles. And when you're in love with a girl, your country and life itself, who's worried about foreigners traipsing around and looking? They smiled at me, calling out greetings I couldn't understand, but could tell were friendly.

'Hoan Kiem – The Lake of the Restored Sword', held the fairy lights of the city on its surface, and as I reached the 'Island of the Turtle' at its head, I realised that I'd been duped and was staying at the wrong end of town. I'd wanted to stay in the Old Quarter, but my hotel was good, even though I was the only occupant, and I was tired - too tired to be annoyed. In China I had been racked with stress, dehydration, diahorrea and stupidity. I had carried on supping beer by the sampan-full whilst writing, and though this appeared to open the doors to creativity, it had shut the windows on my health. I was mentally and physically as healthy as Gorgonzola left in a hot place; it was time to take myself in hand. I already felt that in Vietnam I could do it. Even on my first evening I knew I could go on to better things, and with this in mind, I headed for the Old Quarter and The Old Dahling Café where I knew I would find other backpackers.

I carried my muddy coffee, still filtering in a tin pot, to the table by the door and sat down next to the two lads already occupying it.

'Excuse me - could you recommend a good hostel in this area?'

'For sure.' said the Australian lad, the first of a thousand annoying times I would hear him utter this phrase.

'Ours is OK - d'ya wanna go an' hev a look? We'll take ya, eh Harry?' he said turning to the other.

'Four shore.' said Harry with a Scandinavian accent. The phrase was obviously catching.

The hostel was at the top end of the town, and we walked through the street-life; noisy, smelly and chaotic. The people were cooking, eating, sleeping, bathing and doing everything - in the street. Small hillocks of rubbish punctuated the pavements; the remains of the day. Later, as the people moved indoors, these were removed by ladies in facemasks pushing handcarts, who then brushed the streets as though preparing a dinner table for its next cover. It seemed that every scooter built in Japan, had emigrated to Hanoi, and were happily playing amongst themselves, the bicycles and the people, in streets not big enough to accommodate scooters, bicycles and people. In China, where Hondas don't go to live, the bicycles often crashed into each other, into kerbs, posts and man-size cockroaches. But walking across or along Hanoi streets, you could be amongst a flock of bats. They seemed unable to hit each other or you, through some silent and invisible sonar device. If, when crossing a wide road, a red light winked green, a phalanx of Hondas and bicycles - spokes and pedals linked, came for you; but as long as you carried on moving, they would pass on all sides, maybe tugging faintly at a shirt sleeve or leg hair.

To stop in the middle of this symphony was to cause the cymbals to crash, the trumpets screech and the vehicles pile into one another. The average number of riders on a Honda was three. Whole families of five and six, sardined on the one seat, cantered along on their trusty steeds, on the way to who knows where.

The proudest of the scooters bore two girls, with their 'Ao Dai' dress pressed close to their bodies by the rush of air, waist length chestnut hair waving gossamer in the slipstream behind. Their beauty was unmatchable and their giggling heartbreaking, as they sneaked you a look with almond eyes and let you know they were unattainable. The Ao Dai contrived to be both modest and provocative at the same time. Fitted tight from neck to hip, it accentuated every contour of their slender, willowy bodies, the curve of the back, the budding swell of breasts and buttocks. The sides were slit to the waist, and below this loose, silk trousers cloaked the thighs and calves in secrecy. Sauntering along the pavements in the evening breeze, they seemed like butterflies, flitting under the tamarind trees from cafe to pavement, friend to lover.

Reaching the Bi-Bi guesthouse with Nick and Harry, I was dizzy with desire, noise and smells, and after tripping up the stairs for a quick look at the room, booked in for the next night. The bunks grappled with each other for space, but at least the room was being cooled by a wall fan and a white-tiled bathroom sat cleanly in the corner. I went onto the balcony, and looking out into the glow of the city, saw that we were surrounded by humped red roofs, like a cluster of crabs.

Between these were the living lanes of the city; narrow lanes stuffed with people, vehicles and dogs, washing back and forth like a tide of flotsam, all held down by garlands of thick telegraph wires strung between the crumbling walls. The accompanying noise was a cacophony, jumping up at me from below like a pack of mad dogs. I just wanted to be here amongst it all, and knowing that I would be, the very next day, I shambled back past the lake to my hotel, content, and slept the sleep of a dead thing.

Bi-Bi Hostel was on Hang Chai St, which translated meant 'bottles and teabag street'. All the streets in Hanoi's Old Quarter are named after the trade which they ply exclusively.
  We came to navigate by the trade or craft, and would direct people with... 'You need to go up Tin Street (which was a hurricane of hammers beating tin), turn right into Shoe Street, go along Jewellery, cross over Red Street, (where all manner of furniture sat scarlet in the sun) – and you'll find the market.'

Hang Chai had long ago said goodbye to its bottles, and was now a backwater in which a cluster of families lived around the hostel, and where, we were told, the kids were the worst robbers in the city.

❖

So picture me, sitting in front of the hostel; soft, buttery morning light floating around. With me are winsome Diep, her brother Danh and their friends. Diep is eleven, but looks eight, with a whisper that barely disturbs the air. Her first pair of earrings swing proudly from her pretty little ears. She pushes my nose (for we are long noses to the Vietnamese) tickles my chin (as it is hairy) and as a reward for putting up with this, I get a big cuddle.

I don't know what to think about this, as I can picture her in five years time, flying through Hanoi on a Honda with her flawless girlfriend behind, or trotting down to the lake with her boyfriend, sitting holding the moon between them as it bobbles across the water. But for now she is a child. I remember that she's a street urchin, that this dream may not happen for her and instantly like a sharp unexpected pain, I wish that she could be the daughter I can't ever have.

Without knowing it – my future is set. And this child of delight and most innocence, sees my eyes fill with pain, and reaching behind my glasses catches a tear on her tiny, shell fingernail. It hangs there, like a transparent ladybird and, as though she could carry the woes of Vietnam and the world on her tiny shoulders, her great and helpless eyes fill for me and her little head drops onto my shoulder. I was gone.

If I'd been offered this one to take home, like the many in China, it would have been difficult not to pack her in cotton wool, tuck her into my backpack next to my Walkman, and ask Stevie Wonder, Julie London, Slim Gaillard and the rest to sing to her and care for her until I got home; because to look at her would still my feet and set them in concrete in Hanoi, there to remain with a marble Lenin and a stuffed Ho Chi Minh.

Jiggling through Cha Ca, and then arcing round the lake, I entered a new world to the West. This was 1930, and it appeared that I was in France; promenading down broad and leafy boulevards. Colonial mini-palaces ticked off the route; The Indian Embassy, the Chinese Embassy, the Algerian, French, Finnish, Australian, and as though transported from a film set, the tall, balconied, weather-beaten Romanian Embassy, with perpetual thunderstorm above.

Amongst these tidy, thoroughly beautiful thoroughfares, lay Ho Chi Minh's Mausoleum. It was an imposing but uninspiring marble block, guarded by soldiers dressed in snow white linen uniform. Barred from entering the mausoleum through lack of sleeves on my shirt, I wandered the parade ground. Around a corner, I startled a young guard, who had been leaning, bored, against the cold marble. As I approached, he snapped to attention with a steely grimace, and realising that I wanted to chat, his face cracked; a huge grin that bridged continents.

After some small talk, very small talk, I asked 'Do you enjoy serving here – at the resting place of Ho Chi Minh?'

'No,' he replied, looking worriedly to each side, to see if he could be heard. He explained haltingly but quite clearly – 'I'm bored stupid. I have to stand here all day like an imbecile. It is 100 degrees, and I guard a lump of marble and a stuffed body.'

'Ho Chi Minh asked for his body NOT to be embalmed and displayed; he wanted to be returned to the earth – to his beloved Vietnam soil. Why have they done this to him?'

'But it is so good when somebody comes and talks; they all think I will arrest or shoot them. See this parade ground? it is made to hold a hundred thousand people. I never see more than a few hundred here at one time. Where you stay in the Old Quarter, people have to live on top of each other and in the road. What do you think Ho Chi Minh would say about that?'

He gestured his partner over for a chat, but he declined with a worried look, and shaking of his head.

'He is frightened,' my soldier said, 'living in the past. Me - I don't care about the army, I like Guns & Roses, America number one!'

I shook his hand and photographed the two of them in front of a Vietnamese flag the size of a football field , gold star rippling over red, and at last the other soldier beamed. I strolled happily back into town, though the Vietnam sun baked down relentlessly. I passed by the nondescript but emotive Hanoi Hilton prison; a triangular, windowless structure, ochre-yellow, the colour of the American pilots' skin when they finally emerged from here. The small door set into the larger studded gates was open, and I tried to poke my nose in. A guard appeared from out of the shadows and barred the way.

'Can I come in?' He shook his head and smiled. No, I didn't think so.

Cutting crabwise on a whim, back towards home, Paris suddenly appeared on the left, a slap round the face with a gothic church; St Joseph's Cathedral. It stood alone, a pale-skinned giant amongst mulatto midgets. After circling the building, I found a side entrance, and slipped into a cool silence. Green, arched paths walked all around the cathedral, touching its buttresses and caressing the walls. The hum and buzz of the city passed over the top of this haven, or waited outside the squiggle-iron gates, sulking and squawking.

This church was not built for pomp or show, but worship. This vessel was never filled with the mighty roar of organ pipes, merely a small piano to one side. The priests were not elevated skywards in a demigod position, but preached from the floor, nose-to-nose with the people.

They were arriving for a service at just that moment, and the cathedral was filled with a deafening noise of feet, shuffling in obeyance as they entered. The windows were the only compromise to excess, with colours dancing through Saint Theresa, Saint Joseph and Saint anybody else you can think of, then falling like petals onto the cold floor. When the sun outside played hide & seek behind the puffball clouds, the colours dimmed, waiting to be fired back to life and spattered around the gloom.

Confession boxes waited hungrily for their evening meal; as between 5.00 and 7.00 the locals came in earnest, in taxis and cyclos - to confess; perhaps their clandestine trips to the lake, or bad thoughts of Richard Nixon. Then, as dark darkened outside, and confession boxes swayed, the massed band of Catholic cicadas set off, round and round the cathedral, each and every one a 'Johnny One Note'. I went home.

❖

I was in love again - and this time it was with a city; I loved the morning, the afternoon, the evening and night, and I tried to wrap them all around me - snug. Once again I couldn't see past the place I was at, but I didn't care, and I shared all this with Harry.

First appearances had let me down; or rather, I'd let myself down by judging on first appearances. When I'd approached them in The Old Dahling Café, it was Nick the Ozzie who did all the talking, and tall, skinny Harry, looking sullen, with ice-cold eyes, stayed quiet all evening. I had him down as a miserable son of a Swede, but soon we were walking, talking and thinking on the exact same wavelength. We would spot things that the other had already noticed, and laugh and sigh at the same beauties passing by. When silence and distance were needed between us, they reigned supreme; until, like two clockwork toys wound to the same tension, we would click into action, banging drums and whirring lights and knocking into new things together.

Listening to one of my own compilation tapes – I was hit by a sucker punch. - 'I can't listen to that!' I shouted and flung my earphones down.
 I explained to Harry that it was a taboo record, to be taken in small doses, and never after a broken heart.
 'I have one tune like that also. Four shore.' he said, as he put my earphones on and raised the volume. His eyes widened...
 'Oh faaark! it's the same song, *'Pictures of You'*! I don't believe it.'
 I put the earphones back in and listened to the bass line pumping sorrow with a rock-steady beat, pounding at my quavering heart. Then, the vocals injected the sadness deep into my veins, where it strolled nonchalantly around, and escaped from the corner of my eyes...
 'I picture you - standing silent in the rain - ' oh, oh, oh!
 But knowing that this tune also caused pain for another made it easier to bear, and I played it again. And now, seeing her standing silent in the rain, I walked towards her stronger - with Harry beside me for support, picturing faces of his own. I wasn't to know at the time, but the picture I was to hold one day, would make it impossible to listen to again.

We spent our halcyon days in Hanoi together, wandering her streets, watching and waiting for the next happening; crawling sluggishly through the alleys, not wanting to miss a thing. And when out on solo missions, we knew of the other's position through the network. Familiar now to the postcard sellers, we each had our own favourite. Thuy would wrinkle her nose at me (a Vietnamese insult) as I refused to buy a card, though she knew that I'd would succumb sometime during the day; perhaps paying for a photo of her and a friend, or a glass of Coke.

On a circuit of the lake, lights from Chinese lanterns wavering on the water, or, leaning through a temple door to gather incense fumes, I would be distracted by a small shout...

'Hi Howie, what are you doing? - you want postcard?'

'No Thuy, I'm just walking, and then I'm going to have a cold beer.'

'Harry is in the Old Dahling Café - he said he has bought you one.'

And that's where I would go with my escort, to spend the rest of the day just watching and talking, and trying to get to the bottom of Thuy's real life story. More than once though, she cut me to the quick - with a casual...'Will you be my father - will you take me to England?'

❖

Walking south, checking out the street barbers for a haircut, I saw Thuy approaching, the piece of folded cardboard that held her postcards and guide books pressed to her chest.

'Where you go? Harry at the fire.' she said.

'What fire?' I asked, and she pointed behind me. I turned to see a column of angry, grey smoke, climbing into the sky above the Old Quarter, and suddenly I could smell an acrid burning, taste it on my tongue; caustic.

'The old market is burning, let's go watch.' and taking my hand, she led me round the eastern shore of the lake; the whole of Hanoi seemed to be heading there. Thuy pulled me through the stream, hurling insults here, there, and everywhere - the peoples' shocked faces bearing testimony to the degree of vulgarity, and we pushed through a phalanx of police who had closed the whole block. By now the greasy, black cloud was a pall across the sky. It had spread across the width of the city and was still growing in menace; sooty filaments spiralling down onto the crowd. Harry appeared with his band of followers, face spotted and streaked with black. We watched for a while - talking to other onlookers, who confirmed there were many people inside the inferno. We agreed that we'd seen enough; that watching people die was beyond the pale, especially when we couldn't help. The crowd stayed virtually unmoving for three days, until the last flickers of flame were doused and the smoke-pallid sky turned back to blue. It wasn't that the Vietnamese enjoyed watching the horrible spectacle; I think they just needed to observe and remind themselves, yet again, how close life is to death in Asia - and compose a strategy to cope.

❖

One day as with all love affairs, Hanoi and I fell out; a small tiff, a misunderstanding. Balmy evening beckoning with crooked finger, Harry and I steamed down to Cha Ca Restaurant, and weighed anchor in the corner of this shabby but lively fish restaurant. Expecting a shoal of choices and service, we looked hungrily around and about, and at each other, and at the ceiling and floor, and other face-feeding customers; an hour passed but no menu seemed on offer. Just when hope was a great pretender, a meal arrived - with a bill.
'What is this?' we asked.
'40,000 dong each person.' was the reply.
'But we haven't ordered yet!'
'This is meal at Cha Ca.'
Not taking to the meal, formally or otherwise, we said... 'No want.' Swearing, he took the meal away, and the Vietnamese couple at the next table, thinking we were broke, offered us their leftovers. We thanked them and left, headed straight for the Western style joint by the lake, and ordered two simple meals, in the hope they might arrive the same day. To fill the time before the food arrived, I told Harry of two other incidents that had shaped my day.

As I ambled along Le Loi, locks of freshly cut dark hair span around the pavement in whirlwinds, whipped up by the passing traffic. With a speckled gilt mirror hung on the brick wall at every ten paces, accompanied by a stool, the pavement was a continual hair salon, and this was 'barber' street. The owner of each and every empty stool plied for my trade with giant smiles, simpering grins or outright camp posturing. I wanted a haircut, but which one to choose? I realised that I was being closely accompanied by a youth on a bicycle, who stopped me with the ubiquitous 'Hello...where from?'
'Anh,' I replied - 'England.'
'I speak England.' he said, his skinny chest puffed with pride, and carried on...'You very big.'
'No; I'm quite tall...' I said, indicating a point way above his head, which he looked at, 'but not very strong.' I flexed my very average biceps, which looked huge beside his puny arms.
'No!' he said, pointing straight at my crotch, 'English have bigger dicks than Vietnamese?' and I realised it was a question.

TWO MINUTE NOODLE

Flustered, remembering China and 'saving face', I hesitated as to the answer. I didn't want to insult the Vietnamese – nor make myself look foolish. But who would know. I chivalrously replied...
'Yes I believe that is normally true... but I may be an exception to the rule.' But he still wanted to hold my hand and accompany me home.
I eventually managed to persuade him that I wasn't interested in boys or men, and he pedalled off on his oversized lady's bike, with a smile and a wave.
I was still grinning at the encounter, when I realised I'd strayed into a back-alley, where the words shanty and slum were fighting it out. I was being watched by every window, door and dozens of shaded eyes. A group of cyclo drivers sat cross-legged ahead of me, sharing a pipe, still wearing their Vietcong fatigues and helmets from the war. Coming abreast, I looked for an expression on their faces. The nearest stretched a hand out to his side, where it rounded and closed on a rock. It cracked into my hip-bone, but not wanting to show alarm, I carried on walking, searching their faces for signs of their mood. I could see none and puzzled and hurt, I turned back and spoke to them.
'Thank you,' I said smiling; and again... in Vietnamese 'cam onh.' and smiled even more. They looked blankly at each other as I walked off whistling and trying not to limp.
'And then what happened?' asked Harry.
'I went to The Old Dahling Cafe for a beer!'
'Aaaaarrrgh, you English, so bloody charming; somebody throws a rock at you and you say thank you - charming! I will put this in my book.' and shook his head. I took it as a compliment, but in reality it was easier on the mind and soul than running away.

The food started to arrive piecemeal. At 8.00 - a plate of chips; 8.30 - a beefsteak; 8.45 - my pork chop; 9.00 - a salad; 9.45 - spring rolls; and as we were about to leave, at 10.00, along came, lonely on a plate with no butter - a piece of bread. By now we were weary with it all and still hungry, so it was off to the Tin-Tin bar to fill the holes with beer, along with two huge Norwegians we met along the way. On the tiny TV in the corner the world cup was being played out; Bulgaria 2 - Germany 1.

And as is the wont of the world today, in the depths of Hanoi, in the corner of a small bar, was an English football hooligan. He'd dropped his trousers standing on the table, to treat everybody to a look at his wedding tackle and spotty arse. Jumping down from the table, he'd decided for some reason that we were Germans, and strutted over.

'That's you Krauts shafted eh! - anything to say for yourselves?'

'I got nothing to say to you.' said one of the sons of Norway.
'Alright Kraut... y'wanna know - outside... now!'
'Well cum on then - outside!' spluttered his mate, the one that hard lads always have to egg them on, or hold them back when they don't really want to fight. The Norwegians were looking at each other and Harry - baffled. Even Harry, with his brilliant English, was at a loss.
I decided that a little diplomacy and translation were needed.
'What's your problem mate?' I asked, in my best East London accent... 'Why you taking a pop at us, you're having a bubble aintcha?'
'You're fuckin' Inglish!... fort you was Krauts... you look like one.'
It wasn't the best time to explain the heritage of my companions, and I reckoned we could take them if push came to shove.
'Well give it a rest then, eh geezer?' I said.
'Yeah, no hard feelings chief eh?' they said before returning to the other end of the bar. I explained to the two vikings that they'd just been challenged. They laughed like barrels, and looking at them, I figured I'd done the Brits a big favour, and really wished I hadn't.
So the day had left a slight bitterness on the tongue, a disappointment had crept into my relationship with Hanoi. Could it be rescued?

❖

The blade of the new moon hung sharp and keen overhead, as we rounded the corner into Hang Chai, slap bang into the middle of a game of football. Though way past any bedtime, here were all our daytime buddies, none higher than our waists, chasing an old, grey leather football up and down the alley. Diep and her friends were getting in the way and annoying their brothers. The steel shutters were closed on the hostel and our hammering brought no response, so we took off our shirts for goalposts and joined the game. Choosing Diep's brother as my first team-mate, I said to him...
'We'll be England!'
'No,' he said 'USA number one! always number one.'
Confident – I said...'England - number two then'
'No, Sweden number two.'
'Why?' I asked.
'Sweden help us in the war.' he replied, and I recalled that a large part of the Embassy quarter *was* the Swedish Embassy.
'England must be number three then?' I suggested.
'No, Brazil number three - best football players!'
'OK then; USA can't play football, they've got an almost Swede playing for them, so we'll be Brazil!'
'Yeeesss!' he shouted and gave me a high five, with a slap.

We had an audience of mangy men ranged along a bench, who smoked and heckled the kids and cheered the foreigners' every kick. By the time the alley dust was running down our torsos in rivulets of sweat, the night had been rescued, and a blush of peach was creeping into the early morning sky.

This Hanoi of surprises and gladness; these people of guile and unfathomable depths had captured my heart. It was no surprise to me that, apart from as guests of the Hanoi Hilton, the US military had failed to set foot in Hanoi. For an early Christmas present, they once dropped more bombs in two weeks on Hanoi, than fell on Berlin in the whole of World War Two. Further south, one of the underground villages which 18,000 people had burrowed out by hand, was hit by three specially designed penetration bombs; they failed to explode. The people dismantled the bombs and used them to make saucepans and other cooking utensils. The three entry holes were gratefully used as chimneys - to ventilate the village. They are an indomitable people.
I heard the clinking and clanking of those pots and pans as I drifted off to sleep, and I knew where my loyalties lay.

We sat in the fresh-cool of the Bi-Bi foyer, hiding from the wicked, wicked sun; even mad-dogs were under umbrellas. The burly security guard, naked to the waist, handed me a cassette. He was listening to Nirvana on Harry's Walkman and Harry was reading my Jack Kerouac; oh lackaday. Through the earphones, MC Solaar, Sensor, Cookie Crew and the baddest sounds from deepest dark Chicago, LA, Brooklyn and Brixton, poured forth. What joy. Into this wonderful cacophony of squealing children, adults winking smiles at us - sharing music and food, came the lazy, balding, Australian slob of a landlord, and he swept them all out into the street leaving Harry and I alone.

Once again a room shrank with lack of humanity. The light faded. Little Diep was outside - mouthing 'Howie' through the window, so just to annoy the landlord, I went to the door, crouched on the step and gathered a clutch of gigglers around me. They stroked my amber pendant, my arms and my heart.

'They're all thieves you know.' said the slob...'I hear you and Harry are going to Halong Bay; you don't want to go there... the water's freezing.'

❖

So, I rolled onto my back, swimming lazily in the tepid waters of Halong Bay. I swam through an archway, its stalactites dripping, and into an auditorium. The cliffs rose sheer above, and this natural bowl was flooded with sun that bounced around and plunged in and out of the water like a dolphin. Still paddling backwards with my ears under the water, I was hearing unmentionable clicks and pings. The sky above was an indigo plate, and there - stencilled just off centre was a hawk, each dorsal feather clearly defined. Blinking the salt from my eyes, the plate was wiped clean again.

Harry and I had decided that we needed to see the sea, and had taken a trip. This was a proper resort, where the visitors were wealthy Vietnamese from Hanoi - engineers, doctors and their chubby offspring, sporting baseball caps, American football shirts and the inevitable Marlboro dangling from their lips. Because we were on an organised tour with a guide, we were feeling like tourists. It was like taking a holiday away from a holiday, but we enjoyed the break; the fresh air floating above the sea, playing about on boats, playing in the sea - playing at being tourists.

The trip back to Hanoi was in a tiny minibus, and we tried to relieve the torment by standing, squirming - anything to gain some room for our screaming legs - sticking heads out the window to gulp air. It wasn't a long trip compared with the buses I'd taken in China, it wasn't even hard seat, but it was the most painful trip; the minibus too small for Europeans and I suspect even for the Vietnamese.

As we rolled to a stop in front of The Old Dahling Café and seeing the cyclos scuttling past - all leg room and spinning spokes, the seats open to the damson sky, I embraced my beloved Hanoi with a fond and relieved sigh.

Sitting around in a post trip gathering, the talk turned to the subject of the Embassy parties, to which the English amongst us said - 'What?'

Apparently, the Australians had a gathering at their Embassy every Friday, which by all accounts wasn't quite a wine & cheese party but was still fairly convivial. The French entertained their countrymen with their own rustic cheeses, saucisson, and Bordeaux by the crystal glassful. The Swedes, who had the largest Embassy, encompassing furniture shops, saunas and a swimming pool, laid on a smorgasbord as big as Stockholm. Considering that the British Embassy wasn't even on the map, we speculated as to the nature of our 'soiree'.

We decided we would need to take a carrier bag of Special Brew, so we could get 'lashed' before arrival. This would be necessary to dull the disappointment of limp cheese sandwiches, served with Courage Pale Ale in plastic beakers, by staff with fags hanging from their mouths.

After twenty minutes we would stagger out into the street where a kebab van would have been supplied, to make us feel at home. After throwing up, we could crawl home across Hanoi, leaving a trail of salad and pitta bread along the road, and chilli sauce down our clothes.

Having read many a Graham Greene novel and also having a genuine query concerning the X-Ray machine at the airport, I set out next day to find the *little corner of England in this foreign land*. It wasn't difficult to find - I just followed the trail of salad and pitta bread across Hanoi.

Arriving at Sunday lunchtime, I found that they were of course - shut. In fact they were shut for Sunday and Saturday, and half-day closing on Wednesdays. I almost reached for my ration book. By luck, as I hung my arms through the wrought iron gate, pushing my forehead against the rails in an effort to read the tiny plaque on the door, a Range Rover pulled up behind me. The occupant slid out - in standard issue, tropical Embassy attire; white short sleeved shirt (pen in pocket), shorts, socks and brown sandals. The whole outfit blended with the pink skin to suggest an ice cream sundae. I said 'Hullo.' – not adding the 'old chap', as I thought it would sound facetious.

'Hullo old chap,' he retorted, 'I'm afraid we're closed... Sunday lunch you know; what seems to be the problem?'

I explained that I may have stupidly put my films through the ancient x-ray machine at Hoi-Ban airport, which could detect bombs bigger than a doodlebug, propagate cancer, and possibly explode your films.

He 'hmmmm'd for a long time, pulling on a beard he didn't have.

'Come in and park your behind a moment, I'll think of the right man to have a natter with.' The right person was Terry, at the South China Post, whom he immediately phoned.

'Terry old boy - got a small problem. Actually - have a chappy here with a problem. Rather nervous that he's put his films through a dodgy x-ray machine, any clues?... mmm... mmmmm,' and all the time he was nodding at me with reassuring smiles, 'mmm... yaaass... champion! Oh well done, thank you, thank you.'

He dropped the phone back on its hook exclaiming *'piiingg!'* as though - twenty years earlier, his last English phone had a 'ping' and this one should have one also. Swivelling sideways and leaning back at 30 degrees, hands locked behind head - brown sandal crossing brown sandal, he addressed the ceiling fan.

'Well young man, we can allay your fears. Terry has pronounced the Hanoi x-ray - o-kay! haw, haw, haw.'

I stood up to leave the office. 'Many thanks for your time.'

'Not at all,' he said, pulling the cork from a brandy bottle with a squeak, '...it's my job you see.' The sunlight dashed through the facets of the crystal glass, cherry brown, as the brandy tumbled in. I like to think that he lit a cigar to complete his Sunday lunch after I had left.

❖

Elbows leant on the rusty rail of our dormitory balcony, I looked down through the spider's web of telegraph wires that radiated from a post below, and then to my left - watched two little girls argue; their voices shrill and staccato, like moorhens bickering. A slap echoed along the alley, bouncing off the walls of Hang Chai, and one of the girls' face snapped skywards with the blow.

'Oyyy!!' I shouted down, the sound of it stopping the bout. They stuck their tongues out at me, wriggling their behinds, then laughing, ran off up the alley - arms around each other's shoulders; friends.

Leaning against the wall opposite was a motorbike, a 'For Sale' sign around its neck - like a slave. As had happened in lovely Yangshuo, I was at last growing tired of being in the same place. It was time for me to move on.

With sudden interest, I skipped down to the bar and grabbing a chill glass of lemon, stood in the doorway, all but my toes in the shade, eyeing the motorbike. It had recently arrived; ridden the 1500 miles up from Saigon by an Irishman called Ian; I had an irresistible urge to turn it around and take it back.

A plan had come out of nowhere. It was a ridiculous idea built on a flimsy foundation; perhaps I was turning into a traveller at last! I was going to spend 300 dollars on an old Russian bike, ride it through Vietnam alone and sell it for the same amount in Saigon before my plane left the runway; hopefully without me chasing after it, the bike parked forlorn and ownerless at 'Departures' - crying two-stroke tears.

She was a Minsk 250 - Russian, I called her Minx. The Vietnamese called her 'shit', and as I was to find out... she was.

Harry, looking forlorn, hissed like a pressure cooker. 'Shhiiiitt!... I want to cancel my Laos flight. I should be doing that; riding across Vietnam on a motorbike -goddamn I envy you!' Others in the Bi-Bi bar nodded agreement in French and Belgian - and some in sympathy.

'What an adventure you will have, on your own, going the opposite way to everybody else here - four shore.'

My stomach turned over and I smiled weakly. I wanted Harry's plane ticket to Laos very badly at that moment.

❖

MINX, HIGHWAY ONE

The night guard crept into our room at 7.00am, wearing only his Mickey Mouse boxer shorts, and cooed 'Howie, Harry!'
Our separate trips were about to begin, and though still half-bathed in sleep, panic swept over me.
I had two cold showers whilst packing, and still reached the ground floor soaked in sweat. I tried to force down some food, but it forced me to the toilet, where I sat head in hands, gagging and sweating. I didn't have the courage to set off and even my singular team-talk failed.
'Come on! You're a big boy now; pull yourself together, you can't stay here for ever, you've bought the bloody motorbike!'
But I was a quivering jelly; almost crying like a baby. Harry jumped into his air-conditioned taxi for the airport and I managed to slaughter a goodbye.
'I'll let you know how I get on Harry. I'll see you somewhere.'
'Goodbye... you lucky bastard.' said Harry, as he closed his door with a thunkk! I sat for another hour in the bar, greeting my fellow inmates as they crept down from sleep to daytime Hanoi.
'Not gone yet?' they asked one by one.
'No, I thought I'd take it easy the first day.'

Eventually, after several false starts, I stood up, the plastic chair stuck to my arse, and strapping my bags to Minx, enraptured a growing crowd of Hang Chai dwellers with a performance of 'melting into a puddle' in front of their very eyes. They almost applauded. Flinging out goodbyes and sweat at everyone, I kick-started Minx, who obligingly roared into life, surprising me and terrifying the small boy who'd been sitting next to the exhaust. I wobbled the 50 metres down to the main road, quickly realising that the wobble was Minx - and not me. The front suspension was lethal; so turning with difficulty, I scurried back to the hostel, sweat drying by the second; saved by the suspension. An embarrassed Ian and I watched later, as a bevy of mechanics laughed a new pair of front struts into Minx, and giggled as they pointed out other disasters they had found. As compensation of sorts, Ian offered me some advice over a meal.
'You realise that Vietnam has only been open to tourists for a year?'
I hadn't. 'Up until now, you could only travel around Vietnam by reporting to the police station at each destination and taking a guide along with you to the next. You also had to report out of each town on

leaving. Well that has changed; but they don't seem to have told everyone yet; you will be challenged here and there.' Great.

'Oh, and Policemen will make you stop by waving a red and white baton at you. This means stop. This is when they will ask you for money to let you carry on. You can pay up, or waste a lot of time being interrogated until you pay up; OR you can pretend you didn't see the red and white stick – and hope they don't come after you.' Great.

'Oh... and also keep an eye on your tools; you'll need them.' Great.

But, I had gained another night to steel my elastic nerves, and the next morning the sweat that darkened my shirt was due to the temperature, and not rising panic. I cockily ate a fruit salad, and saying goodbye to the one traveller in the bar, rode out of Hang Chai. I made it to the lake - half a mile away, where Minx flopped to a halt. Tinkering with every unnecessary bit I could find - trying to look knowledgeable, I was joined by an old man who looked young, or a young man who looked old, I just couldn't tell which. He was a bicycle repairman and had a large, oilskin pouch containing dull steel tools, which he laid out on the pavement in a fan.

We cleaned the sparkplug, checked the wiring, screwed in the mixture screw, screwed it out again. The postcard sellers, who'd been steadily gathering, had lost interest in selling cards by now and were also tinkering. The old/young man flew at them when they started to use his tools, and as he wielded the largest spanner above his head, they scattered. They returned though - like carrion to a road-kill, and he gestured for me to push the bike. We wheeled the little bitch round the corner into a lagoon of quiet, and the arms of a proper mechanic. My man and his man huddled over the engine, eventually called me over to indicate that Russian petrol taps worked the opposite way to the rest of the world. I slapped their backs, shook their smiling hands, and we shared cigarettes as they poked and pointed at Minx - looking at me with obvious concern.

I smacked Minx out of Hanoi on Highway One, with shiny sneering Hondas all round me, and set to my task, weaving in and out slalom like - only 1800 miles to go. I bucketed along, trucks bowling by and hitting me with a wind like the blow of a fist.

I had cleverly chosen the hottest part of the Vietnamese summer in which to ride. Huang, the young waiter in Yangshuo, had predicted it graphically to me.

'Huang... is China always this hot in June?' I'd asked, sitting under the Jacaranda tree, where a dappling of shade fell onto me like a cold compress. He nodded, stony-faced.

'July?' ... 'Hotter.'
'August?' ... 'Much hotter. But Vietnam even hotter than August!'
As I left the outer limits of Hanoi, the surrounding crowds thinned in proportion to the increase of potholes. Most of these were avoidable, but in particularly bad patches or lapses in concentration, I would slam into holes big enough to bathe a baby. With the weight of the backpack strapped to the petrol tank, the suspension would hammer into the frame, leaving both the pack and myself momentarily airborne, the shock having travelled up my spine. At times I resembled a Rodeo rider, as Minx bucked and bolted across the road, the engine whinnying when the wheels were off the ground.

All traffic now seemed to be trucks or buses, the latter travelling at the same speed as me. Following close behind, I would be in a maelstrom of dust and flying grit, which would force me to overtake. Travelling at only a few miles per hour faster, I would crawl alongside the bus, turning the heads of the passengers. I'd now be in a desperate race, as the rest of the passengers would be called over to my side to look. This would unbalance the bus, veering it towards me. Many times, with Minx on the grubby verge of the ditch, and the bus inches from my right handgrip, I would wring the life out of the throttle to gain a last morsel of power, and pop out into clear space like a cork from a bottle.

I managed to sneak glances at the passing countryside between traumas. At this stage my goal was to put miles between Hanoi and myself, and keep the gap between Minx and me minimal. The region was featureless, spreading out table flat, with only a faint grey smudge on the horizon to suggest a landscape. The route was ticked off by telegraph poles, none of which were upright. At rare points the road ran through small groves, which hung over to meet above the road and cast cool, green shade. These flashed past in a blink of the eye.

The paddy fields ran right up to the edge of the road, brown stalks sticking up from brown water, held in by brown banks; the odd green shoot - an emerald flash in the corner of my eye - like a diving Kingfisher.

Fifty metres apart, on their own islands, stood shacks, or houses; each one linked to the road by a dirt causeway or a bridge made of railway sleepers. Each one was a family. Each one was a business. At the front of the shack by the road would be a small display cabinet; the top half glass, the bottom tin, with stickers of worldwide brands. In each cabinet could be seen several cans of soft drink; Pepsi, Fanta and Coca-Cola, their splendid liveries faded to pastel from being left on the shelf. These normally shared their shelf with a roundel of processed cheese triangles, a cow on the front, leaping and shaking its bell across long-forgotten Alpine pastures. Once I stopped and turned back, as alongside the usual offerings was a pot-noodle. Someone had anticipated the coming of the backpackers. The cabinets punctuated the whole length of Highway One; the longest convenience store in the world. Each shack was the same.

❖

As I pass by, the smell of dry stones and sunburnt bushes fills my nose; a mother stirs greens in her wok with a SSSSHHHH!! and acrid smoke rises from the burning oil, drawing a veil across her face. A child, from head to toe - the colour of the road dust, lifts his T shirt and scratches his round and stretched belly. The man bends over a wheel, stretching on a rubber tube, using spoons as tyre levers. The transistor radio sits on a shelf with a rusty oilcan, talking mumbo-jumbo and spitting out songs. Gravel from my wheel, peppers a chicken, which flaps into the sullen air - beating it into life with flapping wings. Inside, shaded from the world, an old man lays dying. In the sales cabinet by the road, the carton of cheese slices weeps.

❖

For hour after hour I rode on, leapfrogging trucks and buses. The slowest of the buses lay on their side in the ditches, one aflame - its passengers seated along the verge watching the show. My arms and thighs were burning despite the total sun-block that I'd applied, my shoulders popping at the sockets with the strain of hanging on, and my arse was nowhere to be felt. I had to stop.

Along a deserted stretch of road, I spied a bamboo shelter, and slowing - drove straight through the opening and into the shade. I cut the engine and through red-rimmed and dust-caked eyes, as the gloom lightened, I saw a boy lying inches from my front wheel, legs tucked up to his stomach, hands curled around his head. As cheerily as I could I called... 'Chao Em! - Anh!' (Hello young person – I am English).

One frightened eye appeared from behind the hands and blinked. I busied myself, wiping off the grimy sweat, applying more cream, and bashing the dust from my hat and neckerchief against the bamboo wall. He stood up and watched me, hands twisting together behind his back. Unfolding my decrepit map, (which came free with the bike) I asked him if I was going in the right direction. My sudden appearance had struck him dumb, as did the map of Vietnam, which in hindsight he may never have seen before. He stayed silent. Taking down my shorts, he looked the other way (rather gentlemanly I thought) and I pulled on my trousers to cover my tomato-coloured thighs. This left only the beetroot arms to stare at, and perhaps he thought I needed medical attention fast, as he suddenly pointed in the direction I was going, and after finger-jabbing at the floor, and then me, and the map, showed me that I'd covered less than an inch on a map that could have been used for a tablecloth. I was beat. The boy was an idiot - surely.

I fished my bottle of water (sterilised with a tablet the night before) from my backpack and drank. It was hot, and tasted of plastic and chemicals. I held it out to the boy who drank without complaint or grimace. I sat propped against the wobbly wall and, lighting up a cigarette, offered him a drag. His face broke into a smile and he dropped down to sit next to me, taking the cigarette between dirty fingers and blowing blue smoke into the chinks of light that wriggled through the bamboo. We spread the map over our laps, pointed to names, reading them to each other pointlessly. Then, using the little yellow book, we carried on a phrasebook conversation. He mimed eating and pointed at me, and thinking.. 'That would be welcome.' I read out... 'Yes please.' from the book.

'No.' he indicated, and pointed at my pack; he wanted food. Seeing that I had none, he rose, and after shaking my hand, set off towards Hanoi. I noticed that as he turned the bend he was a diminishing silhouette against a crimson-flecked sky; the sky to my right was a charcoal juggernaut rolling in for the night. It was too late to try to reach Sam Son; I decided to stay put. I watched the sunset until dark swallowed up the hut, listening to my walkman and smoking. I pulled Minx across one of the corners and curled up behind it on the dirt floor - backpack for a pillow. The thunder of trucks passing by thinned, but each one woke me from a half-sleep with a start; in between trucks, the only sound was of reeds brushing up against each other - hissing at the warm night breeze.

I woke with a start, sweating - banging my head on a foot pedal which knocked Minx over. I ran out to the road cursing and stamping and holding my head. The sky, almost a false blue, stretched to receive the heat of the day. It was already hot, and by the time I'd applied sun cream, wheeled Minx out, strapped my pack on and started her up, I was already panting like a dog in the road.

I set off, doubtful of my location, and after stopping at several hanky-sized shadows and asking passing cyclists to look at the map, it was confirmed. The boy had been right; I hadn't got very far. I stuck to my task, basted my arms, and rode on with swarms of bees raging inside my fingers. Approaching a rare bend in the road, I found with horror that the handlebars were no longer attached to the bike. I squeezed the disconnected brake lever, the back end snaking in the loose gravel, and leaning as gently as possible to the left, hit the footbridge to the next shack, missing the ditch. Minx flick-flacked left and right, and throwing me to the floor, ground a tricycle into the dust. I sat up and seeing the cogs and wheels, inner tubes and spokes hung on the outside wall, realised that I'd crashed right outside a bicycle repairman's shack.

He must have dreamt of this day; he was laughing as he pulled Minx from the floor, wheels still spinning. He almost hugged the crushed tricycle, and held it up with glee to show the children, who had now gathered in a row outside the shack. The neighbours had also arrived, laughing and shouting and dusting me down. I was holding up the handlebars like the head of a guillotine victim, the sinews and tendons still attached. My host bore a striking resemblance to Elvis Presley and wore a crisp, white T shirt, but he set to straightaway to fix Minx, with the help of his friends. She was stripped of her outer clothes then her underwear, and was poked and prodded with steel. I hoped it hurt. I tried to help, but they waved me away, made me sit in the shade; brought tepid tea. I decided to entertain the crowd of women and children. I pulled faces, tweaked little ears, sweated profusely for them. Elvis showed me the retaining washer that had sheared off, and then a bicycle equivalent that he proposed to alter to fit. I gave him the thumbs up - relieved.

As they hammered and sawed, cursed and spat, the afternoon wore on. I stood, sat, tinkered with the engine, drank tea, and tea, and tea; translated words from the phrasebook. In this way I managed to explain who I was, where from, how old, what I did for a job - to the procession of spectators that filed past on their way through life. The day dwindled down and with it my hopes of getting to Som San - a beach resort where I could eat, drink and sleep. Flicking through the book I had a sudden inspiration, and under 'sickness' I found what I was looking for. Getting to my feet, I announced to the remnants of the crowd and the mechanics that this bike was 'behn ia chay' – diahorrea! and mimed kicking her to death. It was the best joke I'd told in my life. The crowd were in hysterics; I thought they would harm themselves. I suddenly felt a little better. Perhaps here was a way to help myself through the difficult times.

Dusk fell quicker than a tart's knickers, and they put Minx's clothes back on under a ten watt light bulb. They'd fixed the handlebars, but as revenge for her treatment, Minx wouldn't start. They threw spanners and screwdrivers around in frustration, but carried on tinkering, as I sat, head against bamboo, falling into a slumber brought on by hunger and the ride. Elvis shook me gently awake some time later, defeat in his eyes, quiff flat, 'T' shirt blackened, and indicated that Minx was still dead, by pulling a finger across his throat.

I shook his hand, and then motioned 'sleep here?' pointing at the floor of the workshop. He shook his head. I found 'cheap hotel' in the phrase book. He shook his head. He strapped my pack to the back of his Honda, motioned me onto the pillion, and off we went - south. We rode for half an hour under a cloud-shagged moon, lamps twinkling off to each side in the paddies like fireflies, the only things visible in the dark.

As we approached the feeble glow of a small town, Elvis pulled off to the left and up to a set of closed gates, which barred the entrance to a large hotel. It looked like a communist workers' holiday camp, and there was no other entrance. A chink of light grew into a flood that blinded us, as the door to a small office next to the gate swung open.

From somewhere in the light I heard a gruff request, and gesturing me to stay where I was, Elvis disappeared into it. After a short but lonely time he reappeared, and taking me firmly by the elbow, led me into the office. Although bright in the outside gloom, the room was dimly lit by a single bulb. The shade had a piece missing, as if chomped out by something that ate glass. I took in the bars on the window, the solid wooden bed, the uniform of my interrogator behind the bare desk, and Elvis shrinking into the corner, face agog with fear. The guard asked for my passport and called in a colleague to look at it. They scrutinised each page and indicated for me to open my daypack. The guard shifted through the contents, expressionless, whilst his friend leafed through the phrase book, and then became engrossed with my Walkman. I decided it would be worth losing if I was in trouble.

'I would like to pay the bill.' the guard read from the phrasebook. The other had the earphones on and was mumbling to a tune.

'Where is the shoe shop?' asked the linguist. I looked to Elvis who, holding up three fingers, pointed up the road.

'Is it an express train?' I was hoping Elvis meant that there was a hotel three miles up the road, or a guesthouse for three dollars. It occurred to me that I may be about to get three years.

'Do you have cheese?'

And at this the guard smiled broadly, and handed back the book. He pulled the plug from the Walkman, and taking it from his now sulking friend, repacked my pack. He led me to the door, and pointing into the darkness said 'LOTOBA'. Elvis had already started his bike, and was moving. I hopped on whether he liked it or not and we sped on further into town; a clutter of cafes, shacks and tyre dumps, lit by strings of white lights. Near to the centre, we stopped outside what resembled a communist workers' holiday camp. Elvis came in with me and explained the situation, and though they were shocked by the small amount of money I wanted to pay, allowed me to stay. The owner explained that it was a truckers' hostel, and looking round the motley collection of grimy men, seated around on steel chairs and plastic sofas, all looking at me, I was pessimistic of reaching the morning with my arse intact, or with any belongings.

It was a gem though, a haven, a palace. It was a family suite with a fridge, air-con and fans, bed linen, and a wood panelled ceiling a long way above the Princess mosquito net, which wafted away any strays that had chanced the arctic temperature. It could have accommodated twelve backpackers comfortably.

I hadn't eaten for two days now, and had no appetite, but I knew that I had to get something inside if I was to survive the journey; besides, I needed beer so that I could at least stay sane. I hid my cameras in the mosquito net cabinet, and checking the door-lock several times, tripped across the strip to the row of non-descript cafes. They saw me coming. Each proprietor was at his or her doorway, leaning like dominoes, eager, smiling, hopeful. I had to choose one and quick, as I'd run out of road to cross. Providence lent a hand, and delivered a small pothole into which I could stumble. Falling forward, hands outstretched, I was caught by a tiny lady who'd rushed from her doorway. Thanking her, I sat down on one of the small stools and ordered a beer, to gain some time to work out the food issue. I smiled at the neighbouring proprietors, whose faces were set in stone, and took a little bet with myself that the pothole would be filled in tomorrow.

Before I could even hazard a request, the old crone was shovelling things into a tall glass. I leant across in the semi-darkness and saw the glass filling with cod's roe, olives, raspberry jam, sheep's eyes, and a topping of grated Cheddar. She handed it to me, smiling, and the two police officers at the next table fixed me with a deathly stare, their mouths still chewing. I saw that the bottom portion was ice so, plunging the spoon through all the shit, scooped some out and forced it into my mouth, waiting to gag or retch. It was a fruit cocktail, with coconut topping: but it was like no fruit I'd ever seen or tasted. I also got cold beer, and so, managed to make the meal look enjoyable. One of the policemen reached over and without word or gesture, handed me a cigarette. Was this a reward - or payment for another performance?

My usual audience had now gathered around, below and above me, as Vietnamese stools are only six inches high. This position put my knees up beside my ears, whilst my forearms were still on the floor: a Barbary ape with glasses.

The crowd always gathered in the same order. An eight year old boy would sit next to me (they could always speak some English) and find out where I was from, going to, how old I might be and sometimes how much I earned per fiscal year. His initially shy friends would move in and sit, and then growing bolder, stroke my arm, leg or hair. An adult would then approach, and having got the details from the boy, shake my hand or squat down on his haunches to smile at me and listen. This would be the signal for any other grownups to join in the circle.

At this point (adding more as I travelled down the country), I would do the coin trick that Guy, the Israeli, had taught me in Yangshuo. It was a simple sleight-of-hand trick which never failed to amaze. The men, being great gamblers, would then elbow the kids aside shouting 'Get thee behind!' or something like that. I would do the trick until one of them spotted the secret, and then ecstatic, he would either let on, or clam-up; either way the pressure was off me. The routine carried on as it always did. Stage two.

The initial boy, still holding my hand, now asked, 'You like her?' - pointing to the person now seated to my left, who I hadn't yet seen.

'You want her ... five dollars?'

I turned sideways to look at the beauty that I knew would be there. She was gorgeous, stunning, with head held coy. 'She work your hotel.' Her hair shone even in the dark. 'Four dollars?' he asked.

She looked the most innocent girl in the world. Tearing my eyes from her I asked him, 'I suppose she's your sister?'

'Yes' he said - 'three dollars?' At a quick reckoning she was about the fiftieth 'sister' I'd been offered since I left home, and I'd refused them all. Would this be the first I would say yes to? After two days of fighting Minx and the weather, I was filthy and beat; a hot bath and company would be very welcome, but the cockroaches were going to be packing their bags when I took my boots off. I had nappy rash, hadn't eaten much, and had to get up early, but there was a stronger reason for declining – I would be the only foreigner in a hotel full of truckers, sleeping with one of their girls. I said no.

I retired gracelessly, back across the road, but slept like Valium, in anticipation of Elvis turning up at noon.

He meant nine. Sitting outside honking on Minx's horn, he had me scurrying around at five past, trying to clean my teeth, pack my backpack and put on my stinking clothes. It was a scumbag that walked out that midsummer morning, all burnt and scrawny and raggedy-rawny. The delight on Elvis's face told the story. Minx had been fixed; allegedly. So I thanked him and pulled ten dollars from my pocket, asking 'Is that enough?' with my face. From the look he gave me and the gathered truckers, it was more than enough. I roared away up the road, back on track again, the morning air whistling freshly past my ears: for two miles. Minx hated me. I hated her. We rolled to a halt on a bare strip of road, the exhaust ticking as it cooled; the day warming. I sat on the pillion smoking angrily, as the caravan that was Highway One passed by. A man stopped, said hello, and then passed out of my life for ever. The fields, which here at least were as green as a Somerset pasture, gave off a whiff of clover and the bitter tang of dandelion; but there wasn't a moo-cow in sight. I pushed Minx for a half-mile and rested. I was beginning to learn the nature of the heat, dashing from shade to shade like a Red Indian creeping up in ambush; then standing still, waiting for nothing.

Cyclists trundled by shouting encouragements or insults back at me, and the honking of bus and truck horns alerted the next bicycle repair shop, who came down the road to meet me. They pushed Minx into their workshop, and me into a chair under the fan in the bar next door. Bringing lemon water, they quizzed me as usual, and I spent the next two hours being laughed at, or with, while I worked through my expanding repertoire. Looking on at the gang repairing Minx, I pointed to the largest of the men and gestured for him to hold the back of the bike. I took the arm of the fiercest looking, and pulling him to the front, put his hands on the handlebars. The crowd looked puzzled as I mimed picking it up. The two men did.

'Now,' I mimicked swinging it, 'Mot ... Hai ... Ba ... throw it in the paddy field!' Then pointing at it - 'Litso (Russian) - it is shit!' They suddenly saw the joke, hooted and hollered, took turns pretending to throw it.

'Right,' I said, as Minx eventually fired into life, 'it's been a lovely Sunday lunchtime, but I must go. How much do I owe you?' and unfolding my wallet, the photo of Bumble kept me there for another twenty minutes.

'Five dollar.' said the lemon juice boy.

'Two dollar.' said the mechanic. My patience was wearing thin.

'No sunshine, you've got it round the wrong way, He gets the five, you get two, and that's over the top.' His face flushed with temper, but the mechanic's friends rounded on him for trying to rip me off. The mechanics were happy. I didn't give a shite.

As I rode off up the road, I began to realise why Minx was such a mess. In her trips up and down Vietnam, she'd been raped and pillaged repeatedly and just wanted to lie down and die. I may have to let her do that at some point, but in the meantime, I would coax her like a sick foal as far as we could go.

SAM-SON BEACHES

Minx managed to keep going for another few hours, but arriving at Sam Son, our destination, she coughed and spluttered down the beach road, rolling to a halt with a final wheeze outside a cafe. Lounging in a deckchair to my right, with mirrored sunglasses glaring, his Hawaiian shirt shouting, was a man gesturing me to sit down.

'Can I sleep here, giuong (bed)?' I asked, miming sleep and pointing upstairs above the bar.

He gestured for me to sit down, called the owner over, and offered me a drink using mime.

Putting Minx on her stand I answered - 'Beer... I'll have a beer... a big one.' I offered him a cigarette and then passed them out to his friends, who'd been eyeing my packet of Silk Cut hungrily. I lounged back in the deckchair and let out a long 'aaaaagggghhhh'. He smiled, but was still silent. Anger suddenly shot through me; not a rage, but a cool, deliberate, dull feeling.

'Excuse me,' I said to my companion, putting my beer down on the olive green oilcloth, 'I have to do something.' I walked from the shade onto the burning pavement, which wound me up further, kicked Minx Kung-Fu style into the middle of the road, and put the boot in: one for each tyre. Leaving her there, and ignoring the open mouths, I returned to my deckchair and new friend, who I noticed had a larger smile now. We sat silent together for a long time, watching the holiday-makers parade, his eyes cool and shaded, mine red-rimmed and gritty. If I could have seen them, I would have noticed that a certain mad glare had crept in. Periodically he flicked a casual finger to point out a girl, and once to see off a group of James Dean styled youth who had stopped to stare at me.

The finger told two of his cohorts to go and bring in Minx from the dust, petrol trickling from her tank. Another climbed aboard his new Honda, motioning me to join him. Looking at 'The Godfather', he nodded assent.

'Food.' the driver threw back at me, as we spun through the town.

And then I was sitting alone in a restaurant with his family, their dog watching me with its head cocked to one side. They brought a dish of rubbery chicken; yellow, tight skin, and sticky rice wrapped in leaves. It was good food and I tried to force it into my shrunken stomach. I tried hard, I really did, but I could only manage a little. Taken back to the bar, staggering with exhaustion, I asked again if the place had rooms. The sunglasses flashed and the finger pointed to the hotel opposite, rising five storeys above the street-stalls. It looked like a refugee from Beirut. Nearly finished or almost demolished (difficult to tell which), it had been built by the Russians, and was damned ugly. But it was a hotel, and obviously upmarket, in a resort where it appeared that anything over two storeys would leave the occupants giddy. Sam-Son was a holiday haunt for office workers and families with money from Hanoi, so I told The Godfather that I couldn't afford it; eight dollars was my top price for accommodation (That was actually above my budget, but I didn't want to look too cheap). He smiled, perhaps thinking I was joking, and signalled two of his men to take me over there, one pushing Minx. I thanked him and offered him the rest of the Silk Cut. Shaking his head, he took a packet of Marlboro from his pocket and showed them to me. Of course; America number one! I took my packet back, and pointing to his, said in Vietnamese, 'Shit!' He smiled so wide, I thought his gold tooth would fall out.

The reception was huge, its keeper tiny, with a shock of black curls. He was filling in the register, which was a vast blackboard with the hotel drawn in plan. The occupants' names were chalked into each box with different colours. Stopping in his task, as my minders explained the situation, he grunted and turned back to it. I shouldered my backpack and shrugging at my friends, headed for the door. One of them tugged at my sleeve... 'Twelve dollars for room.'

'No,' I said, 'eight dollars only.' Half way down the front steps I heard... 'Nine dollars!' His face was spread with concern, and I didn't want to make trouble for him and The Godfather so I said ... 'OK'.

He took and me and Minx to the security guard's hut, and explained that the guard would fix her for me and I was to go and leave him to it. So off I went on the long climb to the top floor and my room. I expected to be sharing it with Charles Manson or The Adams family, but no; I had another family suite to myself, albeit devoid of any trimmings - apart from the solid wooden board bed.

I stepped out onto the balcony to view the resort, legs quivering, head spinning, and reached for the rusty railing for support. Below was a checkerboard of simple roofs; clay tiled, tin sheeted, flat concrete, and scattered amongst them like coolies, were straw-hat huts and shacks; the kitchens, food stalls, and bars of the resort, blue smoke seeping through their thatch. From these arose a clamour of a hundred karaoke machines, all blasting their own tune, each one out of tune.

The buildings crept up to the concrete promenade, where ponies and traps clip-clopped along between the holiday-makers, walking back and forth, up and down, left and right. Then a strip of dirty yellow sand, scattered with bodies that lay still in the sun, or moved around like Mexican jumping beans. In the water, which heaved sluggishly, the bobbing heads put up a great shriek, as if they were a flock of seabirds. This clamour mingled with the karaoke, and hit me like a soldier beating his drum.

I lay down on the hard boards of the bed, watching the ceiling fan spin, and when I closed my eyes the bed whirled round and round. I fell unconscious; sounds of Brighton and Littlehampton drifting through the window.

I woke with a start. Where were my cameras? They weren't in the room anywhere, nor were they in my backpack. I looked in my head and there they were; in the mosquito net cabinet at the trucker's hostel - crying. *I* was almost crying. I raced down the stairs, two storeys at a time, trying to get my head straight. Would Minx make it back? What if I broke down in the dark - the lights didn't work. Were the cameras still there? Who spoke any English here?

Lanh, the girl at the bar, apparently spoke a little English. I sat with her in the deep, plastic sofa by the bar, and using the little phrasebook, tried to explain what had happened. I had left 1000 dollars worth of cameras under a bed, whilst chasing around after a 200 dollar heap of Russian shit. It took an hour to try and cobble together the story, throughout which other staff and guests tried to help, some by just standing and staring - puzzled. Lanh pointed in the book to 'doctor', and I assumed this was because of the condition I was in.

'No, I don't want a doctor, I want my cameras back.' I almost wailed.

The doctor, it transpired, was on holiday, and could speak English; they were fetching him back from the beach. He appeared very quickly, still wearing his stripy Speedo trunks under a towelling beach robe. He spoke English.

'What was the name of the hotel?'

'I don't know – can't remember.'

'What town was it in?' I didn't know. It was clear they thought I was a complete idiot. I was.

'It may have been Tha Trung, Hong Trung, Nam Dihn, Tam Dinh.'

'You must sit quiet and try to remember the town. When you have, Lanh will ring the police there. They will go to the hostel and find the cameras as they know they can make you pay to get them back.' And leaving for the beach, he added...

'You don't look very well.'

I sat on the sofa trying to think; beating myself mentally with fist and boots, for being so stupid. Lanh and a friend sat with me, offering gentle comforts.

'Will find camera, police will find - be calm.'
Unfortunately their tenderness led me to the brink of tears, which upset them, and they held my hands; one each.

I went up to my room to give them a break from their vigil. A straggle of kids shouted over and over at me through the slatted door, their bright eyes shining through the gaps at different levels. I was in a dangerous condition. Each time I chased them away, they returned like flies disturbed from a corpse. The last time I almost caught them, but a shout from the woman next door saved them from a plummet six floors to the ground, from the end of my boot. Everyone in the hotel was trying to help, but I couldn't help myself. Everybody had an idea; I was a frigging celebrity. I went outside and sat on the hotel steps for air, the holidaymakers filing in from the beach with towels and rubber rings, and even buckets and spades. I went back to the sofa as twilight slipped into bed to prepare for sleep.

Sitting facing Lanh, a vision suddenly flashed through my mind. I had travelled back in time. I was squatting on a stool, staring at the beautiful sister who worked my truckers' hotel - and there just behind her was a ridiculous clock tower; its huge Art Deco letters stood proud and floodlit in the sky. It had a perfectly round O and the front stroke of the A curved; LOTABA. I looked into Lanh's eyes, so hopeful and sad, and whispered 'Lotaba'. With the biggest grin in Vietnam she squealed 'LOTABA HOTEL... HA TRUNG!' and the words floated over and around, through the whole hotel, and the people passed them down to the beach, where they were wrapped up in towels and brought back to the hotel. Lanh phoned the police, who were going to ring back at 9.00pm. I wouldn't be able to return until the morning even if they were still there, so I consoled myself with a beer. Sitting there, it dawned on me that if I'd lost my cameras, my pictures of China and my first friends, Hanoi and Thuy, Diep and Harry, had gone with them. I groaned inwardly, and achingly sad, went out into the night to try and eat a last supper before sentence was passed on me.

Down on the promenade, I picked the emptiest café, and a seat in the semi-dark, to avoid attention. I found Chicken and Rice in the phrasebook and ordered. By the time the two fried eggs arrived, alone on a plate, I had calmed down, and thanking the owner I tucked in with my chopsticks. My stomach had other ideas though, and only allowed me one egg. The owner looked disappointed when he collected the plate, but returned seconds later with a dish of nuts. I ate them one at a time, slowly, as I watched the passers-by and wrote, head down to hide my face, until 9 o'clock came round. I left, complimenting him on the meal and paying double. I wondered if, when more travellers passed this way, fried eggs with peanuts would be on the menu.

Reaching the hotel, I nervously climbed the front steps to where Lanh stood waiting, expressionless. Facing her at the top, she said...
 'You look happy Howie.'
 'No, Lanh, not happy.'
 'Yes,' she said, and it came - a dashing, twinkling starlight from out of the gloom ... 'camera was under bed in Lotoba!'
 LOTOBA. I loved that word. I loved it in English, I loved it in French, Vietnamese and in Art Deco. I was going to have it tattooed on my dick for luck.

❖

Whole families waved me off early in the morning, and I promised myself to come back later and thank everybody properly. Minx took me the whole way - almost. She coughed a final gasp with that magic word visible above the huddle of Ha Trung. Pushing Minx into the car park, I went in to claim my cameras. The police hadn't bothered to get involved, and left it to the manageress to give them to me. She seemed delighted for me, and handed them over, beaming. The swarthy truckers around the vinyl clad reception area were also beaming.

As I fiddled with the bike outside, a group of them joined in. They took over, and two hours later had found the problem. The key didn't work properly and was continually turning itself off. After I'd thank-thank-thanked them, we rode back to Sam-Son, as happy as two dead beats could, and displayed the errant cameras to the masses. They were all delighted for me. I owed these people something; if only to show my face around for their entertainment. I took off for the beach, a swim and food. Changing into my trunks, sarong wrapped tightly round, I was being watched by several hundred pairs of eyes, and as I swam around in the tepid sea, a vast shoal of little black heads surrounded and followed me, like pilot fish. Dried off by the sun, I walked amongst the lovely boys and even lovelier girls who paraded up and down the beach all day. Being an oddity, I was propositioned by each and every one. Now I knew what it was like to be a film star, a celebrity, public property: on call to all that pass by demanding a hello or a smile. It was damn tiring being a freak, performing a hundred times a day; but at the same time, it could be lovely. Later that day I was to reach megastar status.

I informed the mop-headed receptionist that I would be leaving in the morning and, packing my bag, slipped out for a meal. As I left the hotel

I glanced back, and the evening dusk made mirrors of the plate glass doors, in which I could be seen looking forlorn and skinny.

I returned to the 'fried egg' café and positioning myself at a prominent table, returned all the greetings sent my way. The owner's family had priority on the infamy, so quite rightly joined my table. They brought me a grilled fish, its dead eye staring at me like the locals, with rice and a bowl of chilli sauce, which they warned me was 'Hot hot!'
'Good good' I said.

The hotel guard had arrived and joined the table. He sat silent, and as I bought beers for the owner and myself, I included him as well. After an hour or so he started to look agitated, and rising, put his hand on my shoulder gently and hooked his thumb back up the road. The guard and the owner had a discussion which became heated, their arms and hands flying at each other, like two Sicilians arguing over the price of olives.
'He is arresting you. You must go to hotel -pay the bill.' Laughing, I looked at the guard, he shrugged his shoulders, with a very weak grin.
'Okay,' I said, nonplussed, 'take me in Deputy, I'll go quietly.'

He'd ridden down to the café on a now-fixed Minx, and putting on my Walkman, used my arrest as an excuse to cruise the town. Having paraded himself and me, we stopped at his favourite café. Here, surrounded by his peers, he really hammed it up; I helped him. We sat at a small table, legs outstretched, lounging like hoods. I put my cigarettes and lighter on the table, so that he could help himself without having to ask. As girls passed by or stopped to gawk, we played - 'That one is for you' and 'I'd like that one'. He'd ordered iced coffees, and to my delight, as I sipped it, I realised it was coffee-plus. The sting of a rough brandy cut through the creamy texture and mingled with the bitter tang of the beans. It hit the spot. Several of these arrived while we hung out, and on leaving, I reached for my wallet. He shook his head. They were on the house. We cruised a few more bars, increasing his kudos, and I realised as we wobbled down a fortunately quiet lane, also his drunkenness. I tapped his shoulder shortly after we'd passed the hotel the eighth time, indicating for him to pull over to the left.

I'd seen a flash of colour, and there, sitting in his usual chair, was 'The Godfather' - mouth smiling, but eyes still hidden by his sunglasses. I sat down next to him, noticing that the guard kept a distance. I offered him a Silk Cut, he offered a Marlboro. We smoked one of each other's, and as the waiter arrived, he motioned for two drinks.

'Three,' I said holding up the fingers, pointing at the guard...'one for him.' Three glasses of coffee-plus arrived. The guard remained standing and gulped his down, so I figured he was in a hurry.

Knocking mine back swiftly, I said...'Thank you, but I must go now.'

'What are you doing riding around the town with this idiot?' he asked. They were the first words I'd heard him utter. Shocked though I was, I answered - 'I'm under arrest.'

'What for?'

'I'm not sure.' I replied.

He barked at the guard, growled low in the throat then savaged him with a stream of sharp language... 'Bac dang fa ... fang cho mot an thuc thuc baaaahhh!' ... or something like that. He calmed down though, as the guard explained - hanging his head and muttering to the floor.

'He says that they thought you had left the hotel without paying. He was meant to take you straight back when he found you.'

'But my bags are in the room, how could I be leaving?'

'They don't have a spare key, so they couldn't check. You had better go back now or this fool will get in trouble. I will tell the manager how stupid he is tomorrow. I hope you have a good trip - though with that heap of Russian shit, you probably won't. Stop at Hoi An, you won't be disappointed.'

I shook his hand. He smiled, and although I had never seen them, I knew that the eyes behind the mirrored shades were kind. Crossing over to the hotel, the guard wheeled Minx into his bedroom, pretending to tuck her in for fun, and walked into the hotel with me. Entering the lobby, I saw that a good portion of the guests were gathered around the old TV, watching a dubbed, black and white, English film - the light flickering on their childlike faces. They turned, and to a man, woman and child - applauded. I bowed.

❖

THE RAILWAY HOTEL, VINH

An innocent light radiated over the beach that morning. As though affected by it, Minx pulled away from Sam-Son cheerfully, and we set to the task - knocking off the 150k to Vinh. She was eating them up for breakfast and humming a happy tune. The morning wore on in quite a jolly fashion, and then her smile slipped.

I was riding whole sections standing, to the amusement of my fellow travellers - to ease the pain in my back and my bruised arse. Passing a busy rice field, a whole paddy of workers raised their noses from the water as I bellowed the longest string of curses I could put together.

A policeman stepped out into the road ahead, waving a red and white stick at me. Remembering Ian's warning, I couldn't decide in time whether to stop. I sailed past, and pretending that his shouts were loud greetings, smiled broadly and waved back happily - as his stick waved frantically. I didn't look back, and expected the sirens to catch up with me - speeding on to Vinh; they didn't.

It was on my third breakdown that I rolled into the village. They streamed out to meet me, and pushed the bike and me to the menders. It was the biggest crowd yet, and something was wrong. They crowded round Minx, and I had to push to get through. The children, usually timid, pushed back at me and I saw my tools disappearing. I shouted for their return, and at once I had men each side of me, shouting into my face from four inches, spit flying. I saw then that their eyes were red-rimmed and vacant, and I was being baited. Turning to the phrasebook to explain, a woman - her eyes mad, and her Edward scissor-hands swishing through the balmy air, snatched it away from me. The mechanic jumped up, grabbed it back from her and passed it back to me. She stood, hands on hips, and spat at his feet. She launched a tirade at him and me, worrying at the words like a terrier. Something hit me on the back - hard.

The crowd were laughing, and with frightened eyes the mechanic indicated that I had to get away. We bent down to the engine, heads together as he screwed in the plug cap. He motioned - 'get out' with his thumb and kicked the engine over; she fired. He sensibly kept the throttle open with one hand while I took out my wallet. As they stepped back to make room for me to hand out money, I put it between my teeth and grabbed the throttle. I shot through the stalls and spat gravel over the dress circle, praying Minx wouldn't stall. She ran all the way to

Vinh without stopping. The mechanic? I hope he lives to be a thousand and people the earth with his offspring.

We arrived in Vinh a couple of hours before dark. The people didn't seem to know their way around their own town. I searched for the hostels recommended in the Lonely Planet. I was sent here and there, there and back, and with Vinh having absolutely no distinguishing features, I covered the city several times. I decided that I wouldn't be putting any roots down here.

Then, as the dark grew with my temper, I remembered the station. They had to know where that was; they didn't. I stumbled onto the railway tracks in the middle of a night market, rode along them to the station, and then through the waiting room into the forecourt. As there were a few shouts being hurled at me, I stopped the bike behind a bush, and walking quickly away, headed straight for the hotel that I could see glowing faintly in the corner. After a few sad attempts to ask for a room in Vietnamese, they fetched the owner who spoke some English.

'My son speaks English well,' he said, 'I will send him to talk to you later. This is room. Be careful to lock the door, station is a bad place - you should not be here!' Great.
'Oh stuff them all.' I thought, and went downstairs to sit outside the bar. The cool air was tinged with the smell of steel sparking onto flints, fuming diesel and wooden benches. I tried to calm down and relax with my cold beer, but within minutes three larrikins, hoods, had sat around, examining me. I stared straight at them, silently erupting, as they picked at my boots, pulled my gold ring and fingered my shirt.
'Don't do that!' I said calmly, brushing their hands away. I had my boot on a neighbouring chair: one of them pulled the lace undone. They weren't playing. I tumbled over the edge.
'DON'T TOUCH ME ARSEHOLE!' I was on my feet, 'or you'll be digging this ring out your arse...' I said to the first. I'm not sure how that would have worked. 'YOU can have my boot in your ear.' I said to the second - still seated on his stool.
'...and YOU!!' I shouted at the one who'd stood up first - 'cop this!' and I mimed a Glaswegian kiss. Unfortunately, either the drink or the tiredness had ruined my timing. My forehead smashed into his nose, and sparks flew inside my head. 'Oh shit!' He shot backwards over the stool, and expecting a full attack, I grabbed my beer bottle from the table and swung to face the other two, but they were disappearing away into the darkness. OK, they were just teenagers and I'm a grown man, but there *were* three of them.

I sat down on my stool, leaning back against the wall, and lit a cigarette; and if I'd looked in a mirror I would have seen a cold, grey, manic stare. Three large men moved over to my table. There was nothing I could do with these three.

'Oh ... fuck ... off.' I said, slowly and quite calmly - staring into space. They shot back on their stools, hands up in mock surrender, laughing at me. I smiled back, and holding my bottle to the moon, seeing that it was half full, remembered the Vietnamese drinking game - and said... 'Same same ... 50.' I tipped it down my throat, which meant they had to do the same. We were friends.

The moment that the three men had left, I was joined by Phuong - the owner's son, and his teacher.

'You keep very bad company.' said the teacher.

'Usually, yes,' I said, a bit drunk, '...it's a gift you're born with, it can't be taught.' I offered Phuong a cigarette, but he'd given up when he was fifteen; he'd started when he was ten. The rest of the evening was full of chatter, and their presence kept away any unwelcome guests. I went to bed like a zombie, but still felt enough unease about the earlier shenanigans to get my pocket knife out, and treble check the door lock.

I woke with the knife still tight in my hand, and used it to strip a Pomelo of its skin, pith and pips, which left little substance but tasted great. Shooting out to find the bank, and then a breakfast, I was stopped on my return by the hotel owner - who begged me to join them in a celebration.

Phuong was leaving today. He was going to Hanoi for two years to study English and Electronics, and the whole family were there to see him off. The men had been drinking since 7.00am, and the restaurant was rocking. As each man poured beer into their glass – they would pour an equal amount into mine, shout 'same-same!' and I was expected to drink it down as they downed theirs. By mid-day I had same-samed my head off, but fortunately the women arrived; with them came food. I was seated in the place of honour next to the son.

'One day we hope Phuong will be just like you.' said the mother.

'Poor bastard.' I said.

'Yes, one day.' she wistfully replied.

Dish after dish arrived; sticky rice, greens, chicken swathed in lemongrass buffeted by spring onion; plates piled high with tongue, and more strange shaped chicken with yellowy, rubbery skin attached, dangling, and to be eaten with gusto. The sister next to me, who had a bun in the oven – her third baby despite being only seventeen, handed me a piece with her chopsticks.

'I like this piece,' I said 'it even looks like a chicken.' Holding it by what looked like a comb, I twiddled it clockwise. The dead eye of a chicken looked up at my fingers holding its comb. There was no possibility of my swallowing this piece and keeping it down.

I mimed a chicken strutting along the table and jumping over a bowl of soup. I dropped it in the soup with a splash, and it swam like a headless chicken amongst the chopped chilli and onions; which must have stung its eye.

Rivers of beer ran around the table, most of which seemed to be flowing into my estuary; the drinking game carried on in earnest. The son had retired early after two bottles, but the father was shitfaced and practically cuddling me; 'You're a really good geezer, I really love you ... my son's going away for two years and he won't drink with me. You go to bed now and we will drink together this afternoon. I will come to your room.'

'I don't think so.' I thought, swiftly sobering.

But I was there at the table again, eating with the family, while they snatched dread glances at the clock - its hands marching on to 8.00, when Phuong would leave. They urged me to carry on eating and to ignore the running around, the preparations and the crying of the older sisters and aunties. At last it was time, and Phuong appeared at the door with his meagre belongings in a tin box, a hush creeping over the room. He was only a boy, but he was kind, handsome, clever, and much loved ... and it doesn't come much better than that in any old language. He had a great future ahead. He said his goodbyes and turned into the darkness. The father - next to me, gamely reached for a piece of meat and attempted to remain stoic. The tears running down his cheeks gave the game away, and he reached under the table and held my hand. It was then I realised that he looked like my Dad, and suddenly I missed him dreadfully, felt very alone, and cried like a baby.

❖

I looked out into the station yard with clearer eyes and mind, watching the early morning scuttling of the people. The pregnant sister had put me to bed, and stroked my head until I slept. The madness that had been growing in me over the last few weeks had been washed out by the tears and the tenderness of a stranger. It was time to carry on.

Whilst packing my bag, I saw that there was a great treasure missing. Robert Smith and The Cure had gone a wandering, and taken the whole of the KLF on his back. But I knew where he'd gone. Phuong had borrowed the tape to listen to the day before, and in his rush and gloom, had probably packed it in the tin box with his few possessions by mistake; or perhaps Robert had so enjoyed tripping down the leafy boulevards of Hanoi, he'd slipped himself into the box for a free ride back. I thoughtlessly asked the father if Phuong had given it to him, or left it in his room; but no. He was humiliated by his son's mistake. I told him it didn't matter as I had another three! But they had to save face, and my two days' worth of food and drink were wiped from the slate with a very wet cloth. I was packed onto my bike with kid gloves and cotton wool, and waved away by the whole family. I think even the unborn baby was waving.

And as though she also had been cleansed, Minx took me, trouble-free, through the Demilitarized Zone - to visit the tunnels of Vinh Moc. We sneaked past the Forbidden City at Hue and on to Hoi An. Why I shot past the beautiful city of Hue eludes me, but I was desperate to get to the much lauded port of Hoi An. It only took three red and white sticks, two Lotabas, and one bamboo hut, to get there.

❖

98 THRAN PHU, HOI AN

The ancient and gnarly pantiles lay heavily on each other, staggering up the roof. Foliage tumbled down their steepness, in places holding the broken tiles together in a mutual bond. The buildings below huddled up to each other in a ragged row, discoloured, broken - like an old man's teeth. Frangipani and honeysuckle dripped down their fronts and over the edges of wrought iron balconies, heaping their scent on the earthy, musty air that rolled through the streets from the river.

Hoi An had once been a bustling and thriving trading port, one of the most important in South East Asia, so pagodas stood amidst narrow lanes of shutter-clad colonial villas, Japanese bridges and Chinese meeting houses. The seeds sewn in the cracks centuries before had now matured into a hybrid; strange and beguiling. Tables at the riverside bore baguettes and confiture, spicy crab soup with quail's eggs and pepper, strong black Vietnamese coffee that drip-drip-dripped into evaporated milk. Passing behind the condiments and still warm bread, a fishing sampan could be seen, nets flying out and skywards to land with a thwack! on the water; then sink silent. Hiding here and there in nooks and crannies were artists, bashing out pictures in a Vietnamese style, but painted with a Chinese brush that had run through the Tricolour on a rainy day.

I rammed Minx nastily up the kerb to a stop and winces decorated the faces of the locals I'd parked amongst. I had left Danang before dawn, Minx's feeble headlight failing to reach the three feet to the road, and knocked off the 60k to Hoi An by daylight, with a sense of a mission accomplished.

Driving in, knowing of its ancient history, it seemed to me that it could hardly have changed in appearance since its glory days; though a lot quieter. I liked it already.

'No rooms,' said the owner of the hostel. 'no rooms today I don't think.' My entrance on Minx had definitely failed to impress. So I sat in the front restaurant and drank coffee and coffee and coffee, until I was running along the ceiling. A couple who were leaving hove into view, so I grabbed their key before the lady receptionist could reach it.

'Now you have a room... and so do I.' I said to her, signing my name in the book. I must have been desperate to be there, as that really was quite rude of me.

By noon I had eaten a tasty breakfast, cycled to the beach and was swimming around in the China Sea with a lazy grin and even lazier backstroke. Looking back to the beach through the gap between my half-submerged feet, I watched a herd of cows pass along the sand, driven from behind by an old man, his cane swishing down onto their skinny rumps.

Later, with the sun and salt-water still clinging warm to my skin and dusk approaching fast, I cycled back to town amongst a convoy of old, stiff-backed bicycles. Dusk falls fast in Asia, so the riders surrounding me resembled the bats flitting around above them in the darkness. They called out to me in Vietnamese by mistake error and I answered loudly in English, which silenced the flock for a while. I explained that I was from England, and that my name was Howie. They rode closer then, and from in front and behind I heard my name and country being bandied back and forth. Unseen hands patted me on the back when they overtook. I suddenly felt at ease, and my troubles fell away - leaving me weak and smiling in the dark. I whistled a Monty Python tune loudly (Always look on the bright side of life) and many riders joined in tunelessly, so that as we entered the town, people ran from houses to look and toddlers ran in to hide from the din.

  I lay showered and cool under the mosquito net, which made ghosts of my room-mates, Gregory Isaac massaging my head through the earphones with a Jamaican beat. A thought nosed its way in and I wondered why I hadn't thought of it before. Why didn't I sell Minx? True - I *had* been collecting some unique experiences, but I wasn't seeing much of the countryside away from Highway One and I was taking a hell of a beating. I hadn't met a single traveller between Hanoi and Hoi An; surely that was good wasn't it... or not?

  I decided to let the idea float for a while. It was my birthday the next day and I wanted to be worry free, so I decided to limber up with a meal at the much recommended Café des Amis, on the waterfront.

After a cold beer and a chat in the hostel, I found myself heading out with two Americans, a pony-tailed Englishman and a Vietnamese girl called Ha. She wore the finest silk 'ao dai' to match her perfection and was a doll in all respects. They told me that she was acknowledged as the most beautiful girl in Vietnam and I could see why. Her Uncle owned the Café des Amis, which was full, but they made a new table for us at the front of the café, in full view of the passers-by. We had the standard meal; there was nothing standard about it. Any superlative would have been inadequate apart from perhaps... perfect. The dishes only stopped arriving when we were fit to burst.

So, out of the kitchen came shrimps which had hopped briefly in chilli sauce, wrapped in transparently delicate pancakes. Flamingo-pink crabs, twice-dressed with garlic, marched sideways round a huge platter. A formation of mussels sneezed in - all lemon and peppery. A very smart troupe of giant prawns in sugar-cane jackets heralded a huge grilled fish, which had lemons and bay leaves for scales. Calamari balls stuffed with mixed seafood and herbs brought up the rear, followed smartly by a new wave of crabs - rampant with ginger.

Then cries of... 'Enough, enough!' brought golden crème-brulee to finish the carnival. The mellow night breeze blew in to clear the table, the mind and the palate, and then carried me home to bed and tucked in my mosquito net; already snoozing into my birthday.

❖

I was sitting outside the Post Office before it even opened, fingers and toes crossed in anticipation, eyes crossed and tongue sticking out - clowning for the two children in the middle of the dusty road. There *was* something for me - a thick and battered envelope, which I hugged greedily; my first mail in six weeks. Squirreling back under my mosquito net, I read and re-read them all; a birthday card and letter from each of my parents, a letter from my brother, notes from my niece and nephew with drawings; they all tugged at my heart. I was happy here in Hoi An and hoped that they could feel it. If they'd known what I'd been through since leaving home, they'd have been shocked.

And there was one more letter, forwarded from Israel... from Keren. She'd returned home to great trouble. Her fiancé had heard tales from many Israeli travellers about her affair with an Englishman! She felt less of me now and would I please not contact her anymore. I laughed, genuinely amused, and throwing it in the bin, decided fatuously that the Israelis were a bunch of insecure, self-opinionated, jingoistic, tell-tale-tits; that is, aside from the lovely kibbutzniks.

It also occurred to me how nice it was that the Israelis weren't allowed into Victnam - not have to see their flocks, gangs and platoons marching around dressed as hippies. The travellers I'd been meeting in Vietnam had been alone, or in twos, or at least had open minds and travelled with other nationalities. But then I also felt some sympathy for the Israelis. They seemed unable to leave home behind and be free; couldn't enjoy new surroundings without referring constantly to how great 'their' country was. It had to be an insecurity issue – possibly bred through National service? Anyway - I didn't have time for it, or for ridiculous gossip and conjecture, it was my birthday and I was going to the beach. I stopped on the way for a leisurely breakfast by the river -

eggs, bread and sweet coffee accompanied by the song of flying fishing nets. I paid one of the boat boys a dollar not to take his boat out for a ride and strolled into the market.

Stale odours of melting ice rose up, giving up its fishy captives from rush and reed baskets; ranks of mirror eyed fish - stone cold dead in the market. A paint box of spices were piled in shifting dunes, each one's colour brighter than the last, their fragrances mingling, and clutching at the ankles of passers by. Dogs lay silent - too hot to snarl; their dry tongues lolling onto the baked earth. All manner of roots and vegetables, dwarfs, giants, yellow-skinned, green-haired, gnarled, twisted, reed-thin, bloated - stood in their cliques, still clinging onto the moist, morning earth from which they'd been carefully pulled. A damp, musty aroma hung heavy in the electric dry air. The chattering of questions and answers, threats and promises, chickens squawking, and metal beating, all sounded dull and muffled under the cane and tarpaulin ceiling, but out in the naked sun the sound rose in pitch and bang-bang-banged.

I pushed the bike around the corner, and passing the blazing, flapping flags of the Chinese assembly hall, swung my leg over the saddle and pedalled off to Cau Dai beach.

I'd arranged to meet my room mates on the beach, and there they were - waving me over to their encampment, surrounded by children, who were trying to sell them - Pineapple! Peanut! Cold drink! I dashed across the burning sand to join Jerome and David - two young Frenchmen, and Katherine - a very pretty American. The boys were outlandish and plein de la joie de vivre. They imitated the sounds of birds and animals, which delighted the children. Jerome mimicked their pidgeon English and chased them around the beach, flapping his arms like wings. David painted with watercolours, using sea-water in a gathered shell and an ancient French paint box.
I wrote and swam, and swam and read; played games with the children. Katherine was blond and attractive with a caramel tan; legs up to her armpits. The differing personalities of our little colony had attracted the locals and peddlers alike, and being ourselves was entertainment in itself. The day ran long and light, with sun and rain and laughter. I was wearing a broad smile long after the sun had dipped behind the mountains, and we moved off home in the dark, once again wobbling and weaving on our bicycles, hooting out 'hellos' and 'bonjours' to the Vietnamese cyclists – like owls amongst blackbirds.

Arriving back at the hostel, my companions announced...
'We are going to stay in the room tonight Howie, we are all very tired, we hope you don't mind?'
'No of course I don't.' I said, and I really didn't. As I showered, I thought how nice it would be to sit alone by the river quietly, eating good food and contemplating the past and the future. I was content. Tripping half naked through the kitchen, to the delight of the giggling girls working, I entered my room. There, in a row, stood Katherine - stunning in evening dress and long-brushed hair, alongside David and Jerome - in white T shirts with ties painted on.
'Taraagghh!' said David ... 'only joking you silly Englishman. Did you think we would not celebrate your birthday? We just wanted to test your English politeness; baaahh! Get your clothes on man, tonight we eat and drink and dance. Let's go!'

Around midnight, Jerome was chasing laughing children away from our table into the blackness, squawking and flapping his wings like a drunken crow. The charming thing about Jerome was that he was very handsome, and could so easily have spent his time working hard at being cool on the Rive Gauche, a smoking Gauloise dripping from his lips, self important and shallow. But he got his kicks with games and noises, and chasing children. Consequently, the locals and travellers alike thought he was cool; because he was.

The night tumbled on and we spoke of England and France and America, until at last we swayed home, arms linked, then tucked each other up in bed.
'Thanks for the birthday everyone.' I whispered into the darkness.
'S'ok ... old man!' replied David.

As the sun geared itself up for another busy day, Jerome chased one last posse of kids round the waterfront before jumping on the motorbike behind David. He donned his white explorer's pith helmet.
'I hope to see you in Bali, you silly Englishman.' he threw back, over the noise of the engine. And I knew that if on some beach, I saw children laughing and fleeing from a great crow making machine-gun noises, I would be wearing a huge smile to see such fun again.
'Au revoir mon petit pommes de terre!' I shouted into the distance.

Sitting outside Ha's restaurant, evaporated milk dripping slow into my strong muddy coffee, a summer storm crept up over the roof tiles. They closed up like clams, jiggling together as the rain bucketed down. If I stretched out my right hand, it disappeared through a wall of water; I kept my cigarette in my left. The tamarind trees were humming 'tra-la-la' and turning greener with delight. The storm washed itself out and the street was bathed with the scent of sighing leaves, their blossoms breathing out sweet honeysuckle perfume.

Suddenly, firecrackers jumped and banged along Le Loi, a thousand starting pistols being fired in ragged procession. The retorts jumped through windows onto sleeping babies, crying them. Billowing clouds of stinging cordite swept the street of perfume, and then turning the corner, barrelled along Tran Phu. Then - a Chinese magic trick. As the smoke cleared, each explosion had turned into a vivid, vermilion petal.

The street floor was the colour of a Cardinal's underpants, and petals were still turning in the air - light, then dark, and floating to the carpet to join the fun. The wedding party tripped along this an inch above the ground, with a terrible clanging of bells and a parade of silk, in all the colours of the rainbow and more. As the procession passed by into memory, the petals seemed to brown and tire, limping into the gutter to rest. A strange melody followed along behind - the theme tune to a spaghetti western with a disco beat. It came from two orange-box speakers fixed at each end of a bicycle, and sitting slouched between them - a Mexican Bandido, eyes narrowed to slits, looking each side into doorways and windows for Clint Eastwood to jump out. It was the Ice Cream Man, who had joined the party in the hope of picking up some extra business, and I thought... it's no stranger than Mister Whippy cruising the streets of Manchester's Moss-side, playing Greensleeves whilst selling drugs.

Beside me, in the evening gladness, sat Ha - glowing in the dark, illuminating my writing. She blinked her big eyes and added a sensual but sad smile across her very kissable lips. She held my gaze whilst she listened, trilling, head swaying side-to-side to the music on my Walkman. Having recognised her job at the restaurant - to attract custom, and knowing her mission - to marry a foreigner, I'd been a bit stand-offish with the little 'Crepe Suzette'.

Earlier, her little brother had brought the visitor's book for me to read. Scanning the endless comments, I saw it was full of worldwide praise for the cuisine; but much more for Ha herself. It seemed that her fame had travelled up and down Vietnam like Minx. Each page held many desperate pleas from Europeans, Scandinavians and Antipodeans, promising the earth and asking for her hand.

Some had travelled a long way to Hoi An just to see Ha, and had left proclaiming - 'It was worth it.' Stealing a casual look, I had to admit it was probably true, but to share electric air and sounds and smiles was

enough for me. I think my lack of interest was affecting her. I didn't want her - had nothing to offer, and in the perverse world of men and women, that is exactly why she seemed to want me. I asked...
'Ha - this book is full of men who want to marry you, to look after you and take you to their country... why haven't you gone yet?'
'I wait for the right man.' she said, and threw me a look that nearly burst my trousers. But it would be like marrying a Martian; you see there is something I have forgotten to mention – she was as unintelligent as she was beautiful. There again it still left that nagging question... what about one night in paradise? I knew the answer. I would have to pay the piper.

The tale of my trip down the country had spread around Hoi An like a bushfire, and having casually mentioned my small desire to be rid of Minx, offers started to pour in from locals that I passed in the street, on corners and even in the sea; they must have been circulating my photograph. The amount being offered was much lower than I could get in Saigon, but the thought of losing my burden was oh-so tempting. I could leave rested, with just my bedraggled backpack to look after.

As I sat basking on the beach, I noticed two burly men seated nearby and behind me, wearing mirrored sunglasses and formal shirts. They were watching my every move, and were obviously uninvolved with the beach life. After several hours and dips in the sea I was getting worried, but I had to pass them to leave the beach. I had no choice, I was hungry. Fronting it out, I walked nonchalantly past them, looking straight ahead. 'Where are you going?' The tone was inquisitive, not menacing, so I stopped and looked at the four of me in their glasses. 'Are you going back to town ... you have been in the sea a long time, you like the waves?'
'Yes,' I said 'but the waves aren't big enough. I like to surf.'
'Then I will take you to China Beach, they have big waves there. The best girls are there also, I will get you one.' Standing now, he mimed a 'slow comfortable screw against the wall' which made both of them laugh.
I suddenly remembered the film 'Apocalypse Now' and the mad commander flying over China beach with his helicopter attack force –
'See there, it peels right and left, must be four foot. Get in there soldier! You either surf or fight.'
'But sir, what about the enemy - this is their beach?'
'Charlie don't surf son.'

'How much would it cost?' I asked.

'No, I will take you as a friend. Also, can I come with you back to town, I want to buy your motorbike.'

He explained that he was acting as agent for a young man who wanted Minx, who couldn't speak English and didn't know how to buy her. We wound through the back lanes of Hoi An and into a maze of houses.

This is where the everyday folk lived in crowded poverty; tumble down shacks made from bits - so it was impossible to see where one ended and the neighbour began. I was once again in the dodgiest part of town alone, and although the thought crossed my mind that I may never emerge from here, I felt quite safe with the agent. Crammed into s small room in one of the shacks, were the agent, a commission man, his friend, two friends of his, some men who'd been passing by and come in to watch, and man sleeping along a bench - his feet alarmingly close to an electric fan with blades like ship's propellers.

After some negotiation, we arrived at a price slightly lower than the ceiling under which we sat; one and a half million dong. The lad had been saving for years; each note was of small denomination and carefully folded in four. The agent looked embarrassed and smiled weakly at me. The lad tipped them onto the table from a shoebox.

'That's alright.' I said, watching the possibilities of the afternoon disappear, 'I'm sure it's all there and correct.'

'No,' said the agent, 'it must be counted in front of you.' With checks and recounts, and a lot of elastic bands, it took an hour. It would have been a lot quicker, but the sleeping man, rolling over, put his foot into the fan and sent a blade flying like a scimitar across the room into the neat piles of money.

They shouted and insulted him for interrupting the counting, as he lay groaning in agony and tending his toe. He wasn't happy - but *I* was. Despite pointing out Minx's failings and faults, I'd sold a wreck with no front brake, little suspension, a knackered clutch, leaking oil and petrol - for 150 dollars.

I'd also lost about that much on the deal, but I figured that the expedition had paid for itself. I'd learnt a lot about loneliness, despair, frustration and I didn't think anything could ever stress me again. Also I wouldn't have it on my conscience to sell Minx to an unsuspecting backpacker. These boys knew what they were buying, and knew its value as a hire bike, they were hard to get in the middle of Vietnam. But then the bubble burst. The agent, examining the papers that came with the bike, looked at me suspiciously and said...

'This is a photocopy of the licence... it is no good.'

'Pardon?' was the best I could manage. I hadn't even looked at it before. He explained it to the buyer, whose face crumpled. I felt like a cheat, albeit unintentional.

'Shit! what can I do?'

'You will have to take it to the registration office in the town it comes from. They will give you a proper one.'

'Where does it come from?' I asked, praying it wasn't Hanoi. Scanning the page, he announced...

'Nha Trang.'

Nha Trang was best part of the way to Saigon. It seemed that Minx and I were destined to stay together for a bit longer.

'I am very sorry.' I said, pushing the pile of money back across the table to the agent.

'No.' he said, and shoved it back at me. After a long debate with the whole room he said, 'We will mend the bike so that it won't break down, and when you get to Nha Trang you must get the papers. If you then go to the Thong Nhat Hotel, a man will take them from you and drive the bike back.'

'It's very kind of you to trust me with this money.' I said.

'No,' he replied, 'we will know where you are all the time. I believed him. I knew now that the Vietnamese were very thorough, apart from when they fixed motorbikes of course.

The next morning, while they fixed Minx, we rode up to China Beach on *his* motorbike. As we dodged potholes and cyclists, he gave me a running commentary. Just to the south of Danang, he pointed out the airbase where the Americans had first made a foothold in Vietnam. We were motoring up a section of tarmac road which he explained was made by the Americans.

'My parents helped to make this road. They were Koreans who were brought over to work on the road.'

'Do they still live in Vietnam?' I asked.

'No, they were killed while working on the road - by an American bomb.' About then, as I was struggling for a reply, his bike stalled, and we came to a halt in the middle of a bridge.

'Minx has a twin!' I thought. Trucks were crashing past, horns blaring.

'You might like to stand over there' he said, pointing to the side of the bridge. 'Yes I might just do that.' I said, as he seemed very happy to work on the bike in the middle of the road. It was soon fixed and we reached China Beach. The surf was flat.

As with any surfing beach around the world, wave-starved surfers hung around waiting hungrily for a swell to arrive. The agent took me amongst them, introducing me, and we talked surfing.

'Tom Curren – number one.'

'Martin Potter – number one.'

They asked me about surfing in England, and I told them how good it could be, but how cold the water was. They said the English were mad but I still saw that far away look in their eyes.

I told them that I was on my way to Australia and Hawaii, which was greeted by a chorus of sighs. The agent had been right, the girls were as beautiful as the surf was flat, and they were circling me! As evening drew in, food arrived from god knows where, with cold beers attached. I insisted they took some money and pleasingly they accepted, but handed it to the stunning girl in the middle that my eyes wouldn't leave alone. The sky was darkening, streaked with runnels of pink and orange, when the agent stood up, and putting his hands on my shoulder he said quietly... 'I am sleeping at my friend's house, I will pick you up in the morning.' and walked off.

Dumbfounded, I watched him head up the beach, and when I turned back there was only one person left sitting by me, smouldering. It hit me... another sister, and yet again I made myself say no – it didn't feel right. I ran after the agent, surprising him, kicking myself for my sensibility, yet at the same time I looked back at the beach – the sky glowing, and thought 'just enjoy what you have; it's absolutely wonderful to be alive and kicking.'

❖

NHA TRANG – THE NIGHT TRAIN

So, as though leaving the hotel room after a six day love affair, I slipped out of Hoi An at dawn, clothes awry. I pointed Minx's front wheel south, whispered 'Nha Trang - home' in her ear, and set off, startling a dog who was licking his nuts outside the guesthouse.

It was a cool start. The sky was like a dry-stone wall, all blocks of grey, and the miles fell away behind me. There was nowhere in particular that I wanted to see along the way, and I realised that my time in Vietnam was running short, so I fixed my head to the task. The sun knocked the wall of clouds down and grew and grew with the morning.

Minx broke down. I passed the cigarettes around: electrics.

Minx broke down. I chased the kids - David style: water in petrol.

Each time I broke down, I was helped to get along again. People found me drinks and shade, had a good old chat about me, and I noticed that after each stop, the toolkit that had come with the bike had got smaller. I figured it was a due payment for the help they gave – but was worried what might happen when I broke down with just a cigarette lighter for a toolkit. I found a Lotoba in a nowhere town and stayed the night.

It was a cool start, but not for long. By mid-morning I felt I was riding the rim of a huge foundry wheel, white hot, so I couldn't stop, ashen dust for smoke, scouring my eyes and tearing at my nostrils: the same shack, paddy, flick-tailed lizard, passing by to the left and right.

Above, the sky was one great sun that defied a glance, and beat my eyelids into slits. The road was as regular as a canal but potholed, scarred, beaten, its surface loose and wicked, pulling the tyres into the dusty verge or a hard edged dent, which would hammer the bike into my spinal column, forcing a grunt as it winded me. It followed the path of the railway, holding hands on their walk down Vietnam, sometimes skipping to one side, or crisscrossing, so they could swap sweaty hands. When they reached rivers, they held each other tight so that they were one, and rode piggyback over the swirling brown waters on the backs of creaking, rocking, complaining old bridges.

Tacked on the side of the bridges were narrow footpaths - incomplete, heart-stopping collections of strapped-together logs and river flotsam - seemingly an afterthought, that carried the walkers, cyclists and motorbikes. Minx shied and whinnied at these, through her wasted shock absorbers, and threatened to push her wobbling wheel through the flimsy guardrail, so I struggled to keep her straight and avoid the missing pieces. Back on the road, I kept the throttle open, trying to stay away from the cloud of brown dust that was tied, swirling, to my back wheel.

On a stretch, virtually empty of shacks and sales cabinets, the road bent lazily to the left, Minx didn't; she headed straight for the sole domicile. The handlebar repair was shot. Once again I laid Minx on her side, my leg trapped underneath, and we crashed through the bamboo wall. I came up in cloud of dust, trying to escape the burning exhaust pipe, and as things settled down into quiet, I saw the family backed up against the wall, eyes wide.

'I'm very sorry, Anh! ... English - the bike is Russian - Litso!'

'Chao em' I said to a little girl with one hand in her mouth; she giggled. They ushered me to sit down and poured some tea. I drank glass after glass, whilst slowly explaining my background with the aid of the phrase-book. The mother, seeing me examine the burn on my leg, rushed off and returned with a pot of gunk, which she spread gently on the wound. I'd left a hole in the wall, but unlike in cartoons it wasn't man-shaped. I mimed to the father that I would help him fix it. He shook his head, took me round the corner, showed me a pile of concrete bricks, sand and cement. He was going to build a wall anyway.

'Yes,' I said 'I can lay them for you.' I mimed bricklaying; his face lit up and he slapped me on the back. 'Tomorrow.' I said.

I ate with the family. Grandmother had been brought out to the main room now to listen, and I passed round the photos and explained who all these strange faces were. The little girls looked hard at the photo of Bumble and held him to their cheeks. They went off to bed with Gran a bit later and I stayed smoking with Dad. They put me to bed eventually on Granny's bed; well, they only had two. It was only a bare board platform, but quite large, and I had a piece of it. The little ones snuggled up behind me, falling straight back to sleep, while I struggled against the furore that was issuing from Granny's mouth. It wasn't just her mouth, her whole face snored.

The family were up at first light. A neighbour had come round and taken Minx away for fixing, so we set to the wall. Dad seemed to think that my bricklaying was brilliant, which was amazing, as it really wasn't. It was a long day's work, but I had one of the sons bringing bricks, and one mixing mortar, whilst I just slapped the wall together. The neighbours and passers-by also stopped to watch; I was back in my circus again and the family were puffed with pride. Minx came back late afternoon, just as we were cleaning the tools, and I was asked to stay. I was delighted. It was a very full house that evening, and many a bottle of beer arrived with visitors, who inspected the wall and me, asking endless questions. If Granny had snored through a megaphone that night, I wouldn't have heard her.

I set off early the next morning for the final push to Nha Trang, as I figured that the man waiting for me may be getting a bit worried.
Minx broke down. I did the coin tricks: spark plug knackered.
Minx broke down. I tried break dancing: dirty petrol.
Minx broke down. My fault - no petrol; was given some.

At last, in the early evening gloom, we arrived. Minx, like an eager dog, ran on home sniffing the lights and fumes of Nha-Trang with delight. The man was waiting. Minx and I said goodbye. Dry-eyed.

❖

My time was nearly up, so after a brief tour around Nha Trang, I bought a ticket for the night train; hard seat. But they wouldn't let me into the hard seat carriage. I was ushered into the soft seats and placed next to a young girl who, when she stopped crying, explained that she was going away to technical school in Saigon.

Unlike the Chinese, who liked to turn every trip into your worst nightmare, the Vietnamese made theirs more like a picnic. Cool, wet hand cloths dangled from luggage racks along with spare clean clothes.
The floor was swept every hour by a smiling lady and her perfumed broom, who, just like your Mum, chuckled as she made you lift your legs, man, woman, monk and all. Food wandered in the carriage every couple of hours, and in between, an orange or a bottle of mineral water would appear like magic, when you opened your eyes from a snooze.

Now and then a guard rushed through, a Mr Jobs-worth, barking at the people to put the mesh back down on the windows. Just as I was thinking his behaviour a bit excessive there was an explosion to my left. A rock fragment spun through the grille, creasing my forehead. I leapt up, threw a 'Fuck!!' out the window, and putting my hand to my face, it came away smeared with blood. The mother opposite was sharing her seat with her two daughters, who she'd been lovingly cuddling, stroking, fanning and towelling with a cool cloth. She put her babbies to one side, where they instinctively clung to each other and went back to sleep. She brought her damp cloth over and, kneeling in the aisle, wiped my forehead; spoke soft and cooing to me. It was such a shock to the system I almost pouted with quivering chin ...'Not the iodine Mum!' The rest of the carriage were indignant that a European had been hit. He may be a foreigner, but he was *their* foreigner.

Minutes later, another missile hit further along the carriage, showering a table of four, and powdering their soup with bullock dung. The Vietnamese lady brushed her hair with her fingers and carried on slurping. The monk sharing the table jumped up, and though barely five feet tall, his head was visible above the seat - ablaze with anger. A look that could penetrate steel and rip through mountains, laser-beamed from his eyes back down the track. The young girl next to me explained sweetly that the culprits were only children, that it was a game to hit the white face on the trains. At this point Mr Jobsworth returned, beckoning me to follow. 'Go with him,' the girl said. 'Take your bags.'

He led me to the next carriage and into a sleeper compartment. There was a spare berth, and the three occupants motioned me to it, and said 'Hello'. Two returned to their books, but I sat by the window with the other, sharing a silent conversation, both watching the same things fly past, agreeing on form and colour. We handed each other cigarettes at the exact time we each wanted one, and once, flicked our butts through the grille and reached for our water bottles - simultaneously. It brought a smile across the divide, which was only two feet wide, but also a continent apart. When we could no longer see the dark-cloaked countryside through the inch square steel mesh, we made our beds and lay on them.

I had barely fallen asleep, when the sliding door flew open with a rush. A hearty and husky 'My friend!!' hurtled in, the words dragged out long, containing the whole of Vietnam in one breath. He was well dressed, so much so that I had noticed him on the platform, and had nodded to his smile.

'You like beer?...yes!...come with me!' He ushered me along with great booming sentences, to the compartment next door, and handed me a cold one. My soul went 'aaaaaagghhh.'

There were only two beds. They were three men, a woman and child, a dog, and the best part of a department store; but they still found room to turn it into a party. Vodka and beer flew back and forth, fuelling Vietnamese, English and drunken gibberish. Under the influence I became a writer, because it was easier to say than graphic designer, or photographer. This made me blood-brother to the one that couldn't speak English, as he was a writer in Saigon; the result - another session of 'same-same'. Empty bottles flew end-over-end through the smog of the compartment, across the corridor, and exited through an open window. The woman and child slept on.

During a stop, where the bottles smashed against the station building, my friend slipped, eel-like and hunched, through the chaos of legs, and dived through the open window. He was stopped by his waist, which was bigger than the hole, his shouts muffled as he hollered into the darkness; legs wriggling behind him like Winnie the Pooh in the honey tree. With his friends pushing from behind he popped out, and was gone for several minutes. He shot back in the carriage with a giant laugh, and cut a clearing through the smoke using a whole cooked chicken as a rotor blade.

He ripped it apart at the seams and spread it on a plate of salad that seemed to appear from nowhere. It was as tender as a joke rubber chicken, but it had been fetched for my benefit - as they indicated that I needed fattening up.

The writer fell off his box and stayed where he lay, comatose. The woman, waking, tapped her man firmly on the shoulder. He spoke to her gently and then to me – 'Bed, my friend,' and held my hands between his. I returned to my bed, and though the noise next door must have disturbed him greatly, my room-mate raised his hand in welcome and very generously - smiled.

❖

KIM & SINH CAFE, SAIGON

4.00 am. Saigon was still half asleep and dreaming of a new future. The girl looked as tired as I felt, and very lonely, at the end of the station bench; the same wooden bench you'd find in New York Central or Waterloo; designed to make sleep impossible if stranded at some god-awful hour - which was now. I crossed the waiting room, hoping that she spoke English; she was Canadian and did. We'd both had the same idea; wait until dawn poked its head through the door and gave a shout, rather than cross Saigon in the dark searching for an open hostel.

4.10 am. Having established that at least I wasn't a stalker, or her - a miserable cow, we wearily carted our packs outside, and with a tired barter with the only two cyclos on duty, took one each; it was a bit early in our relationship to cuddle up in a small vehicle. Pedalling side-by-side across town, our drivers swopped notes on us, politics and the World Cup, while that great sky painted itself, splashing colour carelessly onto buildings and roads. Cach Mang Thang Tam Sreet was as long as its name, and ran most of the way into District One, and to Pham Ngu Lao – already laying its foundations as the backpacker's area. We watched it waking up and going about its business as we rode. My driver laughed, as his friend - showing off, went round the wrong side of the roundabout, shaking his fist back at the hooting traffic.

4.40 am. The steel shutters were still across the door of the Hoang Tu Hotel. I pulled them back far enough to squeeze through, which made them squeal, waking the inevitable security guard sleeping on his camp bed in the middle of the marble foyer.
'Do you have any rooms?' I asked.
'One...' he mumbled, without lifting his head from the pillow,
'double... 8 dollars.' He produced a key from under the pillow and held it in space. I looked at her, she shrugged, then nodded. There was neither discussion nor suspicion.

5.00 am. We'd both showered, and in my case shaved, and were lying unclothed in a crisp, hospital-white bed, knowing nothing about each other - yet everything, and if she'd turned and asked for a cuddle I would have given it, with comfort the sole motive. We slept.

I crossed the road at 11.00 am for a late breakfast at the famous Kim Café. I had left a note for her on my pillow, and as I was enjoying a cup

of treacly Mocha, and warm croissant with strawberry jam, she joined me; sat down with a smile and looked for the menu.
'Good morning... my name's Howie.'
'Katherine!' she said, leaning over the table and planting a soft kiss on my cheek. I'd fretted and bothered about all this before I left home. How did this hostel business work? How would I meet people? What would it be like sharing rooms with strangers? It was as easy as pie, and already fitted like a well worn glove.

❖

My Vietnamese visa had only two days left. Katherine also had to return home, so we wandered sprawling Saigon aimlessly, trying to take in by osmosis what had taken two weeks in little Hanoi. Saigon was bigger and wider, brash and bold. Charm was not a word that sat comfortable. The postcard sellers lacked the personality and theatrics of Thuy and her friends. Along Le Loi they looked like the unattractive friend of the girl you really fancied, with scowls that could curdle milk. One boy had a railway-track scar from nose to ear, that pulled his eye into a menacing squint, as he cursed you for not buying... 'Fug yooo!'
But consider this. They were called 'Bui Doi' - a Vietnamese term for kids who were orphans, homeless, or working for a gang. They had a right to scowl, spit, snarl or cry if they wanted, because the term meant 'Dust of Life'. It meant 'Nothing.'

Turning any corner, the chances of finding someone pissing up a wall or squatting in the dirt, were quite high. So, my first opinions of Saigon were negative, and quickly grew. Whether it was by constructing ugly buildings, using the river to collect rubbish, sewerage and slum dwellers, or erecting acres of western billboards to complement the river view, Saigon was quite happy pissing in its own backyard.

My dislike was further fuelled by a visit to the War Crimes Museum. It had seemed to me that in the North the war had been pushed into the background - best forgotten. Here, the intention seemed to be to show what inhumane bastards the Americans had been. They probably were, but I don't recall the Viet-Cong pulling any punches. The Huey helicopter was, for me, a lasting impression of that black & white television war, buzzing the skies like demented dragonflies, on the News at Ten each evening.

Here was one sitting on the lawn of the museum, as though it had been invited to tea. It was a tin can, ugly as sin, with dials and gauges that looked as though they came from a tractor. It had me cold, thinking of its occupants trying to survive, but also the people below, running from the hell and damnation that spat from its cannons.

Inside the museum I found a photo so blurry it could have been shot through a sock in a sandstorm. It showed two US soldiers standing next to a body, and was entitled '"GI cuts off the ear of his victim... will he take it home for a souvenir?' The alleged ear was not visible; neither was a knife. I'm sure that ears were exchanged in the conflict, but pure conjecture don't amount to a hill of beans.

To speed my exit from this debacle, I overheard a party of middle-aged Japanese, who were scrutinising artists' impressions of American torture methods, 'tut-tutting' in disgust. Hypocrites of the world unite.

I learnt one very interesting fact at the Museum of the war between America and Vietnam. For every three Americans killed, an Australian or Kiwi also died: and I hadn't even known that they were there. What *were* we being fed on the nightly News broadcasts? More importantly what *weren't* we being told?
 It was this ridiculous omission of knowledge that prompted me, much later, to start skimming over the history of Vietnam. I was captivated, enthralled, studied its history in detail, and subsequently my views on Saigon and Vietnam as a whole radically changed; as did my life.*

❖

Sitting back at the Sinh Café, the other famous backpacker's café, sugar-dust blowing from my fresh cinnamon doughnut, I held the page of my book down against the wind which was trying to rush on to the last chapter. A man appeared round the corner, on his second circuit of the morning. With no legs, he lay face down on a trolley, nose three inches from the cruel concrete. His stumps rested on a plastic sheet, which dragged behind rasping. He had two rubber blocks tied to his hands to pull his way along this horizontal mountain, hand-over-hand - the summit never in sight.
 The wind brought rain, that first whispered its approach, then roared on arrival. He slithered under a cyclo, which left abruptly; the dry patch it had left was soaked in an instant. Diners fretted over wet newspapers, the rain in their coffee, and having to move indoors, whilst the road filled and become a river.

---

*The epilogue is an attempt to right my ignorance of Vietnam in these earlier writings.

Inching upstream, wheels submerged, the man turned his head sideways every metre to draw breath, his mouth a great 'O' shape, eyes shut. Looking around me, I saw all eyes fixed on coffee, newspapers, light fittings and distant objects. I walked into the rain to share some discomfort with him - handed him some money. It wasn't enough. I wished he could turn into the flow, drift away clean out of Saigon to a merciful drowning; wake up on a sunny China Sea beach with legs to walk up on, toes sifting the warm sand. But it wasn't going to happen; he was a poor man, fighting the great fight.

The rain spent, the sky streaked with blue, Katherine and I crossed the city through a gentle steam bath from the road below. We were heading for Maxim's - *"the best restaurant in Saigon and probably all of Indochina. Numerous enthralled backpackers have reported... absolutely not to be missed - Lonely Planet Guide."*
 We passed Paris, Biarritz, Peking and Brooklyn on the way - in the guise of buildings. The Ham-bu-go Ca-li-pho-nia had no customers. We strolled along boulevards lined with classic French salad trees, but being Saigon, the leaves were limp and dusty, and above were concrete cloud-kissers that the Americans and Russians had thrown up; literally.

Just next to the river the doors to Maxim's were open, to let in the early evening dusk and early diners. We goaded each other to go in first, pushing and pulling each other through the door like two silly school-kids, skitting across the lush carpet to peek into the dining room. Outside again, drawing a circle on the path with my toe, I asked -
 'Shall we book a table then Katherine?' not really fancying it.
 'Do you want to?' she asked, not really fancying it.
 'Not really.' I said. 'Nor do I.' she relented.
 'I don't think I can cope with clean tablecloths and choosing cutlery, it all looks a bit... 'posh' for me.'
 'I'd feel tatty in there wearing these clothes.'
 'I *am* tatty in these clothes – shit... let's get some noodles!'
 'I'm with you - tramp!'

While we walked, almost skipped, to the soup shop, I thought back to when I was comfortable in the *very best* restaurants, and what an extravagant waste it now seemed. We slurped our bowls of 'pho', shovelled garlands of noodles, chewed on chicken wings, dropping the bones on the oil cloth amongst puddles of iced water from the sides of the beer bottles: no glasses. As we chomped and chortled, dark crept over the railway tracks and slunk downtown. Saigon had put its face and glad-rags on and was shimmying into life.

Stepping out onto the street, the advertising hoardings were like costume jewellery, the ornate hotels - floodlit Disney castles, and flying scooters were disco-lights leading the dance around town.

Passing a brightly lit colonial garden, we were hailed by a concierge...
'Please...come in, have a drink and watch the tennis.'
We entered a false daylight, where greens were ultramarine and ferns waved like seaweed. A Vietnamese man in a crisp, white Fred Perry outfit jogged by, swinging his racquet and nodding a loud 'Hello' as he passed. Slazenger balls 'thock thocked' back and forth through the arc lights, landing game, set and match. As if we'd entered a different world, we took up our surroundings and ordered Gin and Tonics. We sipped them gently over ice and lime, as Miss Trung trounced Miss Nguyen... 6-0, 6-1. We applauded as they bent to each other over the net to shake hands and display their frilly pants.

Returning to the piss-stinking street, a mere laurel hedge away, it felt much hotter. The city lights blazed gaudily like a cheap fairground, and a sound crept into my head - a sound I'd been hearing all day. On every road, alleyway and boulevard, street-boys and girls tapped on hollow sugar canes with sticks, while dipping along. It was the rock-steady beat that you hear at The Oval - as England try to survive the onslaught of the West Indies bowlers; no melody - just a tap tap tap, a tocka tocka tocka tocka, tap tap tap; and it gave Saigon a heartbeat that I will always remember.

The 'Dust of Life' were playing up.

Leaving Saigon on the plane the next day, I was playing the rhythm on a Singha beer can with an airline plastic spoon, watching Pnom Penh pass by below me. Was Cambodia rocking to the beat, or still dancing to the Khmer Rouge quickstep? A lot of people I'd met were there, or on their way, and I knew that a trio of English, French and Australians were being held captive directly below me right now - death hanging over their heads like a cloud of mosquitoes. I asked myself... 'was I being a coward for not venturing into Cambodia?' or just Captain Sensible, heading for Bangkok, back-packer's convention town, as exotic and dangerous as Worthing. Perhaps I was.

'But at least..' I said to myself with some pride 'I did go to Vietnam, on my own, pre-McDonalds.'

Tap tap tap, a tocka tocka tocka tocka.

KHAO SAN ROAD, BANGKOK

So, it was down to Bangkok I fear, and the shock was shocking. With my new-found travelling skills, I sat on my backpack outside the terminal, ignoring the touts and taxis, and watched and waited for something to happen: as it always does. I smoked two snouts.

Two girls walked past me - left, then right, then left again. On their next pass they approached me, their backpacks still holding the creases from the shop, but no flag sewn on to show their homeland.

'Are you going to the Khao San Rd?' they asked.

'Yes I am, but I'm not paying the 300 baht that these taxis are asking. I might take the bus.'

'Would you share a taxi with us?' said one of the two extremely attractive girls, who looked like Spanish sisters.

'I would be delighted.' I said, and I was. They were Spanish sisters on a one month trip to Thailand.

'Have you been travelling long?' they asked, looking over my rather threadbare outfit.

'Not long enough,' I replied, 'and too long.'

This produced a heavy silence, and Spanish eyes stared at me as the taxi moved another ten feet closer, a worry growing in their minds.

'It's OK,' I offered, 'I'm just tired from travelling through China and Vietnam alone. I'm harmless – and old enough to be your father.'

We jumped in the taxi, and having seen that Bangkok was concrete and cars and motorbikes, all thrashed together in a huge traffic jam, I closed my eyes, leant a heavy head on the door jamb and sank into a resigned doze. I hadn't really known what to expect from Bangkok - but the reality was a bastard to bear.

❖

The Khao San Road - a theme park for all travellers. You could arrive an English public school child, or the EEC equivalent, and in two hours buy all the necessary clothing to look like a hippy; then you only had to act like one ...man! It was children trying to be adults and adults trying to be kids: a never-never land of blinkered people, travelling to islands and resorts packed full of their like, swapping 'where to buy this, where to buy that' - 'where's the drugs man, the rave, the full moon party?' The real travellers looked on in amazement, with their boring clothes and anything but boring experiences tucked away in their backpacks; memories of getting high on coffee, lemonade, ambience and

conversation. In China and Vietnam the travellers talked: of the moon, rivers, mountains; of home and life. Going to bed was sense and sensibility, not a matter of ridicule or a challenge failed, because the new dawn seen through clear eyes, heralded a great day.
It had been a long time since I'd touched drugs, or drunk ridiculous amounts of alcohol, and was just a bit pleased with myself. I had tried many substances in the past, whereby only huge quantities of Special Brew could keep me from walking on water, and sleep was a fairy tale I seemed to remember from childhood. The after-effects of this were akin to Parkinson's disease with dysentery thrown in, and of course only another bucketful of the hair-raising shit could hit the spot. I was now enjoying life through undistorted eyes, ears and mind, and knew I didn't have to try and kill myself to die happy. I was, at last, being honest with myself.

The Khao San Road bars blurted out Bruce Willis and Whoopi Goldberg videos, and all heads - dread-locked, nap-headed, pony-tailed or braided, stared blank-faced and blank-minded at the flickering screen, having consulted the blackboard earlier to see what was showing at 2.00, and 4.00, and 7.00. I couldn't be doing with it; couldn't see the sense in coming this far to do so little.

The delightful Spanish sisters found me, outside a bar, observing this circus parade, and as though this had been an appetiser to whet the palate, they asked me if I would take them to Patpong – the infamous red light district; to see a sex show. Being an English gentleman, I was obliged to fulfil my duty as a responsible chaperone. Well, I ask you, you would - wouldn't you?
  We shot across the city in a tuk-tuk, its two-stroke engine screaming, and avoiding the sneak-eyed side-street touts, who promised real treats 'upstairs', headed for a large club where we hoped the beer wouldn't climb from $3 on entry to $300 on leaving. We watched paint dry for two hours, until Elise complained to the waiter.
  'We want to see a show, with ping-pong balls and things.' These girls didn't mess around. 'After 12.30.' he replied.

True to his word, the show commenced at 1.00am. A girl ambled, naked, onto the stage, and then lying at our eye level, assumed the birthing position. She produced a string of razor blades from her front bottom - to polite applause and sharp intakes of breath, then used the blades to shred a sheet of paper. Handed a balloon, and feeling silly with all the other balloon holders around the bar, I waited my turn, as she blew darts from a blowpipe - accurate as Robin Hood... bang, bang,

bang!! My balloon burst as it nudged my neighbour's cigarette end, and as she hadn't visibly reloaded, everybody looked to see if she'd cleverly hit mine with a hidden blowpipe up her arse.

She looked over at me with a relieved expression, (probably an unsuitable choice of words), but this was explained, as with just one balloon left, she missed with three darts in a row.

'Come on darlin!' shouted a heckler from the darkness.

'It's tired... you try it!' she shouted almost tearfully.

Then, with an extra last squeeze of the buttocks, she lobbed a dart in a lazy arc over the bar into the heckler's lap, and to finish - burst the last remaining balloon with her left nipple. I never worked this one out, but assume it must have been a 'slight of the teat' trick.

By now I was delighted with the performance, and the fact it was meant to be sexual had passed completely over my head. I mouthed at the Spanish girls across the bar 'It's good isn't it!' Elise shouted back - 'Yes, but I want the ping-pong balls!'

She didn't get them, but we were content with the next performer's impression of a crab circling a giant birthday cake, blowing out the candles with a bushy mustachio'd mouth; although the smell of singed hair did indicate a less than perfect performance.

We left whilst the next girl was halfway down a Marlboro Light, and I hoped she'd heeded the Government Health Warning and left a long stub. The man to the left of the exit, invisible in the dark apart from his card held outstretched in the neon, said - 'We have very nice girls.'

'Yes,' I said, 'and very talented too!'

We tuk-tukked home to the other circus which was the Kho San Road, and I reflected that I'd only been in town for eight hours.

Bangkok ...mad, bad and sad.

❖

RHANEES GUEST HOUSE, BANGKOK

Just one row back from the Khao San Road was a narrow Soi - or alleyway, where I stumbled upon some small guest houses. Peaceful, and huddled around the leafy courtyards, the chalet-like rooms had shade and whirling fans; not a TV in sight. The quiet was excruciating, and I leapt into the first one that had a room. I found later that my little bungalow had bedbugs, but they were quiet, and left interesting patterns on my legs. They left the next day under a cloud of toxic, and probably carcinogenic, insect spray, which left an interesting perfume.

I was sitting, fork poised, about to tuck into one of Rhanee's delicious, towering toasties, when I was joined by a fair-haired Rasta from Copenhagen, whose bloodshot eyes and racking cough, were nothing to do with smoking dope and eating shit food, oh no! He explained that he hoped his business would grow as he was short of money and pointed to his shoes. I looked down and realised that I'd seen these shoes pass by me earlier as I was bent over reading. They were skin-tight and made of neoprene, with the big toe separated from its brothers. They rose above the calf with three buckles an inch apart, and the tops rolled down. They resembled a sub-aqua diver's pirate boot.

'I make these you know... man. A lot of people have approached me about them,' he said '...on the Khao San Road.. lots.'

'Yes,' I said, 'that doesn't surprise me.' which he took as a compliment, smiled a sickly smile and coughed till his buckles rattled.

'Can I ... finish your ... sandwich?' he asked, coughing in its general direction.

'Help yourself,' I said 'I seem to have lost my appetite.'

'That's the heat that does that man.' he said.

I did see a few pairs slosh-buckling down the circus during my stay, and decided that they must have some redeemable quality or practical use, such as holding a joint between the toes when wrecked on the floor, but they didn't quite fit into the Khao San fancy dress party. where Israelis came as Arabian Knights, English as Thais, Thais as Americans, Australians as Indonesians, Scandinavians as Rastas and the French came as the French. The real travellers came in their usual outfit - the scarecrow, with that certain un-coordinated look.

As the evening inked purple I strolled past the Hello Cafe, and was hit round the head by a blast from Exterminator 2 and at the same instant a hearty slap on the back from Doron! The Kibutznik picked me up and whirled me around and around shouting...

'Ta gidli! ta gidli! (Tell all!) Turning, I saw Sharon - those dulcet eyes brimming with honest and real felt tears. We were speechless, but not for long. They were leaving three hours later for the south of Thailand, so we set about catching up with tales. They shook their heads and Sharon moaned 'Howie, Howie, Howie' at the juicier parts. They'd parted company with a very confused Keren at Beijing, as the scandal had travelled ahead and met them there. I felt a bit of a shit momentarily, but then I thought – it wasn't my fault the Israelis were so insecure, and I hadn't done anything.

It was, to use a distinctly out-of-fashion term, a gay time that we spent together. They took me to an Israeli cafe up a side alley where I was the only foreigner. The waiter asked me for my order in Hebrew, to Doron's amusement, and we ate falafel, hummus and chips. Swearing fealty and meetings in Australia, we said goodbye once again. Seeing them onto a coach heading south, and feeling more than a tad sad, I retired to a bar for a disconsolate beer and to reminisce of Yangshuo, but the noise from the circus outside interrupted my thoughts, forcing me to leave for somewhere quieter. Standing up and turning, I looked, stunned, into the face that rose from reading its journal at the next table. I sat down opposite, placed my bag on the floor and grabbing the waiter who was clearing my previous table asked...

'A large beer please.'

'And a large one for me too!' said Harry.

'What the fark are you doing here Howie?'

'Drinking beer.' I said, and in an instant I was back in Hanoi again.

'I just heard about you yesterday from a man in Laos, who saw you arrive in Hoi An and Saigon' he said.

So in my innocent, bumbling way I'd managed to gain infamy the length of China and Vietnam; quite an achievement for a stupid old Englishman; an absolute beginner.

We fell to comparison and opinion, sucked on beer bottles with a vengeance, and when it still wouldn't go down fast enough, tipped the latch on the forehead, flip-topped the head and poured it in from the upturned bottles; which is how we came to spend the last three hours of the night in a bar with no name. A bar for gay Thai head-bangers, who fed us whiskey, crisps and dances, heads pumping to Whitesnake, Aerosmith and Nirvana.

Dawn blinked furiously as we carried our air guitars home and Harry tied the ends of the night off with...'It's Tuesday. Mondays are always such hard work.' We parted again later that same day with the certainty of future meetings stomping over any gloom. He was going to Penang, and without knowing it, I was off to a new, enchanting country called... Chantal.

Having lost my best pals again, I stepped back on the treadmill to find some new ones. I spied... with my little eye.. .something beginning with A. A girl. Alone. In a bar. She was a very attractive girl.

With bashful left behind in England with Dopey and Sneezy, I strode in and took the table next to her. My approach was pretty weak.

'How's the food?' - which came out garbled, as my head was twisted round over my shoulder.

'It's okay.' she said. What magical words.

Somehow, I manoeuvred onto her table. I wasn't looking for a result, just companionship. We were staying at the same guest house but hadn't seen each other. She was Flemish; yes of course I knew where that was... where the hell was it? At first she was cold, formal, slightly aloof; but my first impressions of Harry sprang to mind and I resolved not to make the same presumption again. Her name was Chantal... mmmm. Using my work experience as a clown on a motorbike in Vietnam, and being in the Khao San Road circus, I played the fool to the limit.

This was a side of me that had emerged since travelling and I enjoyed the audience reaction. I noticed now that Chantal's eyes were limpid pools, and I wanted to dive into them naked and splash around. My tomfoolery was adding very attractive crinkles to the corners of her eyes and softening her lips to... kissable. I was reaching the third stage of enchantment, and every time she laughed she reached in and squeezed my heart. Once again, a woman had slipped in the backdoor and was right now strapping explosives to my soul.

She had seen Bumble staring out from my wallet, and with a slender hand over her mouth, was trying to hold in the chuckles. Her eyes gimlet with tears of laughter, she giggled... 'I am so sorry to laugh at you, but I'm sure only you would carry around a picture of a dog.'

I didn't know if this was good or not, but she asked to see it several times during the evening and at least she was laughing. I tend to wear my heart on my sleeve, cuff, collar, lapels... anywhere where it can be damaged so, anticipating a brush-off, I kept away the next day and ate alone, but I joined her later in the same bar for a few drinks and a bowl of beer nuts.

Travelling back across town from the Post Office, on the Chao Phraya Express boat, I realised I was seeing nothing, I had only one thing on my mind. Wats and palaces were passing me by like emperors in their new clothes. I had to make a move of some kind, so I hurried back to Rhanee's where Chantal sat cool and shaded. When I suggested eating out together that evening the affirmative came almost too quickly. I was wavering slightly, but a few shared beers cleared my mind and like a boy slipping his arm around a girl's shoulders at the cinema, I lifted her hand from the table and held it.

'Are you reading my palm?' she asked after a long pause.

'No - I'm just holding your hand.' Her eyes dipped momentarily, and for the next two hours we loved each other madly, bayed at the moon, hung upside down and scraped our shoes on the stars; but old doubts were creeping along behind in the shadows. Was I strong enough to handle a parting - another unrequited love? So we kissed briefly and sensibly before retiring, and I could tell she was frightened as well.

I said farewell to my bedbugs in the pale morning, paused to stare at the flimsy door along the corridor separating me from the sleeping Chantal, and dropped my pack to the floor. I wrote her a note, pinned it to the notice board, promising to meet her in Chiang Mai where we were both heading. I knew Chiang Mai would either be our swansong or duck shoot. The old qualms, inadequacies and doubts were nowhere to be seen. What the hell; like the great philosopher Forrest Gump said, 'Life's like a box of choclits, y'never know whatcha gonna get.'

❖

LEK HOUSE, CHIANG MAI

Enjoying another fine tray of food with wine and brandy, courtesy of Thai Airlines, I touched down in Chiang Mai with an agreeable Australian girl by my side. But Chantal was already inside.

I went straight to the hostel where I knew she was heading, trying to think of a plausible excuse as to why I hadn't gone to the one I'd said I would be going to. But then I thought, if you're skating on thin ice you might as well tap dance - you're going down one way or another.

Chiang Mai was a small version of Bangkok, an ancient town that had all but hidden its heritage with western bars and hotels, and the smell of fried chicken and burgers often rode roughshod over the incense from the hundreds of Wats scattered around the town.

Though the second largest city in Thailand, it was a manageable size, and its air was sweet, rolling down from the mountains, and frequently washed by clean rain and hung out to dry in the ensuing heat. Unlike Bangkok (Venice of the East) whose canals were a polluted broth, the moats around the city had clean water where people sat and fished; languid and hopeful as anglers anywhere in the world.

Just as languid, but not quite so hopeful, were the Europeans banged up in the prison in the centre of the city for drug offences. Backpackers were invited, nay encouraged, to visit and cheer them up - perhaps with a book or some chocolate. I was reading Midnight Express at the time, which wouldn't have made a good bedtime read, they wouldn't have the munchies - so chocolate would be a waste, so I didn't think I'd be much help, especially as I didn't have a lot of sympathy.

The hostel was a peach. I'd arrived by taxi and walked into another courtyard, quiet in the midday heat. Palm trees, hanging foliage and several men, all dozed in siesta. The only movement was a puppy dog's tail, sweeping fallen blossom - glad of a moving person. His 'yip, yip, yip' pulled open the left eye of one of the sleepers, who leapt up with a laugh and hopped from one leg to the other whilst he pumped my hand in welcome.

'I would like a room... a single room.' I said.

'Yes - Room 103!' he shot back, handing me a key attached to a large, smiling, wooden cat. Looking back up at his face I saw the same Cheshire smile.

'That'll do.' I said, to complete the quickest hostel check-in ever.

'No!' he said, 'Look first, you may not like.' I looked, I loved it, and walked back, crunching on the gravel to where he sat beaming.

'You're right...' I said, 'it's awful, horrible.' As the smile on his face disappeared below the horizon, I added...

'Do you know of a good hostel around here?' His mouth, wide open, snapped shut with a loud 'but..' and again... 'but..'

'Only joking,' I said 'it's a great room and you're not having this key back.' and tried to match his smile. Jiggling from hot-foot to other, and spinning around, he let loose a string of squeals and giggles, cuddled me from behind, massaged my shoulders and picking me up, carried me across the threshold; completing the friendliest hostel check-in ever.

There were several others like him. They were the trekking guides, who also served the food, checked in guests and cleaned the rooms; everything at a laughing, hopping jog and 'no problem!' It was an all-singing, all-dancing show, and the hostel was their stage.

On waking, the next morning, I looked across the courtyard through my mosquito net to see Chantal sitting behind a glass of orange juice, head thrown back laughing, with a pony-tailed, olive-skinned man; another piggin' Israeli?

To save face and self respect, I showered and shaved for a remarkably long time, dressed twice, and eventually stumbled across the gravel, stubbing my toe on a plant pot. In a gesture of defiance and perhaps possession, I kissed her hello on the lips. She was still laughing; with me or at me? They'd been on the bus for fourteen hours and I knew how this threw people together. On a Dulux colour chart, I'd have fitted snugly between emerald and pea-green, and home-makers would have chosen me for my dazzling hue.

I'd fallen foul of for first impressions again. He was a Mexican called Oscar - slight of build, but straight and true as an Aztec lay-line. They'd been waiting for a double room to become vacant, but I realised she was shining at me and only glowing dully in his direction. We shared breakfast as we waited for a room to vacate, and when one was offered, we decided that Chantal should have mine and Oscar and I would share the double.

This was a great relief, and I knew it was the right course of action, as I always held that longing was the best part of belonging. As well as that - I really liked Oscar. He asked *me* for advice about travelling, had no pretentions, and was as respectful as any English gentleman. He was also the first Mexican I had slept with; we got on like a hacienda on fire. He'd come all the way from South America to study Thai massage at a school in Chiang Mai; he'd seen a leaflet in Mexico!

'I could qualify in two weeks - and then I could go home and start a business!' Did we think that was a good idea?

Oscar was out, riding with Bandidos somewhere in night-time Chiang Mai, which left Chantal and I watching the stars through beer glasses and shooting the breeze. We wondered at someone's determination to travel halfway round the world for a two week course; and why we, who'd completed more courses than anybody needed, were wandering around for a whole year with no plans at the end. I discovered that we'd both left home the same week; that we'd travelled the same circuit in China and even crossed paths at Yangshuo for a few days; that as I was riding down Vietnam on Minx, she was on the train, and the day I shunted into Hoi-An - she was leaving. Harry and I were scoffing noodles downstairs in the Green Bamboo Café in Hanoi, whilst she was upstairs - ill. You could say we felt a strange attraction. And as bed time came around, Chantal slipped around the other side of my little veranda, on the way to her room, but stopped, and leant over the wall. I kissed her still firm lips, her neck, then across her downy shoulder and back to her...was I imagining it? - slightly parted and softer mouth. We were still working at each other, bobbing and weaving and looking for a clench.
'I am exhausted Howie, I'll see you in the morning.'
'Night Flem.' I said, as calmly as I could, as behind the wall I was hiding a hard-on a cat couldn't scratch. Two feet away, on the other side of a thin bamboo wall, I'm sure I heard Chantal, as I drifted into slumber...purring like a kitten.

Through the leafy canopy, the Siamese sun filtered into our coffee as we broke our fast. Across the gravel came Rak, juggling two bucket-size mugs, deliberately rattling them whilst walking an invisible tight-rope. He bounced them onto the table, not a drop spilt - singing...
'Tea for two, and two for tea... me for you (looking at Chantal) and you for me (swivelling to me).'
'But we already have coffee.' said Chantal.
'Have tea too...ha, ha, ha, ha, ha, ha; no problem - Rak's gift.'
Rak, who was later to take us trekking, was charming and funny; birds were falling out of the trees at his feet.
'I get you a biiigggg breakfast! I know you Germans eat a lot.'
'But we're not....'
'I know.. .ha, ha, ha, ha, ha.'
I'd finished the huge breakfast, and my hand, dangling over the side of the cane chair, was nuzzled by a wet, puppy's nose. I started playing with him, and perhaps with Bumble in mind, allowed him to nip my

finger and bite me playfully. In his excitement he launched an attack on my arm. I saw a thin scratch tracking across my wrist, around my thumb, and turning my hand over, increase in width and colour into an angry cut. I suddenly remembered the French newspaper I'd somehow managed to translate and read earlier. An article had interested me, especially after seeing the scabby mutts roaming Bangkok, stating that over 60% of the dogs in Thailand carried the rabies virus, and should be avoided where possible. The scratch on my hand seemed to turn into a festering wound, and I could almost see wriggly things burying along my veins. How stupid could I be? It was too late to suck the poison like a boy scout bitten by an adder, so I stared at the wound, waiting for the convulsions to arrive. Was I imagining it or was I going blind? No, a cloud had crossed the sun. Chantal arrived, and with a soft, moist kiss - sealed the wound, and put a cold compress on my heart. Hell, if you're going to go, why not rabies?

Numbed by the choice of treks available and stultified by the presence of each other, we whiled away the morning doing nothing.
  Rak brought lunch, asking - 'You two not going anywhere today?'
  'Yes,' I suddenly decided, 'I'm going for a haircut.' Chantal looked at me in surprise. 'I'm having one in every country just for the sake of it, and so I can tell my hairdresser friend Carl in England, how underwhelmed I am by his cutting skills.'
  'Well,' said Chantal, 'In that case, I'm going for a massage to loosen up for the evening.' Gosh.

The tiny lady in Hanoi, who had to climb a pair of steps to do the top, gave me an amazing cut - using a pair of wallpaper scissors and a hand operated pair of sheep shears over an ancient tortoiseshell comb, so I had no qualms when the Thai pensioner donned a surgical mask, pointed an interrogation lamp at my head, and set to, after a loud 'thrump' through his nose.
  I sat, smiling at the absurdity of it all. He took this as encouragement - not knowing that without my glasses I can't see the wall in the opticians, let alone the chart on it. My smile was fading after an hour though, as I couldn't figure out where he'd found the hair to cut for so long; it was already short before he'd started. Eventually, after stepping up to the podium and back many times, snipping at something each time, he removed his mask with a 'thrump' and handed me my specs. It was perfect. It was Steve McQueen in 'Papillon' with a Tin-Tin quiff at the front. I laughed. He laughed; nervously.
  I slapped him on the back, disturbing the cloud of microscopic hairs he'd managed to create. This was a fifty pound haircut; it cost half a

dollar. I gave him two dollars with glee, as I loved it, and had the delicious thought that any traveller following me into the chair was going to get the same... not very hippy man! Pulling my hand forcibly from the old barber's grip, I left his shop. I spied Chantal entering a café after her massage, loose I hoped, and followed in behind her. She turned at the sound of the door, and looked; then looked again.

'Wow,' she said running her fingers up the back, 'Wow.' again.

'Hey, where did ya' get that haircut man?.. that's cool?' asked the traveller at the next table. I navigated him to the shop and described the old cutter. 'I'm going to get one.' he said, and left.

I turned back to Chantal, flicking my locks. Her eyes were blazing above her smile. She loved it, or perhaps she just loved the fact that I'd done it. It had been a good afternoon's work, but later I was to fan the flames even higher, unintentionally but very effectively.

❖

The two of us sat in Daret House, Chaiyofum Road, facing each other over a fantastic fish hot-pot; squid slinking in the depths, while above, crabs chased chillis amongst waving fronds of coriander. I'd grabbed a sneaky head-start at Lek House, while Chantal was getting ready, and sunk a few Thai beers, and was, to put it mildly - fluid; but still in control I thought.

I was being distracted from the heavenly smile in front of me, by the sounds behind... bip-bap-bip-bap ping-pong bip-bap. For some reason, I was turning around every few minutes to watch the locals playing table-tennis. One of them gestured me to play. I politely refused, but turning back to Chantal - she smiled at me to go.

'They will like it if you play with them.' she encouraged.

Without rhyme or reason I left a crab claw in mid air and took a paddle. Now I was quite good at this when younger, and even had a small tin-cup for it somewhere; my solitary cup, that sat among my brother's massed army of tall, fat, silver trophies. It had a purpose though, as it collected all the dust and left all of his sparkling. My mother, bless her, regularly moved it to the front, after the surrounding bully boys had nudged it into a dark corner; she even went to the pretence of trying to make it shine. It never shone - however hard it was rubbed. In fact it was rubbed so much, the crossed bats became a smudge, and my title read 'Table Ten... ham.'

I took on the first player quite easily, and getting into my rhythm, beat the replacements as they came - each one better than the last; until the final one. Stony-faced and cool, he matched every shot as the audience grew, but they were clapping both of us. I was pleased to see that he was as sweaty as me when we shook hands. I was chuffed, as I had beaten him narrowly, and then it hit me - I had left an angel in mid-dinner, to play ping-pong. I returned drenched, bowed and crestfallen to the table and sat down. There again though was that same glowing smile. I'd somehow done the right thing.

We left by the back door, as the bar had closed long ago, and wandered back to Lek House. Parting at our separate doors - we didn't. She leant over, and brushing my neck with her cheek whispered:
'I want you with me tonight.'
'Yes, I do too,' I said panicking... condoms! I returned to my room, where Oscar was asleep under his igloo-shaped mosquito net.
Rummaging in the dark for the packet I knew was there, somewhere, Oscar awoke.
'Hey Howie, how goes man?'
'Very good Oscar, I'm sleeping next door tonight, so lock the door behind me.'
'S'cool man, wondered how long you two would take.' And he rolled over, naked - conchitas waiting for him in his dreams.

We danced on each other's bones; first a fiery tarantella, then a bouncy bossanova, the bed and the bamboo walls swaying to the beat, and finally as daylight was more than newborn, and the morning kitchen sounds clinked and clattered, we'd floated through the mosquito net, past the ceiling fan, and were sleeping spoons on a cotton wool cloud somewhere in the north of Thailand.

We bumped to earth quite sharply when Oscar knocked at the door, and shouted through the bamboo...
'I go to school now bambinos, sees you later!' and left for his first massage lesson. Between snoozes, we massaged each other's egos, hearts and insides, and the dust disturbed from the floor raced around in the shaft of light from the glassless window. The cat had got the cream. I dozed; purring.

❖

Its name was Snowy, a stuffed white toy. In the day it was my friend. Together my bruvver and I rode it, bouncing down the stair-rods and drab paisley carpet. At night the landing light squeezed into the bedroom and lit Snowy, hiding under Martin's bed. Snowy frightened me at night.

Tommy Slater could make great machine gun noises, 'Ack, ack, ack, doosh, doosh, doosh ... pwwhiirrrrr' Mine just went du, du, du, du. Nobody played dead when I shot them.

The sun shone through the primary school window onto the blackboard marked "The Weather Today", and when the monitor banged the dusters together, I thought he was making clouds.

My brother was told off for showing off. He did a handstand and broke my Mum's glasses. She sent him to his bedroom. I hated her. It was his 8th birthday. But I cried 'cos she couldn't see and the red marks on the sides of her nose looked sore.

The Budds were the same age as me, but bigger. Their Dad ran the scrap yard. He had deformed arms but still lifted engines from cars that smelt of old red leather and mould. I pushed John Budd in the stingers and hid in the coal cupboard at home. I got the cane.

If you put dandelions down someone's back, they wet the bed.

If you threw mud pies at the side of your council house, they stuck, and when he came home from work, your Dad went barmy. I loved pulling the ends of the sheets from the mangle, when Mum was turning the handle. The water oozed down your arms from the rubber rollers and into the tin bucket. I put my hands in the mangle once to dare myself. Didn't hurt.

"One, two, three, mother caught a flea, put it in the teapot and made a cup of tea, flea jumped out, mother gave a shout, Dad came running with his shirt hanging out."

Snow was the best thing in the world, until your gloves and balaclava got wet, and the cold made you run indoors, hand and ears stinging with burn and tears; until, to be brave, you went back out again to stick rocks in snowballs and crack your head on ice slides.

We stole Jif lemons from the village shop with the rusty Tizer sign, to use as water pistols. We got caught and Mum chased us with a wooden spoon, and broke it when a wild swing at Martin missed and hit the banister. We laughed, Mum wasn't laughing.

Bonfire night was scary, and we had to put a cloth over the goldfish bowl, so it wouldn't die of fright. Dad said so. Dad was an engineer.

They poured milk on the machines to cool them down, and he came home smelling of metal shavings, until he went in his shed and came out all wood, sometimes with a boat or a fort or a garage with Shell stickers and a ramp that went up and down.

Mum's Hoover switched off at elevens's time; we had orange squash and biscuits, and sat by the radio to wait for the lady to say, as she did every day "Are you're sitting comfortably?" and we would wiggle our bums... "then I'll begin." And as the song began with the Grand Old Duke of York's men marching up the hill to a trumpeting ... or was it a trombone ... or ... I was dragged from Clappers Meadow, Alfold, Surrey - 1964 to...

...the trumpeting, not entirely tuneful, split my dream into pieces. Where the hell was I? My arse ached, and the tugging at my sleeping bag was definitely not from Chantal. Even without my glasses I realised that the wet and snuffling member snorting my bedding was as thick as a man's thigh and - attached to the front of an elephant!
 I touched the yard-broom bristles to confirm my suspicions, and it disappeared out the window with a snort, grey against the dark sky, still half past a moonbeam. I turned to Chantal and even in the gloom, could see her face, innocent and as happy as a sleeping child, felt her puppy breath sweet against my cheek. Disturbed, but not woken, she buried deep into my neck with a warm nose.
 I pinched myself, to confirm that I was in a village hut in the northern hills of Thailand with a lovely girl and the elephant we'd ridden together the previous day. The insane grin that recognised this kept me awake for a long time, and I was glad, as it gave me time to breathe in the perfume of life; freedom, rain-drenched air, elephant dung, lingering opium clouds, sweet Belgian musk - and I realised that this was it. And now I knew at last what 'It' was. Tomorrow I could die happy, knowing that although I'd still be missing a lot, I'd had so much; so much more than most. My candle had burned so very bright through storm and flood, while others' had flickered dimly in a sheltered breeze.

❖

RAK'S TREK

The weather was like a child on an activity centre. It would push the heat button, spin the clouds, and pull the string for rain; often spinning, pulling and pushing at the same time. We took our boots off to cross streams, put them on to climb a hill of mud, took them off, then - just kept them on whatever. When the cloud covered the sun, the fields and hills were khaki, until the sun cracked through, and then the country turned into heaps and mounds of sparkling emeralds.

We trekked through mud and sheets of rain thick as duvets. The slopes were often steep and slippery, but Rak sang, danced and jollied us along, even when we didn't need it. Chantal and I sat in our creaking wicker basket as Rak rode the elephant's head, flapping its ears with his bare feet. He rode it backwards like Pan on a buffalo, sometimes standing up, pretending to mock gallop; the man's store of fun was bottomless.

As we climbed the hills on our bristly juggernaut, Rak explained the problems that opium had caused his country.

'These slopes were once beautiful with red and white and blue flowers, but of course the by-product of this beauty was opium. Over 90% of the population were users, and most of the addicts were cabbages. Work output fell - as people didn't want to work; only smoke. So the growing of poppy was banned, and the government brought in a slash and burn policy to rid the country of the menace. For me it was very difficult as I loved smoking opium, but it has made my country better and now I see the people happier and working. Large areas were de-forested and the people were encouraged to grow cabbages instead of the so pretty flowers'

And there, as we puffed our way up a skid-pan slope, the rain dripping from the penthouse of our backpacks, were the cabbages; laid out in neat geometrics, for all impressions - a graveyard, marking its former victims, spread up and over and around the hills. I stopped, cotton-wool breath billowing, and thought twice about drugs.

Now that the number of users had been halved, a lot of the addicts had been rehabilitated, and it was one of these that I lay facing on the rattan floor, arm crooked under my head, drawing in great lungfuls of opium, whilst he poked in the bead of bubbling resin with a pointy stick. But we knew that this was tourist class, for fun only, and we wouldn't be taking a trip across clouds of flowers and cabbages. Opium has a calming effect that also heightens the senses, and it was whilst floating in this euphoria, with Chantal stroking my forearm, that Rak was persuaded to tell a tale. The light from the oil lamps crept across the floor, up the bamboo wall, and slinked out into the smouldering dusk over the window sills. Rak coughed long and hard into a dark corner and started.

'My first trek was in 1979, when I was only sixteen and not a real guide. A hotel owner had phoned me one morning to say that two Germans wanted to go trekking in the hills. I thought it a good chance and went over there in a flash. In the bar, waiting for me, were two huge German men. Not even knowing what to charge I asked: 'You want to go trekking?'
'Jah, in de mountains.'
'Would you like to ride elephants - it is more expensive?'
'Jah, money is no problem.'
I left and returned two hours later with all preparations made - to give them a schedule. They had gone, and the very happy barman said, 'They very good customers Rak, they spend 100 dollars today!'
'You have robbed them,' I said 'even for that amount!' as I pointed at a table, full of empty beer and whiskey bottles.
'No,' he said, very upset, 'look under the table Rak.' and he pulled the cloth aside, to show many, many, more empty bottles. 'Oh God!' I said.
'They said they go to the silk factory and will see you at one.' said my friend. I went back to the bar at one, and they were there, dressed in the finest silk suits and new handmade leather shoes!
'But we must go now,' I told them 'you must go and change!'
'It's OK Rak, we have more of these,' said the biggest, 'Do we have time to go to beer shop?' At three, they were ready to go, but unfortunately then, in come the elephant owner.
He saw the empty bottles and the size of the Germans and said 'No my elephants cannot carry them.' I saw my first job disappearing, and whispered to him, 'They will pay extra.' We had to pay the man double, but they were happy with it, and we left four hours late.
The next day, still in their fine silk garments, we climbed up a steep hill, one of them in the basket, one on the head, and the legs of the poor elephant were bending. In my stupidity, I stopped to speak to a farmer, but I keep my eye on the elephant going away from me. I did not know that over the hill - slash and burn was going on, and the smoke was scaring the beast, who almost was running, and the Germans bouncing up and down. The owner shouted, and the farmer and me chased after them, and as we went over the top of the hill we saw the elephant

charging down the hill. One of the Germans grab hold of a branch as they went under a tree, and his trousers rip off. The other hang on to the flapping ears, until the beast get to the river and with a big trumpet... stop dead. The German flew into the muddy river. We pulled him out, and all ran back up the hill to get his friend, who still hang from the branch, with no trousers. 'Let go!' we all shout.'
  'Nein!' he say 'the elephant will get me!'
  Now with a big crack, the branch break from his weight. He hit the floor and started sliding down the hill on the mud, and past the elephant who was coming back up. The beast stood up on his back feet as the German went past, trumpeting, and then chased him down the hill. He wouldn't come out of the river until the elephant was gone.

When we got back to Chiang Mai we went to their hotel - which was very expensive. When we walked in, they saw a group of Western people at a table, and with torn and muddy clothes, and bruises and a nose bleed, they went up to them. I couldn't find anywhere to hide, and I saw my new job disappearing.
  The smaller of the two giants, the one with with no trousers said –
  'If you is thinking of the trekking - go wiz zis man Rak. It is great. But leave out ze elephant riding - it is a little uncomfortable.'

Rak tucked the two of us up under our blanket, both chuckling and giggling long into the night; but before I drifted off, I heard our porter - 'opium man' behind the curtain, blowing up a storm on his pipe; a soliloquy to the cabbage.

'Tea my little ones.' was Rak's morning greeting, as we scrambled to wake. 'No worries!' have a cuddle, wake up slow - it's raining.'
  We crossed swollen streams barefoot, showered under pounding waterfalls in underwear, stumbled off the narrow strips of green that held in the water of the paddies - filling our boots. Then, through the rain which was sweeping across like a theatre curtain, a hill village appeared; all stilted bamboo, squealing pigs, and smoke curling damply into the mist. As I heaped my backpack onto the others in one of the huts, I watched a small boy crouched on the packed earth outside, firing a catapult at a piglet.
  This was a 'Karen' tribe - the most numerous of the hill people, and not particularly rare. But we weren't collecting stamps or Brownie points, just having a look; getting a taste. Initially, children were the only sign of life. Dressed in handmade calico clothes and smoking pipes, they had already learned by heart...'5 baht!' which was the rate for anything; a photograph, a friendship bracelet, a brooch.

Eventually however, men strolled into or through the village, invariably sporting Adidas stripes or a Nike logo on their jogging bottoms. Warmed by a rice dinner and tea from a villager, Chantal walked off to the edge of the village - and a small hilltop. I left her alone with her thoughts for a time, and then followed up the winding, slippery path - nervous. As I approached, I looked past her to where she was gazing.

Puffy clouds streamed out of Burma, their shadows plunging down the slopes of cabbage, then slowing as they moved up the hills. She turned to me, sweeping her hair back against the wind with one hand, and taking my hand with the other. As she looked into my eyes, her own were alight; full dark electric pupils - like a cat's.

'Burma,' she said, knowing that I knew, 'I have to leave Bangkok to go there in three days.' And as she said it - her eyes dimmed.

'Chantal... I have a very hard question to ask. It's been going around in my head since yesterday.' I chewed the inside of my lip, and wincing, asked...

'Can I come down to Bangkok with you? When you leave, Thailand will be finished for me also.' She breathed loudly and pulled me to her, nuzzling into my neck, and murmured...

'I dreamt you asked me that in my sleep last night, or perhaps I just hoped you would. Oh yes please!'

And so the sadness of parting was trampled over by another three days with each other. We returned to Lek House entertained, invigorated, and very much together. The storm clouds gathered over our picnic.

❖

SUMPRASONG GUEST HOUSE, SUKOTHAI

With only a brief time left together, we opted for a single stop-off on the return to Bangkok; Sukothai, the first but short-lived capital of Thailand.

It had an impressive line-up of Wats, but after Bangkok and Chiang Mai, I was practically stuffed with Wats. The area around Sukothai had been flooded before our arrival, and the river in the town was lapping at the top of the banks - so thick with mud it looked walkable. We spent the afternoon as only lovers can, and strolling out for an early evening walk; the sky put on a show.

The rumbumptious weather patterns were battling it out above, refereed by a waning sun. The spectacle resembled Van Gogh's palette after a mad canvas. The clouds were every shape from round to square, and the only green cloud I'd ever seen was threatening a purple patch that already looking bruised from the conflict; the river was pink. I was whirling around in the road, eyes aloft, until Chantal pulled me to the safety of the pavement. The mood stayed with me until much later, when we sat in the dark of our balcony, and tongue loosened by beer, I poured thoughts onto the sounds of the night: raindrops, cicadas, cats fighting; our hands holding very tightly - in desperation that our time together was running away down the chocolate pink river.

I gabbled on for hours, dredging up old memories, thoughts and feelings; talking China, Vietnam, Belgium, England. I was drunk with words, and they all wanted to come out. My mouth went bananas. For the first time since I left home, I felt I could pour it all out: I laughed, I cried, my voice went deep and hoarse with the effort, and at last I stopped. There was a silence like after the crash of broken glass.

The rain had stopped.

'Oh god,' I said 'I'm so sorry Chantal... I've been talking crap for hours, you....' She put a finger to my lips and led me to bed.

It was nine in the morning, and the sun was already at it. Seasoned travellers that we now were, we spurned the taxi driver's special offer of 200 baht for a return trip, and headed for the local bus to the ruins – 10 baht.

We had the choice between an open-sided affair - that could have come from Trumpton, or a charabanc that would have been at home on a day trip to Bangor. We chose the latter, as it looked as though it may be quicker. We rumbled out of the station at 5mph and roared into second gear. Several minutes later, just when the engine seemed to be near exploding, the driver jammed it into third, and reaching its top speed of 10mph - stopped suddenly, to pick up an old lady with a shopping bag. Chantal and I looked sideways at each other, eyebrows raised. The driver had converted his area into a lounge. A 1970's music centre sat on a shelf supported by wrought-iron brackets, the speakers above and behind him. A lamp-cover with tassels hung round the light, throwing a shadow onto the picnic chair beside him, supposedly for guests. Between the driver and the chair - resplendent on the engine cover, was a vase of plastic flowers. Real flowers would have been shaken to bare stalks by the vigorous gear changing, and we saw that we too were being vibrated forward. Only by shifting back continually could we avoid ending up in the guest chair. We arrived at our stop at the old town - bums sore, but amused, despite the thirty two stops.

Two bicycles were pushed at us with – '15 baht for day.' We took them and set off around the ruins. The wats and buddhas had been groomed into a virtual theme park, each different area incurring another entrance fee, and the only thing missing was a procession of people dressed in orange robes like a Disneyland parade. Virtually empty of visitors, the only things in abundance were wats, as thick on the ground as fleas on the scabby Bangkok dogs. We took advantage of the situation by using the paths for a game of hide-and-seek on bikes.

I caught glimpses of Chantal between wats, hid behind golden buddahs, and when a hand tapped me on the shoulder, I whirled around expecting it to be her, but found two Japanese girls asking, 'Please, can take picture?'

We cycled to the ancient dam through pampas-like grass, where lesser wats stood derelict as scarecrows, and cows drifted in and out of the shade of solitary trees. We skimmed stones and hearts across the water, making no promises beyond the night to come. We opted for the Trumpton bus for the trip back to town, in the hope it would be quicker. After the exhilarating acceleration to 11mph we stopped suddenly and picked up a bunch of schoolboys. Schoolboy humour and bashfulness caused them to giggle and fight, and being in a childish mood ourselves, we contributed to their state by making faces and winking.

Chantal exploded into laughter - which had them straight-backed and blank-faced with confusion. I shrugged my shoulders at the uneasy line of faces, to try and comfort them, but Chantal whispered in my ear, 'The little one on the end has his money in his ear.'

At that point the conductor arrived and glad of a diversion they all turned to her. The little one prised the coin from his lughole with some difficulty, then gave it to her; we hoped he wouldn't be given any change - as the next coin down was much, much bigger. We rocked and roared all the way to our stop, where the frowning boys and smiling conductor waved us off, and the driver rang his big brass bell. We giggled into the Wagon Wheel restaurant for a fiery Tom Yum soup, which turned our tears of laughter into tears of pain and joy.

At bedtime however, Chantal's eyes brimmed with anguish, cutting me to the bone, and making me wish I'd never started this thing.
　'I want you to come to Burma with me.'
　'I would love to come to Burma with you Chantal.'
　'But we have to go our own ways though, don't we?' 'Do we?'
　'Yes.' I said. If only I could go back and change that word.
We took a last walk along the Willy Wonka river, reflecting on a magical day in Sukothai. We held hands and hearts all the way to Bangkok on the bus, spent one last night together at Rhanee's, and before I knew it, I was standing in the middle of the Kho San Road with a lump in my throat, watching Chantal's bus disappear around the corner to Burma, India and Nepal. My visa to Chantal had expired.

I staggered back to Rhanee's and moved my belongings from the double room, where we had spent our last night, into the single box room - with my old mates the bedbugs. I lay on the sarong that Chantal had given me, staring at the ceiling – trying to find some positive thoughts. It was no good, I had to go and get pissed.
　I walked up and down the Khao San Road, friendless, clueless; passing the empty green chairs where we'd first met, a thought grew from out of nowhere. Harry was here somewhere.
　I scanned the bars with no result, until, for no apparent reason, I returned to the café down a side alley, where Chantal and I had enjoyed our last meal. Approaching the chair where she'd sat, I saw Harry - waiting. 'Hello old friend' I said, 'I knew that you would be here.'
　'Yes,' he said 'I knew you would find me here if I sat long enough.'
　'I go home to Sweden tomorrow.'
　We didn't look for an explanation or a meaning, but merely said our goodbyes over many hours and bottles: went our separate ways.

Bangkok had a pall of melancholy hanging over it that spread to the boundaries of Thailand, so to escape, I pulled my flight to Bali back a few days - grimacing until departure. Despite my inward urgings, when the aeroplane parted the curtains of the Bangkok smog and sliced into clean blue air, the pilot didn't change course to Burma, but flew unwavering in the direction of Bali, with me wavering in my seat.

❖

KUTA BEACH, BALI

The first sign of things to come glided round the baggage carousel at Denpasar airport; suitcases - shiny and clean for their holidays. Backpacks were thin on the ground and pushed together like second-class passengers. I shared a ride into Kuta with a Kiwi, who flew over as regular as a trip to his local Tesco, buying cut price goods for his shop. He sold Australian surf-wear made in Bali, to New Zealanders.

On leaving the airport, it's possible to collect your bags, change into your Speedos in the taxi, apply suntan lotion and wrap around the sunglasses, by which time you've arrived at Kuta Beach, where you can spill directly onto the sand. Then, catching your first rays, you can look through the basting bodies, tits toasting, bums burning - right up to where the sun don't shine, and you may catch a glimpse of the next planeload skimming in to land; practically on the beach. There were more tits to be seen in one sweeping glance, than a year of Sun page threes, which shocked me initially after the modesty of the Vietnamese beaches; surprisingly, hawkers were not allowed onto the sand.

Kuta - half Australians, half hawkers. The latter had been irritating in China but easily ignored. In Vietnam, their extra guile made them harder to avoid, but their charm or looks normally compensated. In Kuta they were dedicated to their craft, though fairly inept, relying on unwary Americans and tourists to fall for their lines and prices. They were downright insulted if you didn't buy one of their fake watches, yo-yos that light up in the dark, or take the boy-girls from the inland side of Jalan Legian for a good time. One day, out of curiosity, I asked the price of a pack of cigarettes; knowing that they were 900 rupia in the shop. I could see this over his right shoulder.

'How much?' I asked, pulling out a pack.

'2000 rupia.' he snapped, hand outstretched for the money.

'1500.' I countered. 'No.' he parried.

'OK, I don't want them.' sliding them back into their slot. His friend, with an identical tray joined in ..'2000 rupia!'

I took the packet out again, and showed them the government price tag showing 1000 rupia. 'I offered your friend 1500 and he didn't want it, so I'm going to buy them in that shop over there.' As I entered the shop I was hit between the shoulder-blades by a double-barrel...'You fucker bastard!' and turning, met four eyes filled with malice; but they lacked the conviction of the Chinese gangsters or Vietnamese veterans, so I laughed.

My friends Kenny and Duggie were due to arrive in Bali in a few days, and I was looking forward to spending a week or so with some mates from home. I was hoping I might be able to persuade them to do some 'real' travelling for a short while, but I knew that I couldn't stay with them, as I was a lone traveller now, and the rewards of going it alone were too great to lose.

Meanwhile, I thought to myself... let's see how you can fit back in to real life - so as to speak, and try to come to terms with the loss of a love. Chantal was summer on my mind.

I spent the afternoon on Kuta beach, basting with the rest, and surfed a rented surfboard on a messy shore break. Coming off the beach, I made a beeline for the famous Surf Bar on Poppies 2. Hurrying past the concrete wave at the entrance, where kooks could have their photo taken - pretending that they're surfing, I settled down to a beer - so cold it froze my fingers to the side of the glass.

Without Happy Hour I couldn't have afforded it; the other customers seemed to think it was cheap. But on the cinema-size TV screen above, Tom Curren - the Rudolf Nureyev of the surfing world, was ripping and slashing some of the best waves in the world. I melted into the screen as Ullawatu (just along the coast), Pipeline, Bells, Kirra, and all the other famed waves rolled by. I was going to be visiting them all. It made me hungry.

Amongst the jumble of side streets running back up from the beach, I sat alone in a restaurant, writing with one hand, shovelling Nasi Goreng into my mouth with the other. I tried to block out the conversation to my left which was grating on my nerves. Gus and Tobes had moved over to the table to join two girls already there. They were English public schoolboys, accent so posh, they could have had the silver spoons they were born with still stuck in their mouths. I wondered why they were here and not Monte Carlo or Cannes?

'Hi gels, mind if us chaps sit down?' They sat down without an affirmative and commenced boring the girls stupid.

'Oh yes, parachuting is just *the* business; did my basic training at Aldershot.. from a balloon, then - gave it the big one at Sandhurst - 15,000 feet free frall.' Gus was a bit worse for wear, and his prey were shrinking back to try and gain some airspace.

'That's right ay Tobes?'

'Yah... but heli-skiing is pretty damn close to it for the old adrenalin. I was just telling this luvvy creature how many harses your family have.'

'Oh Christ! must be dozens of them.'

'Not harses you prat... houses!'

At this point Gus kicked his chair backward to the floor and sprinted for the toilet.

'Must have gone to throw arp.' said Tobes, head swaying alarmingly.

'Sorry about that gels, had to go an' throw up..' said Gus, returning on jelly legs, replacing the chair and sitting down... 'just the four now, and the lodge in Scotland of course.'

The girls had taken enough and took their leave, grinning at me and grimacing at the boys' backs. Gus and Tobes grated on to each other.

'Y'know Tobes, being honest now; never ever in our time together, never, ever thought D'Arcy's jokes were funny, never, ever farking laughed once... ever; though one pretended to of course.'

'S'right!'

'Never, ever.'

'Hey! sis bill correct old chap?' slurred Tobes. 'Surely can't be this much... only had a couple of drinks!'

'No problem Tobes... got m'calculator with me - can add it up.' Gus couldn't.

'Look at this farking loser Tobes, at the next table, writing his postcards or something... think he's a Dago?'

'P.. p..p robly.' stammered Tobes.

'Should be out looking for chicks... get his dick pulled, must be something wrong with him eh?' 'Hyaaa, hyaaa, hyaaa!'

Gus let go a snort that would have won him first prize at a pig show. I didn't want to look across - I'd avoided it so far, but I couldn't help myself. And there they were; Tobes - hefty, with bloaty jowels, and bum-fluff on his upper lip; Gus - weedy, thin nose, no chin; both sporting foppish haircuts, polo shirts, khaki shorts and boating shoes. I laughed as they stared at me with unsteady, watery, and I guessed - 17 year old eyes.

'What's *your* problem Dago?' said Gus.

I very carefully and very correctly pronounced - in the proper Queen's English...'Fuck off... and go to bed old chap, before I call Matron.'

'No need to be like that old chap – didn't know you were English.'

As they staggered out the door, a girl entered through the adjacent one, reminding me of those little weather houses; out went 'wet and windy', in came 'sunny'. She was an Asian girl; a girl of immeasurable gorgeousness. As though time had stopped still, forks, spoons and food hung somewhere between plates and mouths. Kicks were being delivered under tables by wives and girlfriends.

She sat alone at a table directly across from me and sideways on, which meant I could feast my eyes whilst eating. The males in the place were stealing looks, while pretending to scratch their ear, or read the menu. She noticed. So did the girlfriends.

I decided to enjoy myself; after all, I had nothing to lose; I was past embarrassment. I called the waiter and asked him to deliver a note, that I'd quickly scribbled, to her table. This was spotted by all the hungry males, who watched his progress across the room, all thinking...
'It'll never work.'

She unfolded the note, the waiter waiting. She laughed, beautiful hand to lovely lips, leaving only the impossible eyes visible. She asked the waiter who. He pointed at me; the whole room pointed at me. I raised my glass and smiled my best smile, and lo and behold, she beckoned me over. The faces watching me thread my way through the tables had 'Bastard!' written all over them, but the girlfriends were all smiles.

As I bent down to sit, she grabbed my pendant (beautifully), pulled my head down to hers, and planted a soft kiss. My lips exploded with delight. I thought I was in a James Bond movie. A dozen men furiously set about their cooling dinners. Having met at the wrong end of the evening, it was a short coupling, but a meal was agreed for the next night. She was from Singapore. She took my hand and led me from the restaurant. I winked and shrugged at every green face I passed.

We had a fun meal the next night, I don't remember what, but we must have looked fresh from bed, as this time all the males in the restaurant were smiling lewd, lascivious smiles. I felt like explaining that - 'No we haven't - you don't have to you know; but we *had* taken two evenings out of each other's lives... and shared them.'

She was leaving for Singapore at I don't know how much o'clock, so we parted in Jalan Legian after an affectionate hug and kiss.

She asked... 'Why didn't you try to go to bed with me?'

'Because I didn't want to,' I replied, and thought 'that sounds like an insult.' But I also knew that I felt a huge loyalty to Chantal, and had no intention of cheating on her. But there was also the fear of rejection.

'Thank you,' she said, 'if you had tried to sleep with me, I would dislike you. But now I love you and will remember you always.'

Jesus wept!

Oh yes...the note? That would be telling.

❖

I'd rung my brother when I first arrived, to ask him to confirm Duggie and Kenny's arrival date; I'd been here four days now and they should have arrived. I was spending a fortune ringing home and I knew my brother was also spending time and money at home trying to find out what was going on.

I had rested, gained some bodyweight and a tan, and felt more human; but no less alone. I wanted to get to Ubud - the artists' colony in the centre of the island, and from there to Mount Batur - the volcano in the north. I'd heard that there were eruption warnings, so I had to be there soon; behind these, Lombok, Sumbawa and Flores beckoned, tempting me away from Chantal province, who for all I knew had already stashed me away on a dusty page in the back of her passport.

It was time to move myself.

'What the hell's going on Martin?' I shouted down the phone.

'I don't know!!' He shouted back.

We were starting to get annoyed at each other; an irrational brother thing.

'All I can find out is that Duggie probably won't be coming.'

'What about Kenny?'

'I'm speaking to his Mum tonight. Ring me tomorrow at work, and hey... forget about the others... enjoy yourself. What's Ullawatu like?' And it dawned on me; he was working away at home as usual, looking after his kids and trying to help me out whilst I was on a dream trip. I was an arsehole.

'Sorry Martin; I'm going down there tomorrow, I'll give you a full report.'

I booked my bus ticket to Ubud for two days hence, hired a motorbike and bought a toilet roll; act positive. I needed to go to Ullawatu – I'd drooled over it in magazines throughout my surfing life, now here was the chance to see it – to feel it slamming onto the reef.

The Balinese were laid back, as were their road signs - right back in the grass; so it was a long trip. I went via Nusa Dua at the opposite end of the peninsula, and found a purpose-built, luxury resort, of no interest to me apart from a telephone.

I bowled into the hotel lobby and phoned England. Martin picked up, and immediately I watched the rupiah disappearing on the screen.

'Can't speak long Martin, what's the go?'

'Duggie *can't* come – I'll tell you why another time, and Kenny won't go by himself. You're on your own Bro'. Do it... and take care.'

Bastards! At least they could have contacted me. I stomped out of the hotel under a black cloud, a stream of filth fuming from my mouth.

I knew I'd made a big mistake. I should have followed my heart to Burma. Instead, I'd wasted a week sitting in Kuta. I would have to shorten my trip along Indonesia and shoot on to Oz. From there, with money waiting for me, I could perhaps go back and meet Chantal somewhere. In the meantime, apart from hanging a Kick Me sign on my back, I didn't know what else to do. I rode on, a steel band of depression and anger tightening round my forehead; at least I could go and see some surf; that might help a bit.

I passed by the Ullawatu Cliff Surf Beach sign through sheer speed, then the official Ullawatu Beach sign, and confused, turned right at the next Ullawatu Beach sign, which turned out to be Padang Padang Surf Beach. Well...what's an Ullawatu between friends. Negotiating a dirt track that rivalled any in Vietnam, I arrived at the car park.

'Need a guide.' the first of the swarm said. It wasn't a question.

'You have to have guide to go to beach.' another threatened.

'No I don't - not unless it's an eighteen year old Girl Guide.' I said. Walking off in the general direction of the sea, I saw a sign that said 'Don't get lost - get a guide.'

I took a path between some shacks, insults being hurled at me from behind, until it split in all directions. I took a guess and followed the flip-flop marks, crushed cigarette cartons and supermarket bags, until turning left at a patch of dusty, thorny scabbage, I spied below me a magical sight.

Rolling in, bedecked with twinkling sunbursts, were queues of waves, their tops blown back; white quiffs in the offshore breeze. Sitting amongst this corrugated heaven, silhouetted against the burning reflections, were what looked like a school of porpoises, bobbing over green skylark hills. Even from where I was standing, I could see that they measured twice head high. As I watched, one of the shapes broke away from the pack and carved its signature along the virgin face; signing off at the end with a 'whooop!' that steamrollered up the hill to my feet. As a surfer of quite paltry ability, the scene below filled me with an electric gush and I had to sit on a rock to take it in. My surfing was woeful, though much enjoyed, and I could handle a right hander on a beach-break, but this was a left over a coral reef. A sharp coral reef.

I watch the next set arrive from the horizon, the energy that has travelled so far, compressing as the seabed shallows. Then finding a solid reef barring the way, it jumps up, indignant, to show its form, and sucks the water in front back up its glassy face, leaving the reef almost dry and gurgling. Along the unbroken face the surfer dances his tune, and as the lip of the wave curls over to punish the reef, he stays one jump ahead to avoid being used as a missile. Like a matador, he teases the shoulder of the wave, flicking the board away and back, a red cape to the roaring bull foaming behind him. And the ultimate; he stalls the board to let the lip catch up and envelop him in its mouth, then shoots out forward in flying spray and over the top of the wave, which comes thundering down onto the reef.

Having never been behind the green door (inside a barrelling wave), I can only wonder at the feeling it must impart; but I know that even when riding a normal wave, perhaps stealing up and down its face, the energy that it harbours runs through the board, your feet and into your body. The buzz that results is unequalled by any artificial substance, and the only comparison I have is to be making waves of your own with a woman you love.

The injuries passing by me testified to the difficulty of the wave, and I knew that the surfers I was watching were.. hotties. Wandering into their camp, intimidated and awed, I was asked if I was going in.
 'No, I'm not surfing today - just taking photos.' which massaged their egos and muscles. Offered a board, I came clean...
 'Thanks, but I'm only a beginner, I'd either get in the way or die.'
 'Good call mate.' said an Aussie, with a broken board and a gashed head. But I desperately wanted to be out in the line-up, stroke into an emerald hill, rip and slash my own signature. I knew it was beyond me; too old, too short sighted, too scared. I envied their youth and skill, and a great helplessness washed over me. I roamed the shoreline taking photos, dipping into rock pools, and hating myself for not being out there. I climbed back up the hill, often looking back at the joy below. I wish I could say that, 'I surfed Ulluwatu' but I can't. Rounding the last corner and looking back, a broken half of a board was floating in across the reef, alone.

On returning to the car park, I found that they had washed and polished the bike. '5000 Rupiahs!' they proclaimed.
 'That's bloody lovely,' I said, 'I'm sure the owner will be pleased... it's a rental bike!' Their smiles dropped lower than a monkey's arse as I thrashed the bike round the car park, spitting gravel and dust over their good works. It was rude, I know, but - as in Vietnam, I was in a dodgy state of anger, frustration and loneliness. I screamed the bike back to Kuta, determined to leave it empty and knackered like me. I cut up everybody I could, rode through red lights, slid round gravel corners, traded insults with bus drivers and other bikes, and on reaching Kuta - rode the wrong way up the pavement, scattering hawkers, tourists and women with starving babies.

I lay in my room at the Losmen, flat on the bed, trying to calm down. A brief thought of joining 'the stupid club' passed by. There were times when it didn't seem so stupid, but I knew they'd never get me to join; there were too many things I wanted to see and do before I gave up the great fight...

Chantal. My family. An August Bank Holiday. Tommy Cooper. A volcano erupting. Cambodia. Roast Sunday lunch. Bumble. Crisp golden Autumn leaves. Rebecca. Monitor lizards. A crisp, frosty morning. A black run on a ski slope. The Great Barrier Reef. Fog. A Brian Moore novel. A cold Lowenbrau. Harry the Swede. Aunty Gladys. Thuy. North Devon. Tom Yam soup. Another motorbike. Kites flying above Bali. Porridge. Manly Beach. Crisp new snow. Schoolchildren - full of the expectations of life. The Merry Harriers. Hanoi in a storm. A Madness concert. My Volkswagen camper. A great game of football. Doron and Keren's kibbutz. The colour of Spring in England. My backpack - full and waiting. The Vietnamese sky... another birthday.

❖

MERTHA HOUSE, THE FOOTBALL FIELD, UBUD

The white marble table was chill to my hand, which rested face down, fingers splayed, trying to copy the gorgonzola veins of the stone. At the same time my right elbow warmed on the terracotta balustrade that had sucked in hours of sunshine through its emery paper surface. Without looking up from my reverie, I saw a plate slide into the centre of my gaze. And there, puffed up with pride, was the tuna sandwich I had ordered. I looked up at the waitress with surprise. Puzzled, she asked...
'Is okay?'
'Is it mine?' I asked, worried that it may be taken away and replaced with tinned tuna in Mighty White sliced bread. 'Yes sir.'
From a pregnant Pitta bread, tumbled a small feast, which hung over the sides of a barely visible cream plate. The bread, fresh and light as a sponge, was steaming, as inside was a sumptuous slice of fresh tuna; scorched crisp on one side to lie on the salad. Alfalfa sprouts, salmon-pink shallots and feta cheese mingled together round the sunniest dried tomatoes I'd ever tasted. Freshening the crowd with a shower of lemon juice, I fancied I heard the fishing boats lapping in the harbour, under a Greek sunset, but looking up it was palm trees and bamboo that I saw; Monkey Forest Road disappearing away into the paddy fields. Thick clusters of white lotus flowers trod water and stirred the sparkling, jade-green water of the pond that ran up to the temple on my left.
I lifted a doll's cup of thick black espresso - bitter-sweet nectar, and looking over the rim, the scene stayed the same.
Ubud really *was* cosmopolitan.

I'd arrived in Ubud the day before, almost before I could look up the details in the Lonely Planet. I was unused to short bus trips now; there was too much getting on and off, and not enough time to listen to your tape collection. Ubud is an artists' colony in the centre of the island; quite apt I thought, as most artists want to be the centre of everything, even though it might be a strange world of their own making.
Here amongst the traditional Balinese wood & stone carvers, German and French expats of repute had set up school, and mixed Balinese style with Gauguin, Renoir and a touch of Andy Warhol. To their credit, they had remained in the ambience that they'd created. I visited Blanco's House. He was an old French fop - a Quentin Crisp-Picasso, who had painted some pictures of note; notably for me, a portrait of Cole Porter that I'd always admired. I managed to speak to him between his chats

with American and Japanese tourists. He opened with a simpering – 'Oooooohh.. you're English!' and fluttered his eyelashes at me. He followed this up after a pause and a theatrical whisper with...-
'How do you feel about the IRA ceasefire?'
'The what?' I replied.
'The ceasefire... it started yesterday.' He showed me the article in The Times. 'Isn't that great news... peace in Ireland!' I felt a long way from home. The house was as bizarre as his work, with artefacts old and new, Asian and European, scuffling with photos and presents from movie and pop stars, politicians, despots and deadbeats. The shockingly blue swimming pool also looked like a painting, a very wet one, but although I'd been told I may be invited in - I wasn't. But I reminded myself that it was Sunday morning and I wasn't lying in bed with a hangover waiting for the pub to open. I was in Ubud, about to ride up to Tampaksring; 'up' being the operative word; 25 kilometres of up; on a pushbike.

My thighs burnt and the sweat stung my eyes, sticking the once pale-blue denim shirt to my back, navy wet. The reward, when I finally got there, was the most impressive ruin I'd seen since Barbara Cartland, and my favourite so far in Asia; not the size, the intricacy of detail or dazzling colours, but the setting and its balance with nature. Hidden in a deep and steep-sided valley, the remains of a burial temple straddled the rushing water - not quite a river, but certainly not a stream. Pocket-sized paddies climbed up the valley walls, shaded and tended by palm trees and flowered shrubs. Whilst these all reached up for the warmth of the sun, dancing downwards to the cool were waterfalls, sluices and sometimes just rivulets, issuing out of tiny crevices, or oozing through sponges of moss. Verdant is a word that would have fallen limp in this valley. I climbed as high as it was possible and, reaching the top, looked down into Nirvana. Then, I looked further, clear round the world and back, asking 'Where are you my love?' and finding no answer but the babbling of monkeys, great sadness flew out from in every direction leaving me empty and alone.
  I looked back to the temple which wasn't forcing itself onto the landscape to exhibit its glory; it was part of it, and now - worn by time, it fitted snugly into its surroundings. It was one of the things I liked about Bali; every house was a temple and every temple - a house; they built the shrine first and thn the e house around it. Each losmen (guest house) was a gaggle of shrines and rooms, as well as the owner's home, arranged in no particular order. Breakfast was likely to come from around any corner, and it was difficult to place where conversations, laughter or wind chimes were coming from. For the Balinese - religion

is in the air, water, flowers, the house; the kites that play above. The stones that made up the temples and statues, grew ferns and flowers in their cracks, to keep themselves alive and new. This particular day was a celebration of metal, so my rental bike had a posy of grass and petals; a burning incense stick tied to its handlebars.

But now I had the long cruise home - downhill the whole way, my shirt tails flapping. I saw a small boy coming towards me, up the hill, and steered straight for him. He changed course to the other side of the road. I mirrored his movement and he tacked back to the middle. His face had grown a mask of confusion, and then, as time grew thin on the ground, I hunched down over the handlebars, poured a wide smile at him and screamed 'Yaaagggh!' With a child's instinct, he saw the game, and jumping left and right, matched my laugh. As I flew past he shot me with his invisible gun. Looking back I saw him alone, punctuating the middle of the road, a big full stop on a line of dashes, hand waving in the air above his head.

I arrived back in Ubud in the late afternoon, and grabbing a cold beer from a bar full of Hitler Youth, crossed the pot-holed tarmac to sit, legs dangling, in a dried out storm ditch. Discarded plastic bags and reeds swayed together along the ditch in the gentle breeze.

It was time for the daily match. At night, this plot was stray-dog town, the darkness broken endlessly by howls of fighting and fornicating. In the day it was the football pitch. One heavily pregnant bitch had held her ground in the daylight, and was curled up in a depression with lip curled back; a snarling corner flag.

There, in front of me, stood Stanley Matthews; red and white hooped socks leading up to billowing shorts which finished halfway up his back, his collared shirt buttoned up tight under his chin. As he turned, I saw that he was only a teenager and proud as punch of his outfit. He was standing on the junction of centre line and a touchline marked by a row of discarded shirts, which more than once brought down players with sneaky ankle attacks. At its zenith, 43 players raced up and down the dusty pasture, the ball bouncing like a ping pong ball on the granite earth. The ball was repeatedly hoofed into the sky, and under each progressively lower bounce, a Thai boxing match took place in midair, the ball still at liberty, until the flailing limbs sent it flying willy-nilly.

The game continued, the ball's progress marked by a rolling dust-cloud, misty figures inside, the other players disappearing into the squall at intervals. Some were engaged in small groups discussing their boots or shorts, and some in pairs wandering the vacant half of the pitch, hand-in-hand, stirring the dust with their toes, until the approaching dust-cloud interrupted their intercourse, and dragged them into its vortex. After long periods the ball would escape its tortured trajectory. I saw it fly like a bullet across Monkey Forest Road, knock the sign for the Dew Drop Inn off its hinges, and cannon into the hands of a portly spectator on a bench. He stood up, laughing at the coincidence, and hoofed the ball back to the centre pullover. Still eyeing his one contribution to the game, and stepping back, he tumbled over the bench. His chubby brown legs stuck up in a perfect V sign, shaking in rhythm to the hooting that was coming from the unseen half of his body. The 43 players became screeching monkeys, slapping their thighs, backs, and the dusty ground, causing the occupants over in Monkey Forest to quiet, in suspicion. When the ball eventually flipped past a goalkeeper, half blind with tears from the dust, just one player - the closest, would shake the scorer's hand as adequate appreciation, whilst the other 41 resumed their positions, quietly and efficiently.

An Englishman had joined the game, his carrot-top head blazing above his Chelsea shirt. As the ball arrived at the feet of a local, 'Ginger' cut his legs from under him with a tackle that would have shamed Eric Cantona. As the boy lay contemplating life in a wheelchair, Ginger took off down the pitch, dribbling manically, jinking left and right, past this player, round that one, the FA Cup in his eyes. He ignored his team mates and carried on his own path to glory. The opposition were letting him pass, I presumed so that they could keep their legs intact, until he fired the ball past the goalkeeper, who was cringing on the floor. "Yeeessss!!' he shouted, turning and running back to the centre, punching the air. It was then he noticed that all the other players were pointing at the other goal, the one he should have been scoring in. His face coloured; almost matching his hair.

There was no time limit to this game, and only bad light, the arrival of a bus-load of backpackers or starvation ended the game. This day, with light waning rapidly, the dust cloud raced diagonally across the pitch then hesitated, as the ball bounced alone to roll and bump into the indignant, snarling corner flag. After discussion, the smallest boy was sent to retrieve it, and wearing only shorts, he had the least protection.

The boy, anxious to impress his elders, took a running baseball slide at the dog, and flicked the ball away with his toe. Now, with only escape in mind, he scrabbled to all fours, frantically searching for a toehold in the dust. As he came off the ground his shorts dropped to his ankles, anchored in the dog's teeth. He shot out of them across the pitch, his buttocks jiggling, hands cupped in front of his groin, and ran a zigzag gauntlet a sea of players, helpless with laughter. This brought the game to an end as efficiently as a sharp blast from a referee's whistle.

Leaving the post match analysis, I sauntered past the temple on Jalan Raya, the Balinese music a cacophony on the deepening dark air. I guiltily slipped through a side gate, and stood transfixed for an hour as the Legong dance troupe put rhyme and rhythm to the noise, translating the syncopation to movement. With eyes and fingers, they sang of love and loss, sadness and fury; sweet gladness. They were fluttering bees, strutting princesses, their tiny steps tied to the beat master's drum. I fell in love with them all and was joined by Aran from my losman, who asked, 'You like the girls... they are beautiful... yes?' I nodded.

'Would you like to meet them after?' I would. But thinking they might be a little young for me, perhaps only sixteen or seventeen, and probably 'somebody's sister' I asked...

'How old are they? - how old is the princess?'

'She is twelve... the others are ten. He laughed as I winced.

I pulled myself away to a nearby restaurant, where the music followed me in and swirled hypnotically around my table.

Duck in hot sour sauce; Aloo Gobi - sweet potatoes with delicate curry spices, spinach hiding star anise and chilli in its greenery. The sounds were mellowing, and with some persuasion from a bottle of Balinese rum over ice and a twist of lemon, it became a lullaby. Drifting off to sleep in my bed a short time later, I clung on to consciousness long enough to run back over my day in Ubud. How could a day like that be matched - compared to? It was a treasured day, a halcyon day; a Sunday. I fell asleep smiling.

❖

In an effort to equal Ubud, I jumped on the first bus going north to Mount Batur, a spectacular volcano with a crater the size of Guildford. At dawn, the sun crept up, peered over the rim of the volcano, and poured sunshine, like liquid fire, into the lake at the base of the mountain. This was what usually brought travellers to the spot, but I had more reason for hurrying north. The word was out that the volcano had shaken off its slumber and was awake with a raging hangover. I wanted to be there when it really lost its temper, or threw up.

Arriving at Kedisan in the afternoon, I strolled around the lake. Swallows and swifts plundered the upper air, the lower air claiming the surface of the water, whipping it up into the smallest of waves. The concussion from the volcano flattened the ripples and shrouded the shrill cries of the bathing children. I stripped down to my now well-frayed Marks and Spencer's boxer shorts (I didn't want them to laugh too much and drown), and joined them in the warm water. Back on the sand after a swim, they performed a 'Monkey dance' for me, all 'kejak, kejak, kejak!' and giggles, while my toes wriggled in the sand with delight. Further along the shore by an outcrop, their mothers and sisters were washing clothes in the lake, bobbing up and down like drinking hens, shrieking, spraying metallic bursts of speech like bullets - around the rocks.

Sulphur fumes wafted by, acrid and homeless, overpowering the incense which drifted down on gossamer breeze from the cremation celebration in the village, an incantation away. I saw a cotton wool cloud appear above the volcano and three seconds behind it came the 'booooooomm!' Mount Batur was no Krakatoa, but it was bubbling away like a pan of boiling potatoes. On the sonic scale of explosions, it was a single handclap in the stands of Wembley, which of course was now extinct. But it made me wonder -'what it must sound or feel like when something as big as Vesuvius decides to relocate very quickly across country, taking insignificant objects with it, like - towns, a forest the size of Surrey?' I had to get closer.

We left at 3.00am in a race to get to the top before the sun could pull back the covers, and jump up, excited with the new day. Our torches struggled to distinguish the black rock from the coal black night, especially as we only had one between four of us and the batteries had come from my Walkman. On the steeper inclines we were on all fours, scrambling up loose screed, barking shins and elbows and loosening lava onto the people below. Some stopped - exhausted, some terrified, rooted to the spot. The guides' powerful torches could be seen flashing, way above and below our position. They were trying to sell Coke and Sprite to other climbers, who were struggling to reach their wallets on all fours in the dark, fingers straining for a safe hold.

The explosions to the left were growing as we reached the summit, sweating - despite the chill morning wind. Facing the awesome sunrise to the east, I was distracted constantly by the 'crack' and 'booom' behind me, and turned to watch the false dawn of molten lava flying skywards. We had a breakfast of eggs, cooked in smoking fissures in the side of the rock, then carried on over the mountain until we were above the core. The mantle would expand and grow veins, then explode like a red orgasm into the sky. Following this would be a 'woooosh' - until the sky exploded and the concussion waves knocked me sideways.

The guides looked worried. An almighty blast sent lumps the size of a family saloon car skyward, brake pads, and coils and tyres whizzing in all directions. With an insane grin, I turned to see the guides scurrying up the hill as red hot lumps rained down. They eventually persuaded me away from my perch, hunkered down laughing like a fool.

We descended into a now fully lit Tolkien-like landscape, all folds of ugly black rock crushed up upon itself, and everything petrified; and if I'd seen what we'd been climbing in the dark, without aid, I'd have been petrified too.

Having swum in the lake, climbed the mountain, felt the power, seen the sunrise, I decided to move on; the shortest stay of the trip. I was in and out of Kedisan in less than twenty four hours, arriving at Padangbai, to the east, in time for a swim and a walk around the rocks in the sunset.

I was getting around, slipping in and out of beds and rooms quicker than a whore now. Some of this was to do with the The Bible; not the one with a black cover and a cross in gold. No, this one was The Lonely Planet - South East Asia, mine and every other backpacker's bible. Spawned by Tony and Maureen Wheeler twenty years previous, The Lonely Planet had taken over the mantle that Baedeker had relinquished. Without this, many travellers including me, would spend weeks in Canton station, months on the wrong trains or buses, or years at home - wondering how the hell to do it. Its information came from travellers - for travellers, and as a result, is a fairly honest, truthful and essential tool. I had noticed recently though, that some travellers were using it as a bargaining tool, offering good reviews or bad ones as threats. I wondered what the Japanese, Swedes and the like made of it. They had their own versions, but seemed to prefer to read it in English. At times, they must have been confused by the anomalies scattered around the book, and wondered if their English was poor.

"Hanoi – is a drab, sometimes pleasant, charming city." Can these three adjectives live together in the same sentence? If the information on a town or service was inaccurate, it was joked amongst the travellers that perhaps Maureen had PMT that day, or Tony - a hangover.

So they wouldn't win an award for literature; they do deserve the Travel Writer's Award for truth and a hearty Tory slap-on-the-back, for encouraging tens of thousands of recession-blinkered, disillusioned Brits to roam the world. A percentage of these would return home enriched and more worldly, in their absence - disencumbering the social security system and reducing the unemployment figures. It's a wonder there wasn't an MP for Gatwick, Heathrow and Dover, there just to shake the hands of departing travellers.

The Lonely Planet was a currency of its own, sold and bought along the way, swapped and borrowed, its value based on the date of the edition; an old one likely to direct you to a quaint fishing village which has since sprouted a nuclear reactor, its inhabitants - extra legs and heads. At the Minnie Mao Café in Yangshuo, after the gangsters and police had left, I shamefully held the LP in my left hand, and threatened to write a letter with my right. The owner was more scared of getting a bad review than the Triads and spilled the beans - bottom lip quivering.

For entertainment and elucidation, it just couldn't be equalled. The disciples carried the word, and the word was the truth –

'The Lonely Planet'.

❖

LITTLE BEACH, PADANGBAI

P adangbai was a small, quiet, fishing village, where ferries popped in and out from Lombok and Nusa Lebongan, avoiding the reef and passing the beach that the outriggers clung to; each painted in children's colours; lazing in the sun until their night-time work.

My bamboo hut was so small I was wearing it, but it was a weak stone's throw from the water, and good value at 9000 rupia a night. The banana pancake, as it did in Kuta and Ubud, arrived dutifully each morning with the monotony of a metronome in an empty room. My alarm clock was a mynah bird that had no snooze nor ON/OFF button. What it did have, was a catchy little tune that defied recognition or sleep. Waking up abruptly, I sat up, Chantal's sarong twisted around me - my comforter and tormentor, and looked through the open lattice window that let the scent and taste of the sea flow in.

A girl - alarmingly pale, lay on the crest of the beach; a new arrival. Legs bent up, supporting herself behind on her elbows, she was an M, and protruding from the first down slope was a dead heat in a Zeppelin race. Tits, though I'd seen a million of them now, still put a smile on my face. I suppose because my favourite part of a woman is the small of the back or the nape of the neck; tits are comical in comparison. So, 'titillated' I set off for Little Beach, and looking directly to my left - it was still a dead heat. I sang to myself as my toes hit the hot sand...

'Sunshine girl - I'm looking down your bra, (hopping onto the road)...
I see two round things, I wonder what they are? (skirting a sleeping dog)... I ask you brightly - if you'll invite me (stumbling over a boat rope)... to squeeze them tightly (kicking a runaway football back to its game)... my sunshine girl!'

I walked by a shimmering pile of fresh caught barracuda - still menacing, and rounded the ferry quay that thronged with comings and goings, threats and promises. Climbing up the headland which was all solidified bubbles of lava, I looked back down to the bay. Snaking away from the quay was a chalk-white line, marking the trail of the now invisible 12 o'clock ferry to Lombok, which lay sunbathing over the horizon.

Crackling and rustling to the sides and behind me, made me imagine I was being followed... even surrounded, but when I stopped - the sounds didn't: not like in mystery films. The trees, eucalyptus-like, had pods which were exploding like firecrackers and shooting out seeds, leaving the dry husks to rattle down through the branches in a chain reaction.

The falling seeds scattered lizards, who scuffled leaves, so that the whole wood was alive. Viewing the beach before me, it seemed the same, yet somehow different. The Germans were storm-trooping the waves as usual, which, as though in defiance, were tumbling people ging-gang-gooly, filling their swimsuits with sand and throwing them up the beach - breathless.

Sitting with my knees drawn up on my towel, there seemed to be tension on Little Beach. The clouds were playing up, interrupting the sun, which drew scowls from the worshippers. The hollow plunking from the wind chimes tied to one of the shacks sounded discordant, and in league with the breeze, which was flicking sand in people's faces. The hairs on my neck stood out, and I watched goose bumps gobble up my arms. I'd bought a coffee, and the glass tankard sat squat in the sand next to me, with a domed red lid that echoed the sunburnt bodies all around. Lying prone, supported by crooked elbow - opium smoking position, I could line the lid up with the rocks at the end of the beach, where a blowhole sent spumes of water skyward with a bellow. And though I waited, and waited, the acrid coffee grounds refused to sink to the bottom and stay calm.

The only happy thing on the beach was a kite, dancing and spinning above, perhaps oblivious of the troubled air below. As if caught unaware, it spiralled down into a sunburnt leg with a smack.

Angry voices rose above the gloom on the beach. An ugly row had broken out between the hawkers, and machetes were being bandied about. I'd watched one of the women scalping a coconut with one earlier, and as she chased another woman with it aloft, my stomach turned. I prayed the blade wouldn't swing.

I'd befriended a small boy the day before - a drink seller, who was quick and funny, and just a little boy called Ramh - with an engaging smile. He was dodging amongst the swirling arms and legs, eyes wide and scared, until they took his drink box away. He fought them, flaying at them, spindly but indignant; knocked to the sand, over and over. As the tide of trouble swept away from him, he was left on the sand crying his heart out. For a long time, a guilty long time for me, he lay alone, shoulders heaving; sobbing.

He looked up between sobs, and seeing me, he raced over. Arms clinging round my neck, his head jerked under my chin, and I brushed the sand from his back as though it would help. I noticed that hanging on a threadbare string around his neck was a handsome silver ring.

I told him, 'This is a very nice ring Ramh - I would like to buy it from you if you give me a good price.'

TWO MINUTE NOODLE

'He won't sell it to you,' said his elder sister, squatting in the sand a few feet away. 'It's his best one. He found it under the waves and has worn it for a year now. He has two others but that is his best one. When he has two more he will sell them all and buy a bicycle. Many people have wanted that ring.'

I wanted that ring. I lifted the little head by the chin until the helpless eyes fixed on me through the tears. 'Ramh, I want to buy your ring.'

His head bobbed down onto my chest, mingling sun cream with tears as it shook in a silent... 'No.'

'You can buy a same ring in town for 15,000 rupia.' whispered his sister. Ramh looked daggers at her, and warily at me. I slipped it, still on the string, onto my finger.

'Ramh, I will give you a good price for this ring.'

He straightened, snuffling.

'Hold out your hands and close your eyes tight.' He did this, and the tears squeezed from the side of his eyes and rolled down his cheeks. I rolled 50,000 rupia into a tight roll and slipped it through the ring, where it expanded and filled the hole. Opening his eyes, he searched his empty hands and my face. I nodded at his chest and he looked down. The sun cast a shadow from his chin, which pointed to the ring. He unrolled the money, added up the notes, squealed, then grabbing the girl's pineapple knife, slashed the string and put the ring on my finger. I felt like I'd been crowned.

His face grew a sunbeam, and he cartwheeled around the beach, waved the money in the faces of the harridans, shouting 'na na na nergh nergh!' like children do the world over. He was a rich man. He was a boy. He was eight years old. An image of my nephew Russell floated before my eyes. He had computer games, a mountain bike, clothes, a future, but he wasn't spoilt - far from it; he was just fortunate to be born in Guildford and not Padangbai.

It was probably the best 25 dollars I'd ever spent. I gained a silver ring that had lived beneath the waves, sliding amongst the shells, to be fished up by a wee boy, who wore it for a year like a treasure; his crown jewels - his fortune.

He screamed when I hit the beach the next day, and ran over, tumbling to the sand once in his hurry to show me his new drink box. His mum, who cooked food in one of the shacks, had made him buy a new one - so that he could stay in business. He was saving the rest of the money for his bicycle. His sparrow chest was puffed with pride. He had a Coca-Cola box.. blood red and bandage white, not an old wooden one.

His eyes still darted to the ring on my finger and I told him...

'Rahm... you don't need a ring - you need a bicycle and a childhood.'

He made me a kite. It was red. We flew it all afternoon over the exploding trees and the roaring blowhole. I had to say goodbye.

His mum let him walk to town with me, his hand so small and hot in mine, but when the time came to leave he cried, so I had to take him back to the beach to his mum.

I caught the next ferry, two hours later, and leaving the harbour and rounding the headland... Little Beach came into view, a white crescent with a red kite flying above; my red kite. I waved, though I knew he couldn't see me, and said quietly to myself,

'Bye-bye Ramh, take your time young man... don't you rush to get old.' Once again, finding myself desolate and a long way from home, I gripped the rail until my knuckles whitened, in an effort to stop the tears from flying out like poison arrows and frightening the locals.

❖

AMPENAM POST OFFICE, LOMBOK

Ampenam is the westerly of four towns, which over the years joined together into a single high street. The Bible had said. "Ampenam fades out before the old dusty port and grubby beach." It didn't. It was faded from the start of Sweta - the most easterly town, carried on in the same tatty fashion through Cakra, and despite a brief flowering of fancy Government buildings and offices with sprinkler fed lawns in Mataram - it faded all the way to the grubby beach.
"These days, many visitors don't bother with the town at all, preferring to stay on the beach at Sengiggi, or head straight to the Gili Islands." it said. Which was exactly why I bothered; and as always, the surprises kept on coming. I would get to the Gilis in my own time.

Stepping out of the minibus, a man, reclining against a tumbledown wall in front of me asked, 'Where you from?'
'England,' I replied, hoisting up my pack, adding the tired old traveller's joke, 'and are you from... here?'
'No,' he said, 'I'm an aborigine.'
'Ah, you are a native of Lombok!'
'No mate - an Abbo from Australia.' Looking at the lumpy forehead, splayed nose, and eyes set deeper than an opal mine, I saw that he was fair dinkum; my first Abbo - in Lombok! Which really wasn't that odd, as a hop across Sumbawa, a skip onto Flores, and a jump from Timor, would land you in the sandpit of Northern Australia.
A stroll on the beach confirmed that it was spectacularly grubby. The sea was characterless and brown, the sand - grey and brown to match the rusting oil tanks which dominated the top of the beach. Dead fish lay dull in the scummy froth at the water's edge, and as I walked, hosts of flies rose humming, from innards scattered along the sand.
A young boy squatted in apparent meditation ahead of me, and I realised as he wiped his arse with his hand, that this was also the toilet for the ramshackle fishermen's huts. A complete family stood outside their hut, as if being photographed, smiling, until I veered towards them and shouted 'Hullo!' Their smiles turned to stone; one little girl running off into the hut, the other - quite lovely, hiding behind her dad.
I rejoined my footmarks in the sand, and walked on. Finding three more children splashing naked in a lagoon, I decided to stay quiet so as not to alarm them. They spotted me and took to their heels, the smallest one howling as though being chased by a banshee. It struck me that it must be *very* unusual for travellers to stop here these days.

I'd been the only passenger, on the minibus, to get off here. The Germans who'd been storm-trooping the waves at Padangbai, were heading for Sengiggi, and a hotel, presumably so they'd have somewhere to park their towels. A French couple didn't seem to know where they were going. The husband, looked quite enviously at me alighting, as the hardcore, techno dance beat had been pounding from the door speakers the whole way, extracting a regular 'Merde... arretez le musique!' but they couldn't hear him, or chose not to. His wife looked sick. The Germans looked at me blankly, wondering why anyone would want to stay in a grubby hole like this. Well, I had a reason; a big one. Two miles down the road, marked 'Poste Restante - Mataram, Lombok', there could, or should be an airmail letter from Burma.

As I returned back along the beach to the town, I thought... 'at least the sky is blue', and saw a stream of starlings fly, seemingly out of the sand, and head inland like a column of ants looking for a picnic. A second stream crossed the first diagonally, forming a giant 'X' in the sky. 'Perhaps it's a sign or an omen?' I thought, and turned in the direction of the Post Office.
  Ponies trotted by with twinkling brasses and jingling bells, their proud heads bobbing, pulling small traps behind them. These were the taxis, and every other one slowed to my pace asking if I wanted a lift; but I wanted to walk - to think about the letter.

Three weeks had passed since Chantal and I had parted. What had happened in that time? I knew so well now how time accelerated whilst travelling. Routine events, sights, sounds, meetings and partings - that would fill months at home, could be compressed into a single week on the road. It was the most tiring thing about backpacking; fitting all the experiences into a vessel used to far less. If the letter were there - what did it contain? if it wasn't - what would I do? I was nervous. It was like waiting for Christmas to arrive, hoping for that football game that you wanted; but anything would do really - wouldn't it?

I'd barely walked the first two hundred yards before I was joined by the omnipresent young lad touting... 'Where are you from?.. where are you going?' He asked if he could accompany me to the Post Office, to practice his English. I knew that, as in China, Vietnam, and Thailand, English words learn, were a currency to be stored away and used to obtain some kind of a future. A stroll and a chat with the young gentleman might take my mind off the letter, so I slapped him on the back and said 'it'd be a hooter!' 'Excuse me?' he said.

'What's your name?' I asked. 'Hallan' he replied. 'Ah! Alan is an English name.' I teased, and his grin touched his earlobes. All along the route, people on bicycles, hanging out of windows, walking, trotting, or just standing, asked him the same question, to which he replied, 'England... Post Office.'

We talked about his ambition to become a normal human being. He was seventeen. He had no house - so he lived with his uncle; no job - there were none here; no money. Without these he could not get a wife. But despite these obstacles he was hopeful of getting a job at a hotel in one of the resorts, as his English was getting better (it was good), and he could cook! He could do fruit salad, omelette and banana pancake!

'Then you and I are same-same.' I told him.

'What a faintly preposterous, hypothetical comparison of human prosperity.' he countered - in his own words, which sounded very much like a laugh. I explained to him that at home - *I* had no home; no job; no money, and certainly no wife.

'Then we *are* same-same,' he said, smiling...'Broken Wing.'

'Excuse me?' I said.

'People like you and me are called Broken Wing, in Lombok.'

I thought to myself... 'That sums me up perfectly' - brought down from the heady heights by divorce, bankruptcy and unemployment - to flap helplessly in the dust of Asia. Would I find a way to get back aloft? Would I get pan-caked into the road by a ten-ton truck? leaving two tail-feathers sticking up: a last 'V' sign to the world. I carried on flapping. We reached the Post Office.

It was high and wide inside, like Grand Central Station; tidy, efficient-looking, clean air wandering around the marble floor. I headed to the 'Poste Restante' desk in an optimistic mood. There was nothing under 'C' in the box for me, or in the cross-referenced, carefully written journal, which had one clean line between each entry. I was heading towards panic and asked to look at 'H'. She refused, as it wasn't in her journal under 'C'. I tried to explain, and under her stiff scrutiny she found it, sandwiched between 'Ferguson Helen' and 'Jalatasin Horas'. There, in black and white, she had written - in her best handwriting, crisp as her blouse collars, my name. It had never looked so good. In my relief at finding the red and blue edged letter in the box, I helped her sort out the other boxes, all blushes and apologies, horrified at her system breakdown.

With that precious missive folded in my pocket, I gabbled on all the way back to town and I don't think Hallan understood a word. I don't remember a word I said. Back at the bar where Hallan lived, his Uncle nodding his consent, I bought him a Coke, and sipped my cold beer while I read the letter; with incredible politeness he looked away until I had finished. He was too well-mannered to ask me outright, though his eyes were pleading, so I told him who and where it was from and read some pieces out for him. It occurred to me later that to him I must seem to be very lucky, and I wasn't really 'Broken Wing'. I wasn't trapped like him. I was lucky; I had a letter from Burma.

I remember every word it said. I still do now. Chantal had sent it shortly after arrival in Burma. Harassed by locals in the Post Office, she had written it in the corridor. She felt the same as me; desperate. She missed me; terribly. This made it all so much easier didn't it? We were on different continents, moving in different directions; what could we do? No answers fell from the sky; no solutions blossomed from the sun baked soil. Happy to be still wanted, but tragic to be parted from her, I sentenced myself to travelling on local transport to the Gili Isles, in the hope it would occupy my mind.

❖

The first Bemo (a small, covered truck with bench seats along each side) dropped me at a crossroads of no significant purpose. The old lady sitting beside the northern tributary, with skin like a crocodile, stopped her Singer sewing machine, looked up briefly and nodded in the direction she had been sewing. She muttered 'Gili.' and pointed at the dirty, scrubby bush opposite. She followed up with '..bus.' I put two and two together, crossed over, and stood on the patch of sun-hammered grass that most resembled a bus stop. From a hundred feet above the crossroads, it would have resembled a scene from a Quentin Tarantino movie...

Two strangers; one, right foot pedalling her old machine, tick... tick.. ticking along the cloth, sunlight glinting off the spinning wheel; myself standing motionless, opposite. The bus stopped on the southern side of the crossroads and glared at me, the radiator and lights - a grim smiling face. I had an eerie feeling that if I walked towards it, the bus would reverse away; stop if I stopped, return if I returned; baiting me.

But it disgorged a passenger, and drove the thirty feet across to me, jerkily. There was room for me inside but not my backpack so, squeezing through the bodies - man and beast, alive and dead, I gave it up to the conductor. He put it on his back and clung to the outside of the bus for the whole trip. A bunch of chickens, which had been on my seat with legs tied - but very much alive, were now on my lap. I was growing quite attached to them, until one of the four took his profession literally, and started a cockfight; unfortunately the nearest contender was in my shorts. I leapt from the seat and threw the bunch, like a bride's posy, down the bus. They landed flapping amongst a huddle of school-kids, who tossed them between each other, as though they were hot potatoes.

Fortunately, the owner, seated next to me, seemed as amused as everyone else, and offered a small pig as a replacement. I politely refused on the grounds that it may hunt through my pants for truffles.

Our passage through the villages attracted great interest, as it appeared that a backpacker had run for the bus too late, and had hung on for dear life, banging on the doors to be let in. But it was only the conductor signalling the driver to stop for a passenger or carry on - my full pack threatening to peel him from the side and drop him onto the monkeys who lined the roadside of Pusak Pass like grinning, scratching milestones. The trip ended at Pemanang, where the Dokar (pony and traps) waited to shuttle travellers the last two miles to the harbour. I decided to walk, eventually shaking off the persistent Dokar driver, who had been shadowing me - puzzled as to why anybody would want to walk at mid-day in the head-banging heat.

The booking office at Bangsai – a tiny port, was a shed. When there were enough passengers to fill an outrigger, we crossed the choppy strait to the Gili Islands. 'Gili' is Indonesian for Island, so I was heading for the Island Islands - three beauty spots on the cheek of Lombok, and I'd chosen the largest and furthest away.

❖

GILI TREWANGAN

If you held a picture postcard at reading distance; perfect azure sea lapping over coral onto white sand - a single cotton wool cloud in a flawless sky, and then drop it - the scene would still be there, with just the words 'Gili Trewangan' - A Tropical Paradise' missing. But we all know that Paradise doesn't exist, don't we children? The palm tree cropping the left corner of the postcard has a nice line of spray paint at its base, and under - enjoying the shade, is a tired hut. Its wall bears the niceties of the world; 'Don't fuck with the locals', 'Hell sucks', 'No money - no honey', 'Gili boys take it up the arse', 'Shit' (a hidden message in that one I think - or perhaps a succinct comment on life on Lombok!)

To the right of the hut, a goat is chewing away at a black & white striped grocery bag, the tip of a mound of rubbish which will take him years to get through. Behind are ramshackle huts, some so tired they've lain down in the dust, which hangs heavy on the limp foliage. Lying with eyes closed, alone in the centre of the postcard, I hear sleigh bells approaching, and stretch out my fingers soporifically to check that I'm on white sand - not snow.

The pony canters past, high kicking, bells and harness jingle-jangling, the little banana-yellow cab bouncing on its rubber tyres. The swirling dust cloud momentarily obscures the number '28' painted childlike on its side. As the dust settles, so does the noise. A dog barks, so far in the distance it seems a memory.

This was *the* transport on Trewangan, and it was a feast to the ears after the bellowing horns of China, the buzz of motorbikes in Vietnam, or the tone deaf traffic jams of Bangkok. The only noise rising above the gentle lapping of the waves, and a Mosque calling the faithful to prayer, was the put-put-put of the next outrigger - arriving at the harbour. The harbour was a fallen tree that the boys tied the boats to after running up the sand with the rope. This was the signal for the sunbathers to sit up and watch the only entertainment available. Backpackers would have to leap from the boat into the shallows, frequently losing balance and toppling forward or back into the waves, where like a turtle on its back, it was very difficult to regain the vertical. This was great fun for the people who had negotiated the landing previously, and a comfort for the ones who hadn't; their belongings spread out at their hut - drying in the sun. Having watched two soakings in an hour, and tired of sunbathing, I moved on home. I strolled along the beaches looking at the peaches, with two stops for a chat: one English - Carol, fair hair, soft pointed strawberry cones; one Austrian - Isabella, dark hair, wicked eyes, firm and brown. I decided I needed a cold shower, and heading home, passed under an exploding Kapok tree, the banana-shaped pods bursting out a snow-shower of white fluff.

The toilet and showers were combined, and were called Mandies. So I took my clothes off and slipped into Mandy; I'd always wanted to. The water was warm and salty, and was one of the features of the Gilis - no fresh water, and no electricity (apart from a small section of upmarket hostels in the middle of the beach). As I was ladling the water over my head, I heard a shouting outside. It was Ronnie and Man, the two men that ran my cottage. Loosely tying my sarong around my waist for modesty, I slipped out of Mandy and into a dust-storm, and bumping into Ronnie, he grabbed my arm.

'Run Howie! whirly-wind! whirly-wind!' We rushed into the calmer dust of the yard, collecting Man on the way. Looking back, we saw the spout come through between the two cottages at walking pace, but with the force of Mike Tyson. It lifted the corner of my roof like an adult looking into a doll's house. We were all three following it along, smiling skyward. Ronny squealed 'My towel!' and there it was, a hundred feet up - spinning; Bob Marley smiling down at us. 'Come back Bob!' shouted Man through cupped hands. The assorted yard rubbish had been sucked up with it, and wouldn't come down for nearly ten minutes.

I had a favourite goat in the yard, jet-black with a white patch like a border collie. It had a strange bleat that was too human, and looked like one I'd had on my toy farmyard when I was a child. Tied by a washing line to a stake, he wasn't going anywhere. We all realised at the same moment that the goat was in the whirlwind's path and we grinned at each other wickedly; it was too late to reach it anyway. Honest. It pulled his front feet off the ground first, then rocked him back onto them, and picked up his back ones. He was like a bucking picnic table, and at one stage was aloft on his rope spinning round and round; a balloon with legs. Then he spun down like water going down a plughole. We were helpless with laughter now, and Ronnie, seeing that my sarong had slipped unnoticed to the floor, fell on his back kicking his legs, dreadlocks brushing the dust and shrieked, 'White bum! ..white bum!' I joined him on the floor, trying to breathe through the laughter. If the goat had broken his moorings, I think I'd have wet myself, so it was a good job I was naked.

Ronnie's towel never came down, at least not on Trewangan, but a toilet roll - complete and unrolled, fell down onto the goat like manna from heaven, and he set about eating it in the now unruffled air. There were no red shoes poking out from under the cottage, so I figured it hadn't been a dream.

❖

I was reading on my balcony by a hurricane lamp that would have struggled with a gentle breeze, and had been doing this for days; just me and silence, the dark, and words on a page. It was medieval but also medicinal. It was a time of reflection and healing, no thoughts of before or after, or why. But then, as if I couldn't shut the real world out for another minute, I had a new and strange impulse - to sit blankly and stare at a video screen, also with no conversation, making no new friends. So I did.

The bar was full, but could have been empty - every head glued to the same spot, the glare from the screen spread across the faces of the watchers; the soundtrack on mega-bass. I joined in. I pointed at the menu and signed to the waiter, to order my food. I tut-tutted when somebody went to the toilet, momentarily blocking the screen.
  I apologised to the person behind when my food arrived, and sat forward to eat it, blocking his view. When the laserdisc had to turn itself over, there was a thirty second gap, and the screen was blank. The heads all swivelled, indignant, and initiated conversations, but the renewed soundtrack cut them short, and pulled them back to the screen. I realised I was amongst zombies and I was being one as well. The film was a masterpiece set in the times of Richard the Lionheart where a rebellious maiden, teaming up with a circus troupe - leads an army of children against a wicked Baron. Crikey. But it put up some memorable lines. Seeing the Baron bowling a maiden over, the short-arse heroine punched him to the floor with a chain mail fist...
  'Wow!' said the second-rate British cockney actor, 'We sure could do wiv a girl like that in our gang.' These gems of screenwriting brought gusts of laughter from the British in the audience, perplexing the Scandinavians and Indonesians; why were we laughing? it wasn't a comedy - was it?

As the credits rolled, people had to look at each other and talk again, but I noticed that on exiting - they were all going next door. I followed the herd, now corralled in 'Rudy's bar', passing the blackboard at the entrance which announced - 'Party night, dance and get drunk. Free popcorn.' How could I turn down such an event?
  I sat alone at a table on the fringes, slightly uncomfortable being the only lone reveller, and I couldn't see a group that I could, or wanted to

break into. My mind however was soon distracted by a figure hitting the empty dance floor. He was a Gili boy; baseball cap back to front, three vests and bright orange trousers cut off at the knee. On arriving nonchalantly at the exact centre spot of the dance floor, he looked down at his feet, as though to check they were still there and see if they wanted to dance. And there they were in a huge pair of Wellington boots, the toes curled up with age. They shuffled and jiggled, they did the gumboot boogie. They were good; and he seemed to just sway along above them, a sort of helmsman steering his boats around a timber sea.

The floor filled, and I was joined by my neighbour - Laurie. She was half-Arabian, half-American, but had lived in Switzerland most of her life. To her misfortune, she carried the questionable whining drone of the Californian valley girl, which took away the charm of her Arabian features. But she was great company, and we played the nationality game - matching clothes, dancing style and behaviour to the country.

The British danced either with a stiff upper limb or the wild abandonment of Rave-goers. Austrians and Germans danced waltzes and Polkas, twirling each other round - a century behind the times.
The Americans; bad shirts tucked into white shorts, white socks and sandals, danced conservatively like Presidential candidates afraid to make a mistake. The Indonesian whiskey had flown down at $3 a bottle, the game taking on hilarious dimensions. Either of us would race up to anybody round the room, shouting at their sweaty faces...'You're English!.. etes-vous Francais?.. Deutschlander?' and signal across the room at the other - a victory, with a raised fist and a 'Yesss!' or in defeat - a 'V' sign from me or a raised middle finger from Laurie. The loser got a whiskey, so there were no losers in this game; an opinion I didn't agree with when I woke up at 6am on the sand; tongue made of sandpaper. Apparently I'd loaded Laurie into a pony and trap, as she couldn't walk, and forgetting that I lived at the same place, set out for a hostel that didn't exist. I never got there.

The party moved next door the following night, to the Paradise Bar. The same warm-up boy waggled his Wellies. We watched the same people doing the same dance, to the same tape. We grew weary of the video and the tape by the third night and returned to real life, sitting with our hurricane lamps hissing at the darkness. After a quiet meal under a spangled sky, we told each other of our secrets and sadness, happily uninvolved and uncomplicated by each other. Early next morning, through the bamboo wall, I heard Laurie leaving.

'Have a good one Laurie.' I shouted with night croak.
'Have a better one Howie - go back to sleep.' she twanged back.
I slipped away again, but before I lost consciousness, I was conscious that I'd lost another friend. As is common in the early morning, my dreams were vivid, disjointed and disturbing. All of my lost friends flew around and about in strange places, and they couldn't remember me, even though I shouted to them, *'Harry! ...it's me - Howie, where are you going? Remember Hanoi... Bangkok?'* And Chantal said, *'I've never been to Thailand.'* in Belgian, but I understood every word of it.

I woke up sweating, ready to move on, but - counting up my Rupiahs and underestimating my beer bill, found that I'd left it a bit late; I had to leave immediately. I was on the beach half an hour later with my pack, waiting for another fourteen paying customers to gather. Two hours later I had swum and dried twice in the sun, and I was still alone. Knowing that I couldn't afford another night in a cottage, I resolved to sleep on the sand. I was joined by three Javanese men who offered to charter the whole boat and split the cost four ways. It was all the money I had, but I could hitch back to Mataram to get to the bank.

As we were dipping along in the outrigger, I trailed a hand in the water, elbow crooked over the bleached wood side. One of the Javanese pointed at my arm and said 'You are very brown.' I was about to say 'not as brown as you...' when I realised I was; considerably. A flight of flying fish skimmed past on the same course as us, like silver direction arrows; I had a vision of a Cormorant swimming along underwater, with the fish flying above in the air, and then swapping places endlessly in confusion at each other's station in life.

I chatted to the three about my travels, and one just sat staring into the distance repeating over and over, "China, Vietnam, Thailand, Indonesia, Australia, New Zealand, America, England." until I started to think to myself 'Yes, it is a bit dreamlike isn't it.' When we reached Lombok, they asked me how I was travelling to Mataram.

'Public bus,' I lied 'it's more fun.' I walked the first stretch to the main road, alone, but noticed a vehicle following along behind at the same speed, tailing me. It was a black space-cruiser with mirrored windows. Eventually it pulled alongside, keeping pace with me, until I thought... 'Here we go, I am in trouble.' I stopped and glared at my reflection in the windows and heard laughter from inside. The window slid down and a beautiful woman, looking straight into my eyes, said 'The public bus has arrived.' The other doors flew open and out popped my three Javan friends laughing at the look on my face.

'I knew you had no money,' one said 'I saw your wallet was empty when you showed us your dog.' So I rode back to Mataram in air-con luxury in just under thirty minutes, passing the same monkey milestones through the pass, one with his lipstick out - pissing a small arc into the middle of the road.

They dropped me outside the Losmen Kambodja, after I declined their offer of dinner. 'I have things to do.'

They smiled at each other - a car load of very wealthy Javans; I had my pride. When they'd turned the corner, I put my back to the hostel, went to the bank to get the very small amount of money I had left, and slipped along to the post office.

I drew a blank. 'No letters for you Mr Cobb,' said the crisp-bloused girl, as I walked in. Her system was obviously working now.

I still wasn't used to the dull ache of disappointment that came from these unfulfilled trips. I invariably left the post office muttering under my breath and hissing 'Shit, shit, shit!' in time to my heavy footsteps. The doubts flew around like leaves in a breeze. Does she not care? Has she found someone else to hold? Where are you my little Flem?

❖

The next morning, the sky could have been anything; I was in a hurry. I skipped down to Lembar, caught the ferry, and took a lingering look at Little Beach as we sailed back into Padangbai. I raced across Bali, stopping in Ubud to return a book and get my deposit money, and then deposited myself back in Kuta. The Bagus bar was rocking to the Aussie rules football final, beer cans bouncing off the screen, to shouts of 'You're running the wrong way Lambert - y'fuckin poof!'

'Hey mate...' said one man to the waiter scurrying past, ducking the beer cans, 'is the chicken curry spicy?' Either honest, or confused, he answered 'No.' Aaah great.. I'll have that then mate.'

And then – unexpectedly - there was a letter at the Post Office from India, and describing Burma.

'I spent hours on the balcony watching the life on the river, the sunset; drawing. It was wonderful. Hard sometimes, to describe the feelings that these places cause inside of you. In the evening, the Burmese came out of their houses, playing guitar and singing, words which came straight from the heart. I went out and sat with them listening to the songs, of which I could not understand the words, but just through the emotions they put in their voices it was like I understood...was beautiful.

My favourite place was Bagan with its 2000 temples. I biked around these for 5 days, by myself again. Spending sometimes hours on the roof of a temple listening to the silence, watching the sun going after the mountains, colouring with its last light, the temples and the sky with heavy orange colours...it was just so beautiful and perfect and sitting there a feeling of almost total happiness could fall over me that tears well up in my eyes.

I discovered things inside of me, did a lot of thinking. Hope you have a wonderful time in Australia, again take care.

I think about you all the time. Miss you.'

❖

CAPTAIN COOK'S. CAIRNS, QUEENSLAND

Leaving 'the footie' - The Bagus Bar heaving with insults and beer cans, I went to the Garuda office to bring my flight back a few days. I wanted to see Australia in Australia – not here. The flight went in four hours, or alternatively in a week's time. I was packed, checked out, taxied and checked onto the plane in one hour.

It lifted its belly from Bali, and we powered out over the sea in the dark - Kuta's tinsel town lights mirrored and wobbling in the surf to our right. We flew into the sunrise, which was coming up fast, due to our approach. The dull, purple sky glowed red, then burst into lemon-yellow when the sun nudged above the camber of the horizon; first a thin slice, then a segment, and almost too quick to notice, it pulled itself away from the rim of the earth with a quiet plip! And there it was - a new day, blue and gold.

We set foot on Australian soil in the transit lounge of Darwin airport. The security guards, custom men and pilots all wore tight shorts, white knee-high socks and bush hats, on top of their 6-7 foot frames.

The smokers milled together, lighters and matches at the ready, eyeing the 'no smoking' signs. 'Where can we smoke please?'

'Y'can't smoke nowhere mate, not in this terminal, but I'd slip into the dunny if I was you, an' have a crafty one on the crapper. Mind the smoke detectors though mate, else you'll have a soggy smoke!'

Then we stepped outside into Cairns. I quickly joined up with Stacey, an American girl, and finding a row of hostel courtesy buses, chose the first one to offer a room for a decent price; a double room. We rolled to a stop twenty minutes later, beneath the spread legs of a fifty feet high Captain Cook, his lumpy hand pointing to the centre of the town. Checking in we took our prison-issue sheets and went to our 'unit'.

The door opened into the kitchen, with all its equipment in the sink, empty instant noodle pots clustered together. Where the lino ended was where the kitchen finished - and the trashed, sticky carpet of the lounge began. The lounge sported a bum-sweating vinyl sofa, and four bunk beds occupied by bodies, backpacks, ash trays and more kitchenware. The wall was decorated with a dolphin, leaping through Magic Roundabout flowers; very hippy - except that a fat penis had been added in biro, and a speech bubble exhorting the watcher to 'Piss off!' The flowers carried on round the corner - at one stage growing on the carpet, and stopped at an open door where four more bodies could be seen - asleep. Next to the bathroom we found an empty room with a small double bed; or large single. We shrugged our shoulders, dumped our packs, locked the door, checked the door was locked, re-locked it, and took a walk into town.

A weekday. The roads should have been busy; people hurrying to work, ferrying kids to school. They were empty and wide. Then I remembered where I was. Australia had an abundance of space in which to fit the people. Standing on the central reservation, to each side would be two motorway sized lanes, a hard shoulder, grass run-off, storm ditch, more grass strip, a pavement, a wide grass strip that ran up to the picket-fences, and then, set back in the distance of a garden almost naked to the invisible eye - a house.

Looking down one of these roads, it ran clear and true to the blue remembered hills without a vehicle in sight. Turning back to face the way Captain Cook was pointing, the traffic lights were flashing 'Go! Go! Go!' to an empty road. People weren't in gardens, at windows, walking the pavement, cycling, skateboarding, following sleepily behind wide-awake dogs, starting cars, hanging out washing or shouting 'g'day' across the street.

The truth was, there was too much space for me. After Asia, where every inch was occupied by people and bicycles, and rice grew right up to the buildings in every crack, and sometimes crept indoors without knocking - it was alien; it was spooky, and I felt lost.

We sat at a waterfront cafe sipping dusty coffee, which came with two steaming, cinnamon donuts free; my first 'Australian special deal'. The street really began to liven up. A few people moved around; some backpackers crawled out, bleary eyed and slack jawed; but it still resembled an English High Street on Boxing Day.

It was right then, that a depression rolled in from the horizon and formed a cloud around my head. It felt as though my trip had ended; or at least faded. I wasn't in a foreign country anymore. Asia had never really appealed to me - until I got there. I never expected to love it the way I did. Chantal was still tripping on, falling over new sights and sounds, bumping into experiences. So I tried to tell myself - there are things to see here as well, things to write about, people to meet: make the most of it. We returned to Captain Cook's, along the esplanade. The tide was out, leaving the mudflats bubbling and browning to the horizon, small mango bushes punctuating the sludge. I couldn't help feeling that my 'travelling feet' were also stuck in the mud.

The 'unit' was awake. The room had been tidied. There was 'Kik'- a sheila, 'Matt' - a bloke, 'Jill' - an Essex girl, Bournemouth 'Andy', and 'Rory' - an extremely slow Kiwi. Three of the bodies had left, but they were replaced that night by three Essex boys, who struggled to say or ask anything interesting at all. Even Jill thought them – 'fick'; but they soon moved to another hostel. Stories and characters unfolded over the following days, and it seems I'd walked into a soap opera; a theatre. The unit had a harmony and it was our little home. New arrivals were treated like houseguests, until they either gelled, or left.

'Kik' was a reformed heroine addict, aged beyond her years; she still hung out with the dealers, aborigines and shady characters. She'd been on the fishing boats before, grafting hard and fast in the Torres Strait. Kik lived in the odd world of Australian optimism. Plans whirled and grew in her mind, and changed by the day – sometimes the hour.

'Yeh! if I get on this prawny boat Matt, in the Gulf for a month, with a 5% cut, I should clean up 15,000 dollars... yeh! I met Buddah, y'know, the dealer down at the Big 'O'? he accused me of buying smokoe behind his back, cheating his fucken cut, yeh he did! Anyway, this guy with Buddah there, say's I could get into the boatyard... mmmm, mending the fucken nets, starting tomorrow morning at seven. Could you give us a shake in the morning Howie?, I reckon I can get up... yeh! When y'going up to the cape Matt, I might go up with you if this netting falls through... mmmh, that'd be the go... yeh! But I'd have to come back on Monday to see the cops, so I'd have to hitch back, do me community service, and try for a boat... yeh! that'll be a spin.'

There was always a short gap before 'yeh! or 'mmmh' as she thought briefly about the next thing, or what she'd just said. She was a rough diamond, but she was a diamond, sharing all she had with anybody - when she had it.

I settled into the game - 'What can you get for 10 dollars?' To start with, at Captain Cook's you got a bed in a unit, then the choice of two swimming pools, one freshwater - the other seawater; a gym, launderette, television room, the free bus service to town, a travel office - a bar with a disc jockey.

Then there was the food; a free evening meal of meat or fish, two kinds of pasta, potatoes, beans, cabbage, rice, salad, and fruit - plus music and flashing lights. The arrivals from Europe, perhaps with a stop-off in Hong Kong or Singapore, thought it disgusting; the post-Asian travellers and the Ozzies thought it great. I'd been eating Nasi-Goreng daily for weeks, so to me the variety was staggering; and no banana pancake either.

Then, to wash the meal down, the next game was to buy a pot (a small glass) of beer, in the bar - after 9.30. This entitled you to an ink-stamp on the arm. With the ink still wet on the arm, the free bus would shuttle you down at 11.00pm - to one of the clubs in town - 'End of The World' or 'Samuel's' - free entry. Then, when everyone from Captain Cook's had assembled - three deep along the bar, banging their empty beakers in rhythm, a keg of beer was opened - free until empty. Trying to hold your place at the bar, you sculled the beaker as fast as possible, then held it out with your arm-stamp showing for a refill.

Matt and I found that we could manage about seven or eight, in the fifteen minutes it normally took before the shout... 'barrel's done!' and we'd face each other, grinning manically at the childishness of it all, belching short, small burps to relieve the swollen stomach, and avoid puking up. All too soon, we'd be creeping home at dawn along the esplanade, the chirruping wagtails telling us off - like Mums and Dads.

On any night in town, free beer could be found, between 9.00 and 9.30 here, and 10.00 there; free cocktails for ladies at this one, 3 dollar jugs at another. On alternative nights, free beer could be won in our own bar, by picking the right cane toad in the racing, naming the record being played, wearing glasses; it was the hostel hobby. The serious side to hostel-dwelling was trying to find work; which didn't bother me at this point. I was still living on the spending money I'd come away with, but now I was in Australia, I could see that it wasn't going to last the whole trip.

It was time to experience the reason I'd come to Cairns. I'd always wanted to learn to scuba-dive, and it was always going to be on The Great Barrier Reef; which was how I came to be standing in a wetsuit and mask, air-tanks on my back, hangover dissolving, in a Hockney-blue swimming pool. Through the prescription mask, and to the left of my nose, I spotted a sign – "All children (Yes yours as well!) must wear bathers, for obvious reasons."

I chuckled in a snorkel full of water, and toppled backwards into the deeper water, spurting and snorting to get air. As we beginners wriggled along the bottom of the pool, pretending we were in the sea, the swimmers above were joined by four very hairy legs, thrashing along the surface. A muted 'bark!' thumped through the water. I signalled to my buddy, and we both laughed eyes at each other and surfaced. It was a Brindle-hound, his head raised high, but beard still in the water. I guessed that warnings had already been given, as the loudspeaker was still crackling, and then a hard reedy shout from the decidedly old, female lifeguard...

'For the last time, get that fucken' dog out of the water before I drown it myself... excuse my French, but I will!'
As we returned to the bottom, the dog carried on doing his lengths - the bubbles roaring from my mouth-piece and racing to the surface to burst with a 'ha! ha! ha!'

Our boat slipped away from Yorkey's Knob, on a barely wrinkled sea, the sky growing in confidence, the sun bathing in its own glory. The white deck threw the light back up in handfuls, and I had to screw my eyes up tight to watch the land shrink into the sea. Turning to face New Zealand, I saw a glistening hump break the surface here and then there, in front - then behind. It was a blue dolphin, enjoying the company of a giant friend. The dolphin slipped in and out of the boat's churning wake, as smooth as a call-girl and her stockings.

We anchored on a millpond with no banks; below us was the largest living organism on planet earth. Almost before I knew it, the weight of the diving gear, which had me sweating and straining on the back deck, was taken away by a single stride into the ocean. We were bobbing corks, drawing loud breaths raggedly in anticipation. Our instructor motioned us down and we followed, sheep-like, bleating into a brand new pasture, clinging to our buddies; if not physically - at least emotionally. We sunk to the seabed, trying to concentrate on the proper technique, whilst spots, stripes and splotches floated past on the sides of fish. Down from the surface, great spears of sun pinned the sea to the floor. A parrot flew past my windows, its beak opening and shutting in silent song, fins flapping in place of wings. Then I saw a chess-board, a girl's summer dress, a neon sign, an acid trip, a giant striped humbug - all sticking to their cliques or running with their gangs.

We settled on the bottom, a nervous semi-circle schoolroom, and following the dry teaching, I pumped air in or out of the buoyancy jacket until the point I'd been waiting for arrived... I was buoyant; suspended - weightless in a new world.
Now, with a single breath, not only did I carry on living but I also rose up, and exhaling... swooped down. I was flying. Like most people, I'd often laid back on clover-strewn grass, watching skylarks wheel above, or skeins of honking geese returning from bombing raids; envious of their freedom. And now *I* was flying! My breath raced in and out with excitement, sending me bobbing up and down like an errant balloon. We followed our leader for a first trip around this underwater garden. Its shrubs were all packed tight, the borders overflowing, rockery bursting, and all tended by mobs of multi-coloured gardeners, some

lying amongst the blooms, others pruning coral branches. I breathed myself over the top of a huge science fiction brain. Taller than me, it looked indestructible, but was as fragile as a butterfly's wings. A huge wrasse overtook me on the right, slow enough for me to run my hand along its blue-green flank; it stared hard at me, mouthing sweet nothings. A small manta ray flew across the false sky above, silhouetted in the descending sunlight like a Batman sign above Gotham City. Feeling a tug on my elbow, I turned to Melina, my lovely Swiss buddy, who signalled... up! I looked down and checked my air-gauge - which was in the red; beginner's exuberance. We broke the surface, and taking off our masks, hung there looking at each other for what seemed like minutes.

'Howie, that was amazing!' she said, as though we'd just had sex.

'Yes.' was the only reply I could muster. We were wide eyed; drunk with delight. Melina was nervous when snorkelling, so she asked if I would hold her hand to swim back to the boat. Once again, I thought to myself, and to the stay-at-homes... 'I'm snorkelling across the Great Barrier Reef, sun blazing in a lapis-lazuli sky, hand-in-hand with a lovely Swiss girl - a new world just below.'

The Australian visa application had sported the query... 'If you are over 25, explain why you haven't applied before.'

I can't remember what I put in this box, but now I would have to say - 'God knows, I must have been mad!' If you are still thinking of going travelling, don't; just put a pin in the World map, book a ticket, hoist up your backpack, and put one foot in front of the other.

❖

We grew in confidence - diving for two days, then took a written exam. To my surprise I passed - just, and armed with a piece of paper and a congratulatory handshake from the instructor, said...

'Yes, I'd like to do the night dive.'

We were to follow him down the anchor rope by torchlight, into the unknown, and gather on the seabed like glow-worms in the dark. Last to go, I checked with Melina, and we dipped down from a dry dark into wet dark. Almost immediately, I saw that Melina had left the rope and was drifting away in the current, checking her torch or gauges, I don't know what. She was also going down fast. The rule is to 'stick with your buddy whatever', so I dumped the air from my buoyancy jacket and emptied my lungs. Shooting down to catch her up, I was planning to grab her tank, breathe in, and inflate my jacket - which would stop us both. As I reached her, the pressure build-up in my ears was critical. I pulled my hand back to pinch my nose and equalise, but it was too late;

my left eardrum burst. Air rushed out with a squeaking noise. The white anchor line went up, sideways, around; my balance was shot. I saw that Melina was still drifting away below me; I had to go up. I had visions of blood pouring from my ear, attracting sharks. It didn't.

It took the whole night for the seawater to drain out from the back of my eardrum. Every ten minutes, during which the pain built up from uncomfortable to agonising, a single drop would escape into the pillow to sleep. The cycle then started over again. By seven in the morning, the pillow resembled the target of a tobacco-spitting contest. I left my bed in time to meet the divers coming back in from the first morning dive. It had been perfect diving conditions, the sea as clear as alpine air - the fish on full parade. My buddy tried to console me, but I could see the gleam in her eyes from the dive, still burning bright. I was pleased for her, even though it had been her mistake that could now keep me out of the water for six weeks; no swimming, and no surfing.

'If I can't go in the water - I might as well work.' I said to myself back in Cairns. I knew I couldn't last right through to New Zealand without working – money was disappearing fast in Australia.

Looking through the paper for jobs, I came across an advert that read... 'Gay bloke - seeks Aussie bloke, who likes a real good time.'

'What do you reckon that's all about Matt?' I asked.

'I reckon this bloke, the first bloke, would greet the other bloke at his front door with – "Hi mate, I've got some cold stubbies in the fridge" Then they'll watch footie on the telly - swill beer - with the odd trip to the toilet, get a takeaway pizza delivery. When they get to the point of collapsing or puking, they'd go to bed – in separate rooms of course, whispering - 'Yer a good bloke y'know.'

'Yeh! So are you - I had a real good time.'

Matt was twenty five, and been out in the wide world since the age of fourteen. His father was a multi-millionaire, his mother - a money grabber; allegedly. Matt had been put through public school, but had dropped out, and dropped into a dodgy Sydney scene. His CV ranged from drug dealer, marine biologist and diver, to protest organiser for Greenpeace. He'd lived with Hell's Angels, ferals, hippies, academics, Aborigines, scientists and backpackers. When I met him, he was sleeping with Scheharazad - a Lebanese freedom fighter, 35 years old, beautiful and fiery. He asked her, jokingly, if she carried an Uzzi around back home when she was doing the shopping.

'No,' she said coldly, 'Uzzi is Israeli weapon, we carry Kalashnikovs, smaller output - but more accurate.'

Matt could never say her name, so we had to coach him constantly. After my experiences with the Israelis, I was glad to have the chance to talk to their enemy. I could tell from her explanations that her hatred was as ingrained as theirs; no, born in. But it was good to hear the other side of the story; a story kept very quiet by the British press. When she left to return home, I asked Matt if he missed her. 'No' he replied, and meant it; he had enjoyed his time with her, and it had come to an end.
  I wondered... 'Why can't I be like that?' instead of agonising, pining - wishing my time away, but the only answer I got - was that Matt was Matt, and I was me.

  Despite conceding twelve years to me, he had seen and done as much, if not more, than I had, so we balanced well and bounced off each other; Bill and Ben. Walking back to Captain Cook's one arid evening, we passed through Abbo Park. This was where the Aborigines held a permanent picnic, with bottles of pop and radios - for music and dancing; if you looked closer it was alcohol, and the dancing was stumbling, swaying drunk. They pretended to leave at night, but the fact was - they lived there, waiting for their social cheque each week, or waiting for a relative to get better in the hospital, so that they could go home. Lost in conversation, we hadn't noticed the large, knobbly Koorie emerge from the shadows. (Koorie is the respectful name for an Abbo - a name now considered an insult. This traditional cultural name still hadn't caught on with the white Australian people.)
  'This is our fucken land!' he shouted, 'black's land, fuck off y'white freaks, we'll kill you all!' He was one of many in a dark huddle under the slumbering tree and the situation looked ugly.
  'Hey Vincent!' Matt shouted back 'have y'got a light?'
  'Aaaaghh Matt, how's it going mate? ...got any grog? ...smokoe?... no? It's okay. Any black fella trouble you, tell 'em you're a pal of Rocky Balboa, best fighter in Cairns.' and he shadow-boxed in the shadows, his bare feet scuffing up the dust.

  Carrying on home, I suggested that it was quite an exotic name for a native Australian. Matt told me that Vincent had watched a Rocky film when he was a boy and had taken the character's name; that adopting a famous name was a custom for Koories. He'd met John Travolta, Elvis Presley and a very skinny, decidedly black John Wayne down in the Woolsack pub. We reached the giant Captain Cook, and looked up at him, his arm looking weary from pointing down the road.
  'He's a bit excessive isn't he.' I said to Matt.
  'Yeh I suppose ...but we have to have something - he's better than lots of others I've seen.'

'What do you mean?' I asked.
'A big thing,' he said, 'Yas has a sheep - forty feet high, Kew - a big axe. I've eaten seafood in the second floor restaurant of the giant oyster, there's a big banana, a mammoth prawn at Ballina, crab, pineapple; you'll see them all on your way down to Sydney. But as far as I know... there's not a big dick anywhere.'
'Yes there is,' I said, 'He's standing right above us. He made the big mistake of finding Australia.'
'Fuck off Pom!' he laughed, and we walked along to room 106 - arms around each other's shoulders like two school kids in the play-ground; which was exactly what we were. When he ran out of money, I paid for his beers at the hostel bar - so that he could come out for the free keg. I paid him in a nightclub. He smoked my cigarettes. He never asked, just took them, and drank as many cups of coffee or tea I would make him; eat any food I cooked. When his money came through, he bought me a huge pack of cigarettes, a six-pack of beer; he bought the sambucas at the club, the shots in the bar; all out of my price range. When the money ran low, he'd had enough - Cairns was too city for him; he went bush. He left for Cape Tribulation, to set up camp and plant a little crop of dope, away from prying eyes. He walked the opposite way to Captain Cook's pointing finger, bare-footing down the highway, a bag of rice and beans in left hand, his right hand empty, in anticipation to seize the day.

I sat, sipping the chocolate froth from my cappuccino, watching her; a Comanche squaw, proud nose flattening to - flared nostrils, full wide lips, burning eyes. A blue tattoo braceletted her bare upper arm. I left the coffee. She pushed a leaflet into my hand, smiling.

Two days later, I was climbing a steep cliff at Cape Tribulation behind her. Rebecca was half-American, half-Arab, wearing black Lycra mini-shorts, black bra, boots, and a film of sweat. She was frighteningly sexual and we were to leapfrog all down the east coast, her - breaking hearts at every step and smile, me holding onto mine tight.

We'd travelled up for a three day stay at PK's Jungle Village. It was set deep in the forest, but held hands with a white, sandy beach that swept up to a headland, huddling under its tropical leaf canopy. It was really just a transplant of a backpacker's hostel to a different and more jungley location. We were hoping to see Cassowaries - a ridiculous big bird made from spare parts of other exotic birds. We wanted to see Koalas; a soporific blend of live teddy bear – Kangaroo; a mix of giant rat, grasshopper and a handbag - and Crocodiles; handbags with teeth.

Cassowaries had a habit of stopping people stupid enough to be jogging, by head-butting them with the hard crown on the top of their heads. Koalas had a habit of doing nothing; kangaroos - stopping vehicles with themselves; crocodiles - stopping at nothing.

We saw nothing but trees and bush-rats; a rat that looked like it had eaten too many bushes. Even on a night walk with a local guide, the only things moving were the trees; growing... slowly.

For entertainment, I dropped to the back of the line and every now and then threw sticks and stones into the darkness, then watched the rest of the group swing their torches onto an unsuspecting branch.

'That was probably a croc!' Dave the guide would exclaim. The only torch that didn't fall for it was Rebecca's, who, in complete boredom, was making faces with her torch under her chin, shining it through her hand, and signalling SOS to me from the front. The interminable walk finally ended, and we were the first two off the bus and into the bar. Before the condensation had chance to run down the side of the glasses, we were joined by some *real* wildlife - pointy heads or inbreeds, the sort of men seen playing banjos and hunting down Burt Reynolds in Deliverance.

Matt had explained that in the bush, the choice of mating partner was pretty limited, so any relative - however close, was fair game for a root, which led to mutations in appearance such as pointy heads, and eyes wandering round to join the ears.

So, seating himself the thickness of a cigarette paper from Rebecca, ogling her tattoo, was a man whose mother must have mated with a platypus.

'I'm Clem mate... woshers names?' I heard banjos in the back of my mind. Without waiting for an answer, he carried on,

'I've just got out the slammer today!' and let out a cackle that would have frightened Hannibal Lecter. Alarm bells had joined in with the banjos. Looking at Rebecca with one eye, me with the other, simultaneously - like a human fish, he said...

'These is me mates... Jed!' Jed seemed to be made of flesh coloured hot water bottles, blown up to bursting point and tattooed by a maniac. The only hair on his body sat above his lips in a great hairy bush. He said 'hello' by knitting chainmail with his eyebrows and narrowing his eyes. '...and Jonno!' Jonno was tall. He looked like a granite outcrop and stared at me until my sphincter got cramp.

'We're out on the piss!'

It was the news I'd been waiting for all my life. Rebecca was pleading with me with her eyes, to find an escape. Clem explained that they swapped pig skulls for tattoos, and showed me a twenty skuller on Jed's

TWO MINUTE NOODLE

arm. It was a bush pig with a knife in its eye. Clem showed me his killing tool - a foldaway knife from the Vietnamese war. With real concern he hissed, 'Careful mate, it's razor sharp!' Unfolding it, a part transformed itself into a pair of pliers.
 'That's for pulling teeth out mate!' Jed explained with delight.
Clem cackled and Jonno's shoulders shook with mirth. My Saigon T shirt had fascinated Jed, and he asked..
 'Are those fucken gooks still hiding under the ground?' then extolled the virtues of napalm as a skin conditioner. My forced smile was wilting like a chocolate bunny in a heat wave, as they ranted that...
 'All tourists, especially Japs and Poms, bringing their stinking diseases into Oz, should be mugged - or killed.'
Rebecca was visibly shaking, so I turned to the full table behind.
'Make room for two on that table!' I hissed. They looked hard at me for a while. 'Now!' I almost shouted - and they wriggled up. I motioned Rebecca to stand up, fixed a smile, and said to the boys...
 'Well, nice meeting you guys, but we ought to join our friends now.'

We moved over and Clem laughed like a stuck pig.
 'What's the problem?' our 'new friends asked.
 'Those three maniacs behind me.' I said, not looking back.
 'But there's nobody there.' Rebecca looked at me with bottom lip trembling - eyes black with fright. 'They've disappeared!'
The darkness was held at bay by the fluorescent light of the bar; they'd slipped into it; they were out there somewhere. We went back to our huts mob-handed that night, and I dreamt of pigs burning in napalm.

We returned to Cairns; my big friend Captain Cook pointing the way to Samuel's, The Pumphouse and The End of the World, and we raged for days on the free drink tickets that Rebecca was given - for giving out free drink tickets.

We had new guests in our room. Jack came from a small village, hidden under Norwich's skirt folds. He was an Ichabod Crane; gangling, shambling and stooped; with a mop of a hairstyle. He hadn't left the village before; had never left his parents or sister. His sister had given him a photo of her fish to take away with him. Written in childish hand on the back, was the name Lydia.
 'Is that your sister's name Jack?' I asked.
 'No silly - her fish!' he guffawed.
'That's really sweet Jack... how old is your sister?' I asked, imagining a pigtailed schoolgirl with horn-rimmed glasses, hair like Jack's, hiding her shy face.

'She's twenty two.' he stated proudly. Jack had come to Australia with no shorts, but six pairs of heavy trousers - neatly folded. Jack had no idea how to converse with people or integrate - which made things difficult for him in a cramped dormitory for ten. But he had party tricks; he could wobble his eyes like a prisoner in the electric chair; he could regurgitate whole slices of bread. Jack got mugged by a koorie in Abbo Park, whilst kindly walking a girl from Sydney back to her hostel. The girl was raped. Jack had been away from home for seven days and now he was going home. Who the hell let Jack out?

Anders, from Sweden, came into the evening meal at Captain Cook's as usual, but this time the side of his face resembled Elephant Man - the colour of beetroot. He'd walked home through the park. He didn't see it coming, or his ten dollars going, but just before the foot crashed into his eye - he saw it belonged to a koorie; Ricky Balboa... allegedly.

The unit was stuffy, someone had stolen my shoes from the washing line. I had a hangover and I needed to clear my head. Stepping down from the hostel bus, I set off for the esplanade - and the fresh air that blew onto it from across the mud flats.

Strolling north from the pier, carefully avoiding the cracks in the pavement, I pushed through the smoke from the bushfires that were burning across the bay, and mentally photographed the scenes that passed by.

❖

The tree hung full of screeching and scrawing; the birds resembling government-grey doves which had flown headlong into a set of children's paints.

❖

The rainbow was complete across the silent Sound, a multi-coloured Sydney Harbour Bridge. There was another, fainter, adjoining it - basking in its glory.

❖

The two old labradors had led a dog's life, and were sleeping it off. The owner sat between them, sporting the longest face in Australia. It stretched from Cape York to the bottom of his chin. His Panama suit was crumpled, hiding some of the stains but showing off the rest. It was the same colour as his skin and the dogs. The notes squeaked from his old flute, the tune as thin and stretched as his frame.

❖

Hammerhead clouds stood guard over the distant bushfire like smoke detectors waiting to go off.

As Lake Street went its way to the left, four pelicans sailed by on my right in Quadrille, dipping their outlandish beaks in perfect time with each other; Prima Ballerina Pelicanus.

❖

The day trip boats were coming in, gleaming white; catamarans, diving boats, dinghies, full-rigged yachts, glass-bottomed boats; all straggled into the harbour like sheep into a pen, the approaching night a vast black Border Collie driving them home.

❖

The Japanese man, playing the saxophone, was facing the sea, throwing manic scales across the mud. His buddy sat cross-legged beside him, counting the notes and catching any bum ones that fell to the floor.

❖

Pausing, while handing the fish and chips to the backpacker, the girl serving nodded to the salt, vinegar and sauces, and asked...
'D' ya want heaps of shit on y' dinner?'

❖

Across the road from the Grand Hotel and the wedding reception, the groom and best man sported red bow ties and bottles of beer. Passing close behind, I heard the best man say...
'Yer married now mate!' as he pounded on his groom's extra wide and shiny lapels.
'Congratulations.' I offered.
'Aah yeah, thenks mate - thenks heaps!' he said, sweating in his penguin suit. I walked on with a smile for his day and his pleasure, but before I'd covered the length of a cricket crease, I realised that I'd cleared the hangover from my head, but my eyes were full - for my own marital failures.

❖

I stopped dancing, suddenly, in the middle of the club. I'd just heard the same three tunes they played every night. Despite our best efforts, Rebecca and I couldn't keep up with the drinks vouchers: they were building up. It was 4.16 am: I had to leave Cairns for my health. We'd been living high on ten dollars a day; costly days were ahead. I was on the bus in the morning - waved off by room 106.

THE EAST COAST TRAIL

With a Greyhound pass to Sydney, I decided to leapfrog down the coast on the Backpacker's trail - to see what the attraction was.

The first lily-pad I landed on was Airlie Beach - gateway to the Whitsunday Islands. It didn't have a proper beach; it didn't really have anything, just a half mile strip of cafes, shops and hostels. But it did have a post-office, and I was expecting a letter from Chantal, so I was stuck there until Monday, when it opened.

I stayed at the Whitsunday Beach Village Hostel, which, if cleared of backpackers and the room occupancy reduced, could rate as a four star holiday village. There were three of these on the strip, and Chungking Mansions seemed an awfully long way off. Although cheap by English or tourist standards, at fifteen dollars a night with no free food or beer - it made Cairns look like a soup kitchen. I realised that my meagre stash of dollars was actually paltry - chicken feed; I'd spent as much money in one month as I had in four, in Asia. I had a cash-flow problem that only working, somewhere, sometime, would solve. On the way down, I'd listened to the horror stories told around fruit picking. Stone Island, Rockhampton and Bundaberg were all being raided by police regularly, backpackers without work permits being ejected from the country.

On top of this, there were 'poisonous spiders in the bananas', 'picking with pointy heads high on dope', 'snakes', and 'bad pay'. I made a half-hearted effort to get a photographic job in Airlie itself, but the owner wanted papers, and I had none. Meeting two girls who'd caught up with me from room 106, we carried on where we'd left off - but dancing on tables wasn't allowed, unlike Cairns, where it was encouraged. I tried to enjoy it, but I was hearing those same records over and over again.

I sat on my porch, a spit away from the kidney shaped pool, and greeted my new neighbours - three Swedes. One of the synchronised spending team introduced himself. It was Anders, and I saw that his eye had vastly improved since I last saw him at Captain Cook's. His friends wanted to go out on the town but Anders seemed to want my company. We talked about travelling, our lives and loves, and he grilled me about travelling alone. He was tired of being one of a group.

I picked up my letter from Chantal on the Monday morning, and took it to the beach that wasn't quite a beach - to read.

There was a stiff, chill breeze blowing up my shorts as I stared at the stamp of Ghandi. The letter was, as usual, edged with red and blue - but this time also tinged with frost. It was a brief note informing me of change to her travel plans, and a promise to write soon. There was no tenderness squeezed between the lines; no affection scenting the paper. The panic buttons didn't start to ring, as they might have done once, but the white flag was starting to run up the mast. It had been a mere six weeks ago that we parted company, but hope was starting to fade.

There was a Greyhound leaving the traps; I jumped on it, and ignoring my own rule of not taking reviews at face value, bypassed Magnetic Island. So many people had said it was crap, I figured it must be – I just hope it wasn't offended by my lack of attraction.

Instead, I landed with a plop at Hervey Bay, with the intention of a side trip to Fraser Island on a four-wheel-drive adventure. I went to all of the hostels looking for work, but within hours I had drawn a blank, and was now signed up for a three day trip to the island. I went to the get-together to meet the eight in my group; old friends after ten minutes; seven were English and one - Belgian; a Flemish girl actually.

The highway on Fraser Island is a hundred mile beach, the inland roads - sand and stone tracks. We had two tents, eight slabs of Victoria Bitter (Vitamin B), some food - and ourselves.

We perched on Indian Heads, and way below in a sea as clear as air, watched turtles swimming with the grace that land takes away, manta-rays swooping and gliding, and reef sharks darting here and there - menacing the innocents. Rejoining the highway, we scooted north, the ozone so thick it slapped you in the face; the only obstacles - the soft sand at the top of the beach, the wet sand at the waterline, and the streams that trickled down into the sea. We waded up the immaculate water of Ely Creek, until the overhanging foliage threatened to strangle, and then floated down in its current over pebbled shallows, past limpid pools and under rickety bridges; like a game of human Pooh sticks. It was still only mid-morning but in celebration of an already colossal day, the first slab was pulled from the jeep.

'God I needed that!' said Hilde - the Flemish girl, as she sculled her first and cracked open another.

'Are you joining me?' she asked.

'That's my kind of girl'' I thought, and replied 'Madness not to.'

'You're beer monsters!' John exclaimed, and grabbed himself a tinny.

We managed to avoid the other jeeps full of backpackers scattered around the island, as we swam in champagne rock-pools, scaled ten-storey sand dunes – to slide down; walked, talked and bodysurfed. I was persuaded out of the waves by a reef shark (or a lump of seaweed), and came out with a jellyfish sting from ear to ear, like a clown's smile. The trip drifted along on the breeze, picked up and moved from lake to river, forest to sand-dune, by an untiring sun. Below it, we moved from strangers to companions, and some of us went the whole way to friendship, in that unknown way that you do.

We built a carefully shielded fire, cooked up, kicked back, and cruised - the moon smiling at us cheekily. Hilde and I cruised long after the kiddiwinks had retired to their tents, the canvas billowing with their snores and dreams.

We were lying in our sleeping bags, watching the stars make eyes at each other, emptying cans of Vitamin B. The dingos starting coming in, wearing the darkness as cover. A rustling from the barbeque snapped Hilde upright - 'What's that?'

'It's a dingo...' I slurred back, 'turn on the torch.' The feeble beam crept over the twigs, pebbles and empty cans, and raised its weary head to rest on a startled dingo with a mouthful of silver-clad potato. Several more milled around in the background, like extras in a film, then slunk away into the dark. Hilde turned the torch off and as the darkness returned - so did they, padding around us to snatch blackened sausages from the still hot griddle. John came out of his tent in the murky glimmer of dawn, and saw Hilde and me amongst the pack of dingos and a hill of empty cans.

'Shit!' he hissed, as I raised a bleary head, 'Are you mad? - have you seen what you've been sleeping with?'

'Yes...' I said, 'it's Hilde.' and went back to sleep, as her hand, warm from sleep, found mine and held it.

We returned to Hervey Bay, as tired as a group of children after a day at the zoo, and handed back the jeep. We were suddenly no longer a unit, and were slotted into our allotted dorms. We clustered back together for the evening – retelling jokes and reliving moments of gladness, and as the plot of the day thinned and tired, the kiddiwinks retired to bed. Hilde and I were the sole survivors again.

'I don't want to sleep in my dorm, I don't like the girls.' she said.

'Don't then - sleep with me.' I suggested.

'Yes I will.' she said, and we walked to mine.

There were two lads still undressing as we entered, one leg in and one out of their jeans, hopping to pull them off. I could see them doing sums in their head - one bed, two people, one of them a girl.

'It's that one up there.' I nodded, as Hilde slipped out of her clothes and into the top bunk. Looking round the room, the lads were still half dressed, books left mid sentence, jaws dropped. I dropped my trousers, shrugged my shoulders at them and leapt upstairs. We were Siamese twins - soul mates, and we fell straight to sleep, gorged on comfort and the warmth of two people who had no idea what they were to each other yet; and didn't care. Hilde cried out once in her sleep, but it was only a night bear. I tumbled back into sleep.

Roast potatoes were better than boiled, but not as good as mashed with butter. 'You've got potatoes growing in your ears.' Dad always said. The Beatles were better than the Stones, mods than rockers, Fruit Salads than Blackjacks, Tizer than Dandelion and Burdock, Saturday than Sunday, Littlehampton than Worthing (It had a funfair, even though we weren't allowed in it)

Life was black and white; in books and on TV – black people were sambos, piccaninnie, or pigmies, and unknown to us in our rural outpost - they were flooding into Liverpool, Bristol and London to make a new life. A life that I would eventually become a big part of and enjoy; find no more unusual than rain and cricket

On Sunday morning we had to stay in bed until 8.00, reading books and comics. (Only the Victor as it had stories, not just pictures) Me or my Bruv would go down and make a cup of tea, take it in to wake Mum and Dad, then squirrel back into the still warm bed, reading and farting for another half hour, until the smell of eggs and bacon and the local butcher's chipolatas crept up the very steep stairs.

At the breakfast table, Family Favourites was on the transistor radio - Puff the Magic Dragon, Three Wheels on my Wagon, My Boomerang Won't Come Back and a host of other such crap, squeaked from the speaker. But sandwiched in between were The Kinks, The Animals, Amen Corner, and best of all - The Who, ripping apart the cosy world of British pop with R & B.

'You're not taking the bikes out until they're clean, until the morning's wood is chopped, the fire grate cleaned out, the fire laid, the lawn mowed!' said Dad, mopping up his last bit of egg with a chipolata.

I went through a martyr stage, where I would go out and chop sticks, fingers blue with cold, all the time thinking - 'they'll love me more than Martin because he said no and he's in our room in the bad books...but also in the warm.' But I was chopping sticks like a madman; I was the best woodchopper in the history of the world, and if my fingers fell off with frostbite... it would serve them all right.

If the bikes were clean we could go out - anywhere! We had no boundaries. Our village and the surrounding countryside, was our playground. We weren't restricted by abduction, rape or murder. Did it go on? Probably; but we didn't know. So it didn't matter; everyone kept an eye on kids, whoever they belonged to.

Kevin Jelly had drunk too many Brown Ales. He was older than us and fat, and got served in the pub. We walked home with him, to see if he would fall over or puke. He said he could smash a window with a punch, and not cut himself. He stood in front of the cigarette machine that had three wired windows - Piccadilly, No.6 and Guards, and punched the middle one, which was strange as he smoked Piccadilly. He showed us his knuckles, fist closed – 'See!' At first we didn't, then a red spider's web appeared, getting fatter, and the blood dripped from his hand. 'Yeah - good one Jello!' we shouted at a distance, as we knew the fat prat would wipe it on us. 'Do the shop window with your head.' I hollered, running away. Some stitches put the tendons back together, but you could never get No.6 from the machine again, which was Kevin Jelly's contribution to the downfall of that atrocious cigarette.

God, I thought, as I crawled into consciousness, I was dreaming about my life in 1970 - most of the people I'd been travelling with, hadn't even been born. I peeled myself away from Hilde's back and went to the toilet. I looked in the mirror, and looking back was an old man. I don't know who he was, but by gum it wasn't me.

The core of our group trundled south to Noosa together; where John and I checked out the surf that wasn't there. I attempted to bodysurf in the wishy-washy waves but, leaving the water to join Hilde, found that my chest was feeling very tight. I tried to walk straight, but left a 'Teach yourself the Foxtrot' pattern in the sand, eventually reaching them on a wide stumbling arc. I had another jellyfish sting, which had wrapped itself round my front and back like a bandolier. Hilde was worried; I was touched. After a couple of fruitless days waiting for some surf, I wondered what to do next. Hilde had decided to move on. I felt slightly attached to her and asked if I could come along.
   'I'm going to North Stradbroke Island.' she said.
   'What's there?' I asked.
   'I don't know, but it sounds nice, are you sure you want to come?'
   'Are you sure you want me to come?' Did she want me to? Did I want to? Why was I asking questions?

❖

Straddie. In Ozzie tradition - North Stradbroke Island, almost a whole sentence, has to be shortened to two syllables; as though any more than two would be far too difficult for an Australian to string together. By the same rule, Tasmania is shortened to Tazzy, Bundaberg – Bundy, Rockhampton - Rocky; Alice loses her Springs, and Sydney - with the correct number remains Sydney, apart from in Melbourne - where it has totally silent syllables. To keep the balance, any names foolish enough to have only one syllable, are instantly allocated an 'O' to get them up to the right amount - Johnno, Davo, Stevo.

Straddie is sensibly anchored off the coast of Brizzie and Surfer's, which to us, passing through, resembled satellite cities of Tokyo, in appearance and population. Booking onto the Straddie ferry, we backpacked aboard, and having deposited the packs in a corner, joined the other passengers loading boxes of groceries from the jetty. The bus to Point Lookout, Outlook Point, or Point Outlook, a name I never got to grips with, carried a mixed bag of school kids going home, office workers, shoppers and two backpackers.
'You two's going to the hostel?'...my name's George.' said the driver. The bus trundled off and we listened to the chit-chat of a close community.
'Hev you f' gotten me today George?' piped up an old lady wearing Dame Edna spectacles.
'Agghh, sorry Ivy.' said George, chunking the bus into reverse, and driving back two houses - until the door of the bus was in line with the white picket gate. George sprinted ahead of Ivy with one of her grocery bags, and opened the fly screen door while she entered.
'Bang the door when you go George!' she flung back, her voice fading as it disappeared inside, and George finished the unheard half of the sentence...'Cos it clears the screen of fly shit!'
After Ivy's, we stopped in front of wire gates, shop doors, the steps of caravans, and Point Lookout hostel. We checked in at what looked to be a family lounge - the TV blaring, a five and a three year old blaring at each other. Welcoming us, the mother shouted...
'Stop it Tim - Edward will get hurt!' just as Edward's head hit the wall with the sound of a hammer hitting a cantaloupe. Holding a squawking Edward on one hip, and our sheets on the other, she said...
'This one is Seek and the one looking all innocent is Destroy... here's your room.' It was a dormitory, and without doubt the nicest I'd seen in all my travels. There was a lone girl in the next unit, but apart from her we were the only backpackers on the island. We took the separate room, which was curtained off for privacy.
'Yes we are a couple.' I'd had to tell the owner on the phone.

'We don't like any funny business.' he'd said.

We awoke in the morning to the sound of a vacuum in the kitchen. This grew louder as the Hoover attachment came through the curtain, closely followed by Edward, who, intent on his job, had reached the end of the bed. Spying us there - he just stared, while the Hoover cleaned one part of the floor, immaculately.

'Hi Edward.' we said, as he stared a gazely stare.

'Edward!' - a shouted whisper from the kitchen '...get out of there!' Edward stared on, the Hoover straining to find more dust. As we stifled our giggles, Edward smiled a very naughty and knowing smile.

'Edward get out here... now!' His smile drooped, but he stood his ground - staring.

'Edward...you wanker!!' his father roared, out of sight, and pulled him out - the corrugated pipe tight under his arm. The coloured plastic blinds swung back together like a grass skirt.

❖

We wandered the cliffs and beaches, slunk into gullies, lazed around Blue Lake and Brown Lake, revelling in being the only visitors. We sat outside our dorm and ate pasta with lashings of garlic, whilst the night grew loud and dark. A trio of kookaburras cuddled up on a telegraph wire above, telling each other jokes before bedtime. They would giggle, until the punch-line, and then burst into laughter until their sides split. As they eventually ran out of steam, got to a low chuckle and...

'Oh dear.. no more.' one would tell another joke and set them off again. We laughed along with them.

'Wotcha eating?' said a small voice from the blond head, almost eye level to the table.

'Pasta. Do you want some Edward?'

'Naarrgh - bums.' he said.

'What do you like to eat?' I asked.

'Cake.' he drooled.

'What sort of cake - chocolate, birthday, Christmas cake?'

'Naarrgh - bugger cake.' He stated. I hoped it had nothing to do with chocolate starfish.

'And what do you make those with Edward?' Hilde enquired.

'Bloody beetles 'n bloody cockies, and red and black icing, 'n bloody eat it. And if y' can't eat it, y' squash it with y' foot, and y' spit on it.'

It made the pasta seem quite dull, so spotting a mean looking spider scuttling up the wall, I pointed to it and asked Hilde...

'D' ya want that in y' bloody pasta, or shall I just spit in it?'

Heading back for the ferry, we thought we were on the wrong bus, but there was George driving as before. Apart from us, the only passengers were toddlers; here - a group of three, there – two, sitting silent looking at each other, and single ones spread around, unworried, unabashed, unwashed. We stopped outside a gate with a huge daisy logo on it and the word - Kindy; kindergarden was obviously far too long a word.

The children trooped off the bus, some in a hurry to get to school, others still at home in their minds - cosy in bed, dreaming of rabbits and bugger cake. The teacher tripped down the path like Julie Andrews and leapt aboard the bus.
 'Any more down there?' Feeling as though we were late for school or skiving, I answered – 'No miss.'
 'Could you look under the seats, they sometimes go to sleep.' So we became seat monitors and reported 'No there's none left.'
 'OK George, full body count, y' can go.' she said, and I swear George said -'Yes Miss.' We trundled off to the ferry, and then left the place where five year olds can cross the island unaccompanied without fear, and still imagine cakes made of creepy crawlies; where the only two people sharing the beach with beached jellyfish - were the two of us.

❖

We crossed to Brisbane, shot through the transit centre, where I had a cup of coffee with the lovely Rebecca - also in transit, and raced down on a Greyhound bus to Byron Bay; another hostel.
 'Two beds please.'
 'Yes we can fit you in - are you a couple?'
 We looked at each other and said 'Yes' in unison.
 'Right then, you'll be in the double room.'
 'Oh no, we can't afford that, a dorm room will do.'
 'No, it's the same price as a dorm, but you share with another couple - two double beds y' see." We didn't at first, but entering the room, we did. The other couple, Tim from South Africa and Anna from Norway, were in bed, with the sheet not quite up to their nipples. Anna left the bed naked, dressed while we chatted sociably, and then left. She came back while we were still talking, removed her clothes and got back in the bed. While Hilde visited the toilet, Tim asked...
 'Are you two going to be hanging around a while?'
 'Just a few days.' I answered.
 'No, I meant this afternoon.'
 'Oh, ah, oh, no, well - we were going to go for a walk along the beach.' I replied, thinking that we were in the way.

'I just thought, if you two wanted to spend the afternoon in bed, *we'd* go for a walk along the beach - wouldn't we Anna?'
'Yaah.' she said through gritted teeth.
'That's alright, we've already got clothes on..' I said, as Hilde returned to the room, 'we'll be about an hour, will that be long enough?'
'Plenty.' said John - Anna looking daggers at him.

Byron was cooool man! a half surfing - half hippie town. We checked out the surf that wasn't there, and then the hostel with the art gallery, log cabins and tee-pees. Rebecca was there, with a man in tow like a lost puppy, and we agreed to meet in Sydney, soon.

We sat on the rocks of Cape Byron, the easternmost point of Australia, and watched the whales migrating past, breaching, and slapping their mammoth fins on the sea like giant backhanders.

We cruised the surf shops, me dribbling at the thought of the waves to come. Leaving a bottle shop fully laden, I spied a very Swedish looking man sitting on the kerb, scoffing down a burger.

Anders *had* taken the plunge and left his friends in Airlie. He was having a great time going solo - his eye healed. We agreed to meet in Sydney, soon.

And then it was Hilde's time to move on; she had to visit friends in the Sydney suburbs before heading home to Belgium. I wouldn't see her before I got back to England, but we said... 'It's only six months.'
I had a word with myself... 'What the hell are you doing - what about Chantal? The answer came the very next day.

I saw Hilde off onto the bus, and to take my mind off her, traipsed around the town looking for work. Optimistic - I asked in every bar, pub, hotel, cafe, restaurant and surf shop; drawing a complete blank. I started to feel dismal, very much alone again; I was almost broke.

On cue, the weather came to town and unloaded its suitcase, the wind blowing the rain off the sea into the town centre; not a rabbity, choppy wind, but a full blown head of steam - with a thousand mile push behind it. As moody and restless as the sky above, I slunk into the post office for shelter, and finding myself right next to the Poste Restante, asked if there was anything for me. I wasn't expecting anything, but there was Ghandi staring back at me again; this time he looked a little guilty. Stuck halfway between town and the hostel, I found myself a bus-shelter and read the letter in a dying light.

It was India, painted in technicolor words, vivid and alive. Temples, people, the River Ganges and mountains, all hurried across the pages in a tumble. And then the colour drained away and all I saw was grey, and perhaps a little red.

'I'm just a memory to you, I'm not even the same Chantal you met. I don't mean to hurt you, I know I will - by writing this, but please forget me. I still wear your sarong, it's very precious to me... and we do still think about you. Anyway... everything what begins has to come to an end, the bad things and the nice, and relationships too, whether it's death or other things what separate two people. Take care.'
Chantal x

I stepped out from the shelter into the rain, which swept across like a theatre curtain, and stood there for the longest time.
 'Shhhiiitttt!!' I cried out, in a great bellow. I stood there, oblivious to the stinging rain, lit up by orange streetlamps and the whining headlamps of the odd passing car, then walked home like a question mark; desolate.

❖

The likelihood of decent surf arriving stood hand-in-hand with the chance of getting a job, so I rang Hilde in Sydney.
 'Hilde, I've given up on the idea of working here, would you mind if I came down to...'
 'Yes - yes please! how soon can you...' I was on the Greyhound. Except that this time, it wasn't a Greyhound - but a McCafferty's. The only difference between the two was the lettering on the side. In all other aspects, the experience was the same; always the same.

This was my fifth bus trip. They usually started with a dreadful video, the sound inaudible, too loud, or drowned out by the driver and his relief - talking. Sleep was not a viable alternative as, even if lucky to be sitting next to a vacant seat, your legs - out in the aisle, would be stepped over all night. Stretched vertically up the window, or squashed into your chest by the seat in front, cramp would gnaw at your bones; so you would try to sleep sitting up; what the Chinese call fishing - your head drooping down to the chest until the neck pain wakes you, and your head bobs up, to start drooping again.
 And then there was the neighbour. They could be drunk, boring or smell; sometimes all three. I seemed to attract old ladies. On my trips, I'd had fat old lady, dribbling old lady (who used my shoulder for a pillow), non-stop talking lady, and scared old lady. *She* had her gear packed up and clutched tightly in her hand - fifty miles before her stop, rising up and down out of her seat to see if it had arrived, eyeing me suspiciously, through the sides of her X-ray specs. I didn't move an

inch - for fear of her crying rape or murder. She peered out of the window away from me, until, passing through a dark tunnel - the window mirrored my face and she started, with a gasp. I offered her a sweet, but she just stared at it as though I'd pulled it from my pants.

I couldn't make any movements next to fat lady, as my right side was pinned to her as though stroke-ridden, soaked with thermo-nuclear sweat. She was quite comfortable during the night, on her waterbed arse and half of my seat, and I slumbered between the aftershocks of her snoring. She never spoke.

Mrs Talky never stopped. From Byron Bay she talked me through to Grafton. Her son - Kevin, hadn't taken after his father, who was a pilot, but gone to Melbourne to study medicine; he always worked hard at school. 'Was I going there? Perhaps I'll meet him!
  By the time we reached Coffs Harbour, Kevin had got engaged, married Sally, and given birth to two children - Stephen and Eleindia. 'E.L.E.I.N.D.I.A...such an unusual name, don't you think?'
  A film started, and despite my staring hard at the screen, and leaning forward straining to hear the dialogue over the details of Stephen's education, she rolled on with the bus, and worked her way through Eleindia's dance career - 'Good toes, naughty toes!'
  'Oh, I'm sorry my dear, you're trying to watch the film. I'll shut up!' She didn't. Kevin Costner had super hair, the wolf was just as loyal as a corgi she once had - the Indians were so cruel at times, but then it did look very cold where they were. And when Kevin (the actor – not the son) rode off round the hill at the end of the film, the real life Kevin was now galloping into middle age as we rode into Port McQuarie.

Her husband survived until Newcastle, though he'd been ill for years, and just outside of Sydney I almost asked if I could marry Eleindia, as she sounded perfect in every way imaginable.
  'Are we there already...' she said 'gosh, the journey goes so fast when you have someone nice to talk to, doesn't it?' I felt like I'd been on the bus for years; no wonder Kevin went to Melbourne as soon as he could.

The coach trips had comfort stops. This was where you emptied your bladder, filled your guts, had a cigarette, and a break from your neighbour. The choice was - to eat in the restaurant or buy fast food from the service station. The former were normally themed, so you could eat for example - in Vienna, pictures of the Danube behind your head, schnitzels, sausages and strudels waltzing away behind the glass counter - the waitresses in lace dresses and mobcaps.

Next door in the service station they had buttons. Press button to release Mexican meat pie. Remove packaging - press red button for squirt of sauce - press 'add creamer' (as you've pressed the Cappuccino button by mistake) put in microwave - press button marked Mexican Meat Pie - press Cappuccino button for luck, juggle the nuclear-hot pie on its pathetic paper plate - then pay the man. After first scalding bite, press the 'press' sign on the bin by the door, deposit the pie; go outside for a cigarette.

Arriving at one comfort stop, I felt as though I'd wandered onto the set of a science fiction movie. Spread around the car park, orange under the sodium glare, were a dozen figures - each facing a different direction, shuffling from foot to foot like zombies, looking down to the ground or heavenwards. Each had six shadows like umbrella spines surrounding them. To the left - a vast mutant sheep was giving birth to a small restaurant. These were the smokers, drawing in desperate lungfuls of smoke before re-boarding their Greyhound.

The next stop had a big thing, a big Merino sheep, shielding a theme restaurant - Hungarian. I ran into the next one at Newcastle, but this big thing was small - a miniature Ayers Rock. And as we all know - Ayers Rock doesn't have windows, so nor did the fast food and souvenir shops inside, bathed in a fluorescent glare day and night.

Outside - the zombies shuffled and smoked until it was time to join the sensible passengers who'd stayed on board, avoiding Austria, Bulgaria, Mexico and the Twilight Zone; they'd also slept undisturbed for forty minutes.

On the lemon side, the Greyhounds had a toilet, drinking water, two drivers, no hard seats, 41 people on a 41 seat bus - and curtains. They didn't break down or slide into paddy fields. The drivers always had friendly names like Bob, Bill, Tom - even a Nobby, so when I felt cramped or tired, I thought of China and laughed.

❖

GLEBE VILLAGE HOSTEL, SYDNEY

I entered Sydney by the backdoor, and checked into a hostel in Glebe. Glebe reminded me of Brighton, one of my favourite places. It straggled over the slopes above Darling Harbour in terraces of villas, their wrought-iron verandas smothered in geraniums and honeysuckle. Miles Davis and Charlie Parker tunes fluttered out of record shops into the coffee bars, milk bars, and bars - where beatniks, punks, fashionista and travellers caressed their copies of Kerouac, The Face, or the Lonely Planet. Glebe was busy doing nothing, just allowing itself to be preened and restored by its new owners, and keeping quiet - so that Kings Cross and the like couldn't see what a good time it was having. Hilde was staying across town with friends and the hostel was a silence of cliques, so I set out downtown to introduce myself to Sydney.

The old lady's nose, supporting a pair of Grouch Marx glasses, was squashed against the pawnbroker's window, and she was hurring up the glass with her false teeth breath. She grabbed my arm and pulled me over.
'You look like you've got good eyesight young man, how much is that ring there?' '80 dollars.' I replied.
'..how many carats?' 'Six.' I said.
'..and that one?' '110 dollars - 12 carats.'
'Do you think that blue one's nicer?' I priced and assayed nearly every ring in the window, and had it narrowed down to four before I started to lose my patience.
'Look I have to go now.'
'Oh thanks lovey.' Something intrigued me, so I turned back.
'Aren't your glasses any good lovey?'
'Oh no dear, I bought them in here a couple of weeks ago and I can't see a bloody thing.'

The wino staggered backwards across Central Park at a trot, pleading...
'It's Wullie's buthday... and he'd love a cigarette!' Correcting his passage, he shot past me at a gallop. Willie's top half however, rocked back and forth, but his legs stayed put - as though stuck in clay. His eyes were also stuck - askew.
'Wull y' have a drrrink with us ter shellerbrate hus buthday?' he slurred, as he passed me on the right, in an arc, desperately trying to get

to the spot in front of me. Willy spun the lid off the new bottle of whisky he'd been holding, and it flew off into the long grass.

'Fug it Wullie, we'sull huv t' drink it orl noo.'

I handed him two cigarettes as he passed my left shoulder - crablike, and pushed away the bottle Willie had pushed in my face.

'No thanks Willie, I'm going to meet my girlfriend - she'll give me shit if I smell of booze... but Happy Birthday mate!'

'Aawwh! s'awright Wullie - if it's his hen's buthday, th' man shoo get along - giv hur a buthday kiss f' me orkee?'

I'd been in Sydney for two hours, and I'd only spoken to a madwoman and two Scottish drunks. As I walked through the city, shoppers shopped, tourists toured, and the businessmen scurried up and down wearing self-important frowns. I felt small amongst the glass and marble monoliths, and then I walked out of the shadows into the light.

The coat hanger straddled, and the nuns stood up to their necks in the wind-choppy harbour, posing for the Yashicas, Minoltas and Nikons. These are the affectionate nicknames for the two iconic structures of Australia – the Sydney Harbour Bridge and the Royal Opera House; and I was delighted that they were as impressive as I'd hoped.

Directly in front of me a litter of harbour ferries suckled the quay, water taxis skimmed the surface, and helicopters flew like dragonflies across the botanical gardens that crept out into the bay. I shuffled through Sydney's history as I walked through The Rocks. This led me to the bridge itself, and a long climb up its steps, where I watched the harbour craft skywriting on the water, a long way below.

A noise rose above the honking of the streets and the hooting harbour, and spun me round by the shoulders. I looked down on a playground; its wall painted so that the colourful balloon, the sky, and the mountains it glided across, appeared to be made from bricks.

The kids were quite small and were playing a variation of volleyball for people not big enough to hit the ball back. The teacher counted down from ten, and the ones holding the ball at zero were the losers. There was one player who caught my eye, dashing around his friends with great excitement, shrieking and laughing. He had short sleeves, but they were empty, and flapped as he ran. And once, as the ball dropped from high, he followed it down with rounded eyes and headed it back over, just as the teacher shouted 'One!' His friends slapped'high fives to his sleeves and hugged him.

I crossed to the other side of the bridge and looked down on my own past. Right there were the customs sheds, where the ocean liners once

TWO MINUTE NOODLE

docked - nudging up to Oz, disgorging thousands upon thousands of over-dressed and over-awed British families into their new home.

We had one trunk each, in which we carried the whole of our English life and some souvenirs of Egypt and Ceylon
We arrived on Christmas Eve. It was 102 degrees. My Mum cried. My brother and I had a tin car each; just one. I think we were happy with that. I think we were scared. We lived in two rooms. The Polish landlord was the only snowplough dealer in Australia.

I went to the big-boy's fence in the playground, and cried for my brother. We ran around Sydney playing truant, and looking in other schools' windows; I was seven. One day Sydney disappeared under a flash flood. Martin and I paddled around in the flood instead of going to school. Alan and Terry shared the room next to us and caught us sneaking in. They dried us off and looked after us until Mum and Dad came home. 'Sorry boys - had to tell them.' said Terry. We didn't mind. Alan and Terry were from Chelsea, they were groovy. We lived with a distant relative for a while; somewhere. My Mum packed her bags and we ran after her crying – 'Don't go! don't go!' She didn't. She wouldn't have; ever. She just wanted to. She had to work in a chip van at the Oval. She looked very hot in the van frying chips. It was 95 degrees outside the van. The teacher asked for a word starting with 'F'. I said 'Fag'. She told me off and all the Ozzie kids laughed at me.

We moved to Manly; a new school. My friends were Yugoslavian, Chinese, Canadian and Ozzies. We started surfing. We rode the ferries across the harbour; it was better when it was rough.

Luna Park had a wobbly walkway, that blew air up girl's skirts - showing their knickers, a revolving barrel and an upside down house. You walked through a huge clown's mouth to get in.

There was Luna Park opposite me now, the gaping mouth entrance had a smashing new set of ivories; and further out, like a child's arms hiding its test answers, were the Sydney Heads. We would drive up there some weeks, to wave at friends on the SS.Oriana and SS.Canberra, sailing home to England - the streamers still hanging from the ship's rails like a gipsy girl's curls. Though I loved Australia - I wanted to be on that boat, waving at us.

It was soon our turn, and we sailed home to a bleak English midwinter; I wished I was back on the Heads again - waving someone else off.

I headed across Sydney to meet Hilde at her friend's house in Miranda, realising, as the train closed the distance, that I was heading into hell - suburbia.

'I couldn't possibly change the seating arrangement Peter - I've planned it!' said Susan; who seemed to have something smelly under her nose.
 'Howie - would you like to have a shower - freshen up before we have dinner?' she simpered. I didn't, but I had one just to mess up the visitor's towel for her.
 'Would you like to see our wedding video after supper?'
 We had three desserts, as well as strawberries dipped in chocolate; they tasted of straw. I wasn't invited to in one of their numerous empty bedrooms, and was shown to the station at a civilized hour. It took me two hours to cross Sydney on the post-pub midnight train, through the areas that had been recommended to avoid. The last time I felt that uncomfortable was sharing the buffet car to Guildford with the Manchester United fans – who'd just lost to Arsenal and the Pompey fans – just thrashed by Chelsea. The buffeting was energetic and then the claret flowed - thick and fast; but I made it back to Glebe.

An embarrassed Hilde escaped the next day - her sanity barely intact. Meeting her at Circular Quay, I rang for the job that I'd seen advertised on the hostel notice board.
 'Yes I am a painter and decorator.' I lied.
 'If I had dollar for every Pommie or Paddy, who told me that - I wouldn't have to work. Have you got trade papers?'
 I didn't even have cigarette papers. 'Yes.' I lied.
 'When did you get those?'
 'About twelve years ago.' I lied.
 I was grimacing at Hilde, who was smiling - hopefully.
 'Alright I'll give you a start - I'll pick you up 6am Monday.'
 Hilde was happy for me, and we had the day left together.

We went back to Glebe, where everything was shining and laughing; it was 90 degrees and sunny, and it was 'Festival Time!'
 The people filled the road, stretching up and over the three hills of Glebe Point, in and around and about the stalls; where people with imagination had laid their creations on trestle tables. The smell of cooking rose - hissing, bubbling into the air; Chinese, Nepalese, Lebanese, Thai, Indian, Indonesian, Turkish, Yiddish and English - leapt from every utensil imaginable. At each road junction a different band played, their notes shimmering and floating on the heat - which washed between the people. We sat in an open-fronted bar, taking our

Vitamin B, while the sweat cooled; until outside, a Samba band drummed by - beckoning with insistent finger.
We tried to ignore it, but Hilde was as much a slave to the beat as me. We emerged blinking at the brightness, and threaded our way to the junction, where I watched Hilde take to the road and sway to the rhythm, her back impossibly arched, hips swaying, finger-popping. She returned - glowing, and we moved off up the street to the next delight. She was pressed close behind me in the crowd, and I felt her kiss me, a soft cat's paw on my shoulder.

Gaining some breath in The Toxteth Pub, a million miles from its Bristol namesake, the riots started again; this time in the sky. As though irked by the fun that had been dragged out below, the sky hit back. It used every trick up its sleeve to cow the people – but the rain just egged them on. The pub emptied into the street, soaking up the deluge as a treat, whooping and hollering with the bass drums above, and cheering the electric show in the sky, which dashed about - trying to be menacing. The crowd was tight; ecstatic.

But Hilde had to return to suburbia; school-sock grey and just as uniform, as 'supper' had been planned. The 'Burbs' must have cracked though; found some empathy, or noticed Hilde's sadness, as, after a meal of - '..it's only leftovers', they drove us back to the city, dropping us under the Harbour Bridge for our goodbye.

We sat on the harbour wall, the full moon crashing through the bitter steel lattice of the bridge and falling in pieces onto the water; facing each other, our hopes and our fears. Hilde clung to time and me - tightly.
'Goodbye Hilde,' I said - pushing her into the parting we had to do. She lifted her face to me like a newly opened bloom, crying soft, silent tears. Dropping her head back onto my damp shoulder she clung tighter.
'Goodbye Hilde.' I said again, and as she released her hold, I heard her arms drop heavy. I kissed the top of her head, and she staggered like a drunk to the car, which stole her away. I wasn't heartbroken; not this time; just hopeful. I had work to get on with the next morning.

I tried to stave off the nightmare, but it wouldn't go; it was my alarm, and it wouldn't leave my wrist. I was out of my bed by 5.20am and walking out into the dawn drizzle at 6.00, wearing a pair of charity shop boots - two sizes too big. I swung them into the cab of the white van, which was waiting for me - 'The Dan Van'.

Dan was big; he was wearing the van like a sleeveless pullover. His eyes were slits, his nose - lumpen, and the hair that stuck out beneath his battered cap looked like rough straw. We rolled through suburbs, cutting corners, mounting kerbs and racing lights. As the next light ahead glared red, Dan looked up at the sky above, the peak of his cap bent against the glass. Ignoring the light, and still watching the plane coming into land above, he growled –

'Another planeload of fucken' backpackers!'

I could hear my sandwiches curling at the corners in my lunchbox.

'I don't know why I take on Poms and Micks, I should stick to Asians; they don't spend all day talking about which pub they went to last night, or who they're going to shag tonight.!' He turned to me, and the lower part of his face cracked into a smile that could freeze a running stream. I knew instantly that my job description was: whipping post, scapegoat.

But Dan was mostly wind and piss, the proverbial headless chicken, lurching from cock-up to disaster half-hourly. We were renovating eight units, eleven hours a day - half hour for lunch.

'How are you with bricks?' he would ask.

'Well I've laid some before.'

'Go round the building and brick up all the holes.'

'OK Dan, where's the spirit level or line.'

'Aaagghh don't bother with that, just chuck 'em in. Haven't you finished yet?'

'How are you with plastering?...render those chasings in.'

'OK Dan, where's the float?'

'I'll have to go buy one.'

Dan went out to buy something ten times a day, and each time he came back he would be panicking.

'What've you been doing, where are you y'slack-arse Pom?'

'How are you with electrics? Y've got forty minutes to disconnect all eight main fuse boxes, everyone on site's waiting for you.'

'OK Dan, where are the blocks so I can isolate all the wires?'

'Aaagghh just wrap insulation tape round them.'

'OK Dan, wher...'

'Oh shit!! I'll go get some; get all the ceilings painted while I'm out.'

'What've you been doing you sad old backpacker bastard?' –

'Painting some ceilings like you asked.' - 'Well get that wiring done!'

So it rolled on for a month. He threw people off site by the collar, walking them to the bus stop on the end of his ham-sized fist. I took others from my hostel - desperate for work. I warned them... 'You've got to be desperate to work for Dan.'

He sacked them all. Michael - the Paddy, put so much paint on the new door - it ran down in waves; bus stop. Dave got vertigo going up the ladder; bus stop.

I learnt to abuse Dan back, although a playful punch to my stomach, that left me breathless for five minutes, almost put paid to that. We rubbed his nose in his mistakes whenever possible, and set him up with pranks. I found a tin of cream emulsion.
 'What colour y'painting that fucken ceiling y'bludger?'
 'White.' I said, innocently.
 'That's not fucken white!!'
 'Yes it is.' I said, stubbornly.
 'IIITTTSSSS NOOOOTTTT!!'
 'That IS white.' said the kitchen fitter, cheekily.
 'It's white.' said the smiling, professional painter Dan had brought in.
 'Aaaggh - I must be going colour blind then.' said Dan - a really quite fetching shade of puce.

Graham, an Englishman, had been in my room for a week; ears like a wing-nut, he only left the room once a day - to get the bread roll and cheese that he ate every day. He stayed in the kitchen all day reading books, and sat in front of the fridge - so I had to get him to move every time I wanted to get to it. I wondered why people like him bothered to come away, and why he didn't do something about his atrocious breath. Similarly, there were the Brits that had come over, some getting no further than Sydney - and had simply transplanted their life. They watched the Simpsons every evening, went up the pub, followed the rugby and cricket, kept to themselves and took dead-end jobs.
 Resting after work one day, I heard through my window...'There's no point getting to know the backpackers, they always move on.'
 It was *their* Hostel; they thought they were 'Big Fish'. In reality, they were minnows hiding under a pebble in an ocean. But Glebe Hostel was good place. It had a rapid turnover of travellers - great for meeting people. Monday night was Welcome night - with free wine and cheese; Sunday night was barbecue - with free wine; and any other time could be a trip to the beach, to a pub or club.

I had a new room-mate - an English boy. Although he looked relaxed, I could see something was wrong. He was fighting back tears.
 'How long have you been here?' I asked.
 'Eight hours.' he replied. 'What in the hostel?'
 'No, Australia... I flew from England this morning. I want to go back; I miss my mates. I don't know anybody... or what to do.'

His lip was quivering, and I suddenly saw myself standing in the reception of Chungking Mansions... alone.

'What would you be doing if you were at home with your mates? You'd be down the pub, talking about the same things you did last week - and the week before – and what you *might* do next week?'

'Yeah... probably.'

'I'll make you a promise. Go down to the bottle shop and buy a slab of beer, take it out to the front of the hostel, find a busy table with a seat free, and say 'Hello, do you mind if I sit here?'...and I guarantee that by Friday, you won't want to go home.'

❖

I swung my old boots out of the Dan-Van, shambled into the hostel forecourt, paint-spattered, filthy, and sat down at the table.

'Have a cold beer Howie, I think you have earned it.' said Anders, who'd turned up the previous week, and had been doing this every evening.

'Cheers old mate.' I said. As I tipped it up, a form peeled away from a group that was rushing past, and approached me...

'We're going up the 'Tockie' for a few beers and then onto a club, d'you guys want to come along with us?'

'No thanks,' I said 'I'm too knackered.'

'By the way' he said 'I don't want to go home now, I'm having a blast. I've met loads of people... thanks.' and rushed after his new friends.

'You did it – I knew you could!' I shouted after him.

'So - still helping us beginners Howie... ay?'

'Nope; I'm still learning myself Anders.'

Then it was the last Friday on site, and I was the only one to have lasted the course; the carpet fitters were coming early Monday morning.

'Did'ya finish painting the last unit Howie?' Dan asked from the van.

'Yeah' I said '...all locked up.' and threw him the keys.

As we arrived back at the hostel, he squeezed his head out the open van window and shouted – 'Thanks Howard, you were the only one I could trust, y'done a really good job - call me if y'ever back in Sydney.'

As he sped off into the distance, scattering pedestrians, the other Pom who'd finished the job with me, opened his pay packet and asked...

'Have you seen Dan's company letterhead - it was in my pay packet?' There it was in black and white... Panic-O General Builders.

Still laughing, I swung my big, smelly, painful boots into the dustbin, and with a chill can of Vitamin B, soaked in the bath, while the rain fell outside to clean the day; looked forward to my sleep - with no alarm at

the end. I had a thousand dollars in my wallet and was rejoicing in the fact that when Dan got to work on Monday, he would see that the two rooms I told him were finished - still needed a lot of painting, while the carpet fitters hung around waiting. And then he'd see the note that I'd pinned to the wall, with a pot of paint and brush below...
 'Paint it y'self Dan, y'slack-arse bastard!!' Ho, ho, ho.

I woke uneasily, trying to think what was missing; it was the alarm. I wasn't working and had two days to enjoy, so I hunkered down into my bed - drifting in and out of sleep. The hostel intercom awoke and the magical trumpet of 'What's up?' by Miles Davis, floated through the building. My smile was wide as the pillow. The tune was cut off by Colin, who was manning the intercom that morning, and still had the peaty soil of County Cork clinging to his boots.
 'Would de tree cleenin girls com to reception please. That's moy burd, the one oy shag sometimes, and de udder one from Noo Zealand. It's noin tirty – checkout toim. If you'se wanning t'leave dis dump t'day, you've got foive minutes t'get yer leezy feckin arses out of y'feckin beds. Udderwoise yer stuck wid yer man here anudder night, and youse all have to listen to dose crappy Canadians, a brayin and hollerin orl day. Boy the way...if yer wannin ter go to the ciddy, the hostile bus leaves in foive minutes...where's dose cleenin girls?'

I lazed the sunny morning away at the front of the hostel, chomping down coffee and chatting to three lovely girls. Matt came jogging past - a Pom who was working at a boatyard in the harbour. He was from Devon, a sailor, with English oak growing in his bones and shooting from his head in the form of a shock of dark hair. His eyes were still narrowed from the sea winds that had striven to scrape them out - like a whore in a bitch fight.
 'I'm shooting over to Bondi Beach in the car, you want to come?'
I looked at my watch - 1.58.
 For some reason the time stuck in my head.
 Sigrid - a Swedish girl, looked up with an engaging smile and said...
 'I'll wash your cup; go and enjoy yourself, I will see you later - yes?'
 'Most probably' I said, hopping in the passenger seat.
 'Tart!' Matt said, and it rhymed with the door shutting.
 'She's alright' I said.
 'No, not her - you.' said Matt. 'She's been giving you the glad-eye for days. Now you've run off for the day, and left her to do your crockery!'
 'I don't think so Matt; anyway, I'm leaving Monday.'
 'So is she, but I think she wanted a souvenir from Sydney – and not one she can show her folks.'

I thought about it – briefly. 'Set sail for Bondi, before I jump overboard.'

We took a walk along the Big-Top that was Bondi. We were passed by four shapely brown buttocks, one pair chewing toffees, the other trying to spit out a piece of dayglo string. They passed a gang of Italian Ozzies, who were lounging on, around and against the railings. They were too busy watching other Italian Ozzies to notice the girls; comparing their own muscles, tans and trunks.

Skateboarders grabbed air in the half-pipe, padded and helmeted against hamburger knee and cabbage head. A Samba band, all drums and whistles, came towards us, and behind, swinging his arms like an ecstatic soldier, came a man with full moustache and shaved head, on the back of which sat a fur hat. He had on a sling-back lycra top, pleated green skirt, black tights and nurse's shoes. His name was Crystal - apparently, and had a new outfit every Saturday. He waved cheekily at the little dog that passed him sporting a sun visor. We sat on the wall with a bag of chips, watching the bodies - there with the sole intention of being watched; didn't want to disappoint. Strains of Forest of Dene', 'Donegal' and 'Gravesend' floated across the sand, hopping over tits and bum, the noise rising up like a host of locusts.

The Bondi Hotel was full, but we found some space outside to watch the show. A platoon of 'the Barmy Army' shuffled past, wearing their uniform of Union Jack trunks, hats and towels; a day off from the test match at the Oval; a practice session for Christmas Day when there would be 20,000 other deadheads on the beach, waving their jingoistic cloth. Two 'braves' broke away from the mob to get into the hotel. They were twins, carroty topped - the colour of sunburnt Spam, strong as cowslips. The bouncers were trembling.

'What's wrong with ar money y'fuckin Penguin eh?'

'Run along now Sir, there's a good boy.'

'What' choo looking at mate?'

'Nothing' said Matt, then turning to the twin '...and nothing.'

The irony was lost on the Brothers Dim, as was the second step that they stumbled down; drunk, and dumb as a box of hammers.

'Do run along now Sir.'

'We'll be back.' 'Yeah we'll will back we will... yeah!'

'There are two fit girls on a table over there - checking us out Howie.'

'The only girls that check me out are hotel receptionists.'

'No, they are! Shall I ask them over?' I didn't really care.

'OYYYY! - would you like to join us?' he bellowed.'

I nearly choked on my beer, and looked at Matt who was smiling.

The whole veranda was laughing. They shimmied their little butts, shook their hair, and joined us. The veranda stopped laughing. The girl with eyes like a solar system bracketed me, and told me she was a Czech, living in Bondi with relations. The afternoon passed in a blur, as we were sailing on a sea of empties, both unfazed by our catch. Matt was an old salt; I was just old.

We quit the hotel when the dark had driven the posers home, leaving a bitter-lemon sunset on the horizon, and crossing the city - beached the car at 'The Rocks', the original and restored Sydney. We hopped from pub to pub, band to band, eating here and there. The girls wanted to go back to the hostel with us.

'Sorry' said Matt 'we're not going home tonight; Howie's leaving tomorrow, so we're carrying on.' They held hands and went to the toilet for a conference, weaving slightly. We met them coming out.

'We're going home... now.' they said stiffly.

'Oh that's a shame...' I said - a bit drunk, 'nice meet you it was... good luck back in Checkinslonvarkiang, and wherever *you* come from.'

'Australia!' she spat at me; and left.

Ordinarily I'd have been embarrassed at my behaviour, but this time I was chuffed. We hadn't played their game you see.

We rolled down to the harbour and sat on the wall, giggling like village idiots. The bridge and the moon, however, took my smile away and snuffed it in the water - leaving me quiet. We sailed our thoughts in different dinghies for a while.

'Hey Howie, what are you thinking about?'

'I'm thinking about Hilde.'

'I thought so... I know how you feel.'

And I wondered what secret thoughts and story Matt had hidden away in his bilges.

'You're a strange one Howie; you've seen off a Swede and a Czech today, haven't you heard of having a girl in every port?

'Yeah... but a port is a refuge from storms. Girls are normally where my storms start to brew!'

'Ah bollocks... let's mutiny the Bounty!' said Matt, jumping down off the wall - onto now steady feet.

The Bounty was a replica of the original, faithful apart from the restaurant below, where the Japanese 'ah-soh'd' around the harbour every lunchtime, stuffing canapes and potato-salad. Matt knew the crew, so we were asked aboard and invited to join them in the crew bar. I leaned against the bulwark, trying to imagine this little tub – which was dwarfed by even the modest sized harbour ferries, sailing the seven seas in terrible storms.

We spent the night on the deck, talking and supping whilst the moon threaded its way through the upper rigging, arced across the planetarium sky, played peek-a-boo amongst the office buildings of the city, and then settled itself snug into the folds of the Sydney skyline - roughly where Glebe lay sleeping. The blackness between The Heads was fading to grey, as Matt and I rolled back into the hostel. I fell into a deep sleep, my bed floating over the waves of halitosis issuing from Graham in the bunk below.

❖

The sun, the Sex Pistols, and a tongue like a furry seat-cover, woke me before checkout time and I staggered to the front of the hostel, where Sigrid nursed me for an hour with coffee, orange juice and smiles. When I could see through my eyeballs, I noticed that she was wearing a very fetching outfit. It was set off by honey brown limbs, hair the colour of honey, lips like bee stings and a smile as warm as toast; aside from the ice-blue eyes, I could have eaten her for breakfast. I could eat her twice a day, and three times on Sundays.

'Would you like to come around Sydney with me - as it's my last day in Australia?' she asked. How did a washed-up wreck like me, deserve a day with a piece of loveliness like this? I didn't.

'Yes please.' I said.

We strolled into the city together, to pick up her air tickets to someplace else: this seemed to have become a habit of mine. We rounded Circular Quay, where the wash from the ferries lapped against the pylons like thirsty dogs. Shapeless, stinking humans in countless layers of clothing, stirred into another day of hell on their park benches; hot dogs leapt down tourists throats, barking mad with mustard; the Opera House bared its cute side to the Japanese cameras, which flashed - although a hundred yards away and in bright sunlight. The jugglers juggled; the didgeridoos did; the businessmen were busy. The harbour shone; so did Sigrid.

A tractor and trailer passed us in the Botanical gardens, and we jumped on the back like kids on a hay-wagon - the driver pretending he hadn't seen us. The gardens passed by on all sides: bushes, flowers and parts of Sigrid blurring with the jigging up and down of the trailer. He slowed the tractor , when we moved to jump off, and then waved. We chatted on, through clumps of formosa, gardenia and honeysuckle, which cuddled up to each other and climbed sun-burnt walls; we painted pictures for each other with words.

We spent time in Sweden, in Sigrid's home, and on the family skiing trip, where the air reeked of pine resin, the trees were sugar-iced and the skis ran with a 'swissshh' along the railway tracks of previous skiers. I joined them for mulled wine and pickled herrings on Christmas morning.

I took her walking around Hambledon Hill in Autumn, kicking up layers of parchment leaves; surfing at Croyde Bay in Devon, carving righteous turns along blue-green waves, whilst above on the hills - the trees grew sideways from the winter winds, like Elvis' quiff.

We skied together under the same indigo sky, but on different snowy mountains, racing down slopes pell-mell and sharing chairlifts

She talked of a life ahead, hopes, unmarked paths; asked which roads to take. 'There's no map.' I answered, and explained the wrong turns, slippery and bumpy roads, dangerous bends and dead ends - that I had taken. Holding hands, we sashayed down the steps of the Opera House like Fred Astaire and Ginger Rogers.

At the bottom, she twirled her Doctor Martens on air and kissed me.

'Thank you,' she said, her iceberg eyes melting to hot pools...'you have given me a lot of hope. I know now that I don't have to worry which way to go - just to do it.'

I wish I'd known that when I was her age.

We were passing the open-air restaurants of The Rocks. The 'suits' were lunching on Italian, Thai and French cuisine, Armani jackets decorating their seatbacks as they grazed through salads dressed with sun.

We looked at each other, knowing what the other was thinking.

'It *would* be nice, wouldn't it?' We carried on - looking for a cheaper café to match our budgets. A road back from the water, we passed a small Italian restaurant with three wrought iron tables outside; on the sunny side of the street. The chairs flung out their legs and barred our way, so to keep the peace - we sat down, and before we'd even thought once about it - the table grew a platter of calamari rings, roundels of sauté-potato and an organised jumble of crisp salad, shining in virgin oil - speckled with mustard seeds. The golden carafe of chilled wine shone like a beacon in the centre of the table, as if announcing our extravagance to passing travellers. We sauntered through the meal with naughty smiles, and finally, leaning back quiet, replete with the food and company, I looked at my watch and watched for the display to flick over to... 1.58. What a joyful 24 hours I had spent.

Yes it was expensive and 'out of budget' but we all deserve a bit of what we fancy. And though I *did* fancy her – rotten, we didn't exchange 'souvenirs' that night - just addresses; Sigrid left for Perth at dawn.

I was leaving the next day for Melbourne, so I decided it was time to revisit my old home – Manly. I hid my bags in someone else's room, in case Dan came a-looking for me, and headed for the ferries.

As the ferry came in to Manly, I saw the shark enclosure to the left, that used to have a gangplank around it, a diving board and, in our imagination, sharks nosing up to the net while we swam inside. Now it looked like a children's paddling pool and there was a new shark enclosure to keep them in - Marine World, an contemporary styled aquarium. I walked through The Corso, which could have been a Croydon shopping mall, except that at the end it led onto Manly Beach.

I remembered it shaped like a longbow, lined with pine trees; Shelly beach and Fairy Bower at one end, the sea pool at the other - into which the waves washed on rough days, and big boys (stupid boys my Dad called them) dived - to show off. Aside from a few less trees and a few more buildings, it looked just the same.

I took the long, long walk adjacent to the river to get to my old house; it was only two hundred yards, and there was the pine tree that had hoisted me up in its arms to watch the circus unfold like a pop-up card in the field: the circus I wouldn't go to, as the elephant looked sad and tired, and the tiger - as though it had been scraped from some dusty floorboards. The midgets scared me. I never went to a circus.

I looked for my school, and found a building where it should have been, but it rang no bells. Then I remembered that, around the back, there used to be a cloakroom, painted in crayon blue, where we each had a peg for our brown satchels that held black gym shoes, and sandwiches wrapped in paper. Tupperware was still awaiting its visa before entering from the US, so each day by break-time, a line of ants would file under the door, up the slatted bench, and choose a satchel. There was no rhyme or reason for the choice, as we all had Vegemite, but for some reason they never picked on the same one on consecutive days. I went round the back of the school, being careful not to tread on the lines in case the bears got me, and there was the cloakroom. Cupping my hands to the side of my face, I looked in, like a burglar: the pegs were still there above the slatted bench, now in crayon yellow. Before teacher could catch me, I padded on down to the beach and mingled with the Manly surf.

I leaped over the waves salmon-like until the water was too deep, then duck-dived out to the unbroken waves. I bobbed over the plundering green hills, until a snow-capped peak came thundering towards me, in ten-league waders. Stroking hard for Ayers rock, I felt the elevator carry me up to the heights, and as the door opened, I planed down the face like a skimming stone, slashing up and down on the palms of my hands, until the washing machine behind me caught up and put me through full wash and spin cycle. I went back out, again and again, hollering with delight and fright. In a lull between sets I heard a shout, and saw another bodysurfer heading out fast, so I followed. He was holding a body, and I saw it was an Asian man, mouth open, eyes closed, body senseless, and then the wave hit us - the first of the set.

We came up separately, and lunged for an arm each. I knew the next wave would be bigger, and as it hit, we pushed him up above us to keep his head near the surface. As we broke through the spume, we were pulling him up by the fingertips from below, and hauling him skywards like a prize catch. His eyes were open, but the body was on early closing. Kicking for shore, each wave snatched him from us and we dragged him back, like a ping-pong game. It was 18-17 and service to Manly, and I felt fear spreading through my limbs. I shouted to my companion – 'Are you Okay?' 'NO' he mouthed, as the next wave hit, washing away his reply. And then, fighting in the maelstrom for air, it hit me for the first time - I was going to have to leave a man to die if I wanted to live. 19-17. I decided to leave him after the next wave. I kicked hard for shore, hoping it would take us further in, but I'd made my mind up – as I was drowning.

'We're in!' my partner shouted, and my foot touched sand, the fear washing away into shore around the ankles of the paddlers. We hauled him, now flapping like a fresh mackerel, onto the sand, where his friends reclaimed him, bowed courteously and took him away. We sat at the top of the beach, shivering, and my stomach was full of dead butterflies.

The loudspeaker burst out 'All swimmers in front of the Corso - move between the flags, you are in a dangerous area - move between the flags now - please!'

My Australian comrade asked me – 'Were you going to leave him?'

'Yes.' I said. 'So was I.'

And we sat feeling sick, and looked at the spot where we'd been - dead centre between the flags, the safe part of my childhood beach.

MELBOURNE

Melbourne wanted a big thing. It had a lot of money to spend. Sydney had its bridge, opera house and a tower. Melbourne wanted to build the tallest building in the world, to put itself on the map, but how long would it remain the tallest?

Melbourne was selling itself short; it was very big on one thing - style. It had oodles of style; coffee bars hissed, steamed and frothed with it; trams rattled, banged and clanged with it. Girls wearing precious little, were swathed in folds of it. Sydney girls knew how to take off their clothes and look like sex; the girls on Bourne and Spence St, put clothes *on* to look damn sexy. They looked past you, but if you caught their eye, they smiled; Sydney girls looked straight through you as if you weren't there. The two cities bickered daily across the fence, trying to better each other, but were in fact the same - just different. Their botanical gardens, lakes and parks, street-art and monuments, would grace any city in the world - and improve most. They both put London to shame, with its filth and laziness; its saving grace coming with the night, when it twinkles - the crap hidden by the dark.

Melbourne was a Monopoly board, set in a square, the City Tram clanking round the board passing 'Go' every twenty minutes; a station in the middle of each side; a gaol in the top right corner with a picture of Ned Kelly peering out. Its savoir-faire came from the bloodline, a heady cocktail of Australia, Greece, Italy and coffee, and a trickle was allowed to flow intravenously out to the suburbs, where I stayed at a hostel in St.Kilda,

The drinking games were good, as was rollerblading along the seafront in the summer sun. There were also some 'choice' bands at the big hotel on the front; but St Kilda seemed isolated, and it was tiring dodging the dope-dealers and dossers from the homeless hostels.

The Nunnery, although in the city, also seemed isolated in its own way, a solitary and tiny island of travellers amongst a city busy doing its own busy thing.

Olembia, Enfield House and The Nunnery – the backpackers' hostels, all seemed a bit too cosy for me: stain glass windows, petrified flowers arched over doors, mirrors held in by cupids, cornucopia and strands of ivy. Reading rooms shusshhed! at the comings and goings of the backpacks, the clinking of cutlery and bubbling of snack pots in the kitchen. They seemed to subdue the travelling spirit with their quiet flock wallpaper, soft mossy carpets, and massed folds of curtain: clocks ticked slow and loud in the scent of old books. The travellers, like so many Aspidistras, bent their heads to books or sent streams of zzzzz's to the ceiling. The thought of spending Christmas here in front of the fire and twinkling tree, with ho! ho! ho's and pulling crackers - just like home, terrified me.

Looking out over the 'Victorian garden' from our veranda, I pointed out to my room-mate that the cicadas were quiet today.

'It's not time yet.' He said.

'What do you mean?' I asked. 'They start in 4 minutes – at 6.10.'

I looked at him sceptically, then studied my watch. At 6.10 there was a single 'chirrup'; silence. I looked at him, and was about to smile, when a deafening CHIRRRRUUUPPPP!!! hit me from a million insects.

My jaw dropped; he shrugged his shoulders.

The penny also dropped; I needed to spend time in the 'real' Australia, where insects and animals live precariously alongside humans.

Whilst travelling down the East Coast, that old chestnut kept cropping up... 'This is not the 'real' Australia.'

I would just say – 'Really?' because that's the same as saying... 'Manchester? Bognor Regis? they are not real England... go to The Lake District, The Cotswolds.' Of course they're real piggin' England!

Brighton - baking on a Bank Holiday Monday, Walsall - Friday night on the town, a football match on a Sunday morning in Gravesend - the ball sticking to the mud. My stomping ground is nothing special, but at the same time, as beautiful as anywhere... if you open your eyes.

Hambledon - famous for nothing, is one of the villages that orbit Godalming - one of the towns that slowly circle Guildford, which in turn sattelites London.

Narrowly missed by a busy motorway, Hambledon is thirty minutes down the line from where the sodium glare of London fades to night; the night of owls hooting and animal rustlings. It comes in shades of soot, jet, coal, pitch and any other colour - as long as it's black. When the moon hangs full and bright, and the poachers wriggle, it's said that the 'parish lantern' is out.

At a cricket match, played out like English theatre in the lush folds of the village green, I asked two Australians and a Kiwi why they'd come to the other side of the world and spent a whole year in Hambledon.

'Look around you mate! It's a beautiful place, the locals are friendly and interesting - and the pub's great. This is 'real' England - this is what we came to find.' And they were right; it was time for me to repay the compliment. I was off to Caramut. Of all the Australians I'd asked in Melbourne, not one of them had heard of it, or knew where it was. Perfect.

HOPKINS HILL, CARAMUT, VICTORIA

I met Calvo, when he and his friend Duffy were working around Hambledon; drank with them in my local pub, The Merry Harriers - or the Hairy Mariner, as we called it. Three months after my first night in Chungking Mansions, he'd flown home to the family farm. His father had been unwell and Calvo thought 'it was time'. I was going to stay with them at Hopkins Hill. It was the legacy of generations, a huge spread of 20,000 acres which had now been parcelled, leaving the Calvert family just 2,000 acres and 'The Big House'.

The red dust drive shuffled past the veranda, with its slender colonial columns holding up the roof that jutted out like the peak of a Yorkshireman's cap. It crept round the box hedges, dodged past the thorny roses and, fading to brown, tumbled into the paddock - mingling with the beat grass that was just burning for water.

The sky above most of Australia played a hard game with the ground below, bullying, teasing, sucking up the water into its cheeks and holding it there. Meanwhile it fanned the flames below by flapping its skirts. Whilst the locals moved water around in tankers, chasing across country after anything that even looked like smoke, rainclouds sat pregnant in the distance.

I eventually gave up asking the boys... 'Is that rain on the way?'

'No,' they'd reply without bitterness, 'that's rain over the coast - it won't come inland.'

Mrs Calvo - Jane, managed to keep the veggies growing, the box hedges in shape, and the roses still flourishing. As was usual in Victorian times, their ancestor had pioneered his way here and created a little bit of England in the middle of bone-dry Australia - in preparation for the later arrival of the wife.

It had once taken a small army of workers to keep the estate in trim, but Calvo and Don - his father, worked the whole farm now, helped by his sister and younger brother Jack, when on holiday from boarding school - as they were during my visit.

Jack – stocky and bushy-haired, had a sewer for a mouth, which often prompted a 'Moderate your language Jack...pleeeease!' from Jane,
but 'F's and 'C's and 'B's flew in all directions. He came from the same mould as his father, ample and rounded, as was their sense of humour and fun; both had stare-eyes that twinkled with barely concealed glee. I was also to see those eyes burn with a dangerous light when challenged. In all the time I was at Hopkins Hill, Don was a complete

TWO MINUTE NOODLE

gentleman - and treated me as a friend. Calvo thought it was because I was writing, and that was something beyond his realm. I think it was because he was a top bloke.

Don didn't 'drink' stubbies. He didn't pour them down his neck. He sucked them dry in one long pull, until the sides of the can caved in. Then whilst replenishing his lungs, the next would be cracked, and on its way to his mouth. Such is the way for a farmer toiling in the heat; but quantity never dulled his senses or his humour.

A knock at the door at 1.00am had Jack and I leaping from our chairs, as this normally meant a fire that needed fighting. Rattling the flyscreen open, we saw a bug-eyed Don leaning forward on his toes, peering in, the pickup running behind.

'Where's the fire Don?' asked a worried Jack, as we'd been on the beers all evening...

'Fire?' and louder, 'FIRE?...we're going possum hunting!' Don was shakier than us. 'I'll get the rifles.' said Jack, turning to me - grimacing.

'Rifles?' and louder, 'RIFLES?' - get the bastard shotguns, this is fucken' war!' he growled into the darkness. Jack shouted into the dark...

'I'll throw a couple of bales in the back of the Ute to sit on.'

'BALES?' and quieter as he crossed the yard... 'Bales?... put some deckchairs in there... we'll wage this fucken' war in style!' as the Ute door thundered shut. It cranked open again... 'and bring along a slab of beer... shit yeh!'

Jack looked at me. 'You grab the beer, we're in the army now - Don's army... the old bastard.'

When |I'd arrived, I made it clear that I was there to help out with anything that needed doing, and not for money. There was always something to be done - but it always seemed to be just enough for the two or three of them. After a week of resting and writing I was beginning to feel in the way. I suggested to Calvo that it was a shame the big house was showing signs of wear and tear, and I could do something about it.

'That'd be great,' he said, 'but it'd be a whore of a thing; last time it took a team of five blokes a whole month just to paint the fucken' outside. I'll mention it to Don though.'

It was three more days before I got an answer. No; but if I could paint the house we were living in, that would be great... if I was sure... and really had the time... just write down your hours .. and we'll pay you.

Basically, the sun was shining, positively beaming - blindingly out of my arse. I would have done it for free; I was working for Don this time, not Dan.

'Don't start 'til after Christmas though - enjoy y'self for a while!'

We'd already started the Christmas decoration in our house. A pyramid of empty beer cans was steadily growing above the fireplace - alternate green VB and red Toohey's beer cans. It waxed as Christmas waned, and by New Year's Eve had hit the ceiling.

I'd pinned my sock to the mantelpiece - one of the three pairs I was making do with, and put in my note to Santa.

'Please could I have Sheryl Crow... thank you. The Pom.'

On Christmas Day I woke to a head full of crows, a mouth like a sock, and a Christmas sock bulging with VB.

'Happy Christmas!' I said to myself, from my mattress on the floor.

'Happy Christmas mate!' I said to my backpack, which lay in the corner, licking its wounds.

Outside, the sun shone brightly, and the dust and gum leaves lay deep and crisp and even. I'd never felt less like Christmas in my life, but at least I was with a family - the raggle-taggle family in our house and the whole Calvert clan over in the big house.

The young cousin had the body of a siren, and was barely dressed. Across the Christmas dinner table, between each mouthful, she pushed out her chest - which looked like two plum puddings in a flimsy muslin bag. Young cousin Hugh, sitting next to me, with a hangover, looked at me with each thrust - and groaned. Walking in the yard after dinner she pulled Jack's cracker - by bending over straight-legged to pat the dog, crooning 'What a good boy', displaying tiny knickers which had all but disappeared between two butterball cheeks. Later, walking back into the kitchen, Jack stumbled to the floor theatrically. She was sitting legs akimbo by the demonic Aga, demonstrating that the front of her knickers had followed the same course as the back.

'Too much drink Jack?' asked his mum.

'That'd be right Jane.' he said, winking at me from the floor.

Don and Jane gave me a generous gift; they told me to use the phone as much as I liked. I phoned home, and spoke the Christmas garbage that you always do to the family. I was chuffed to hear my mum say...

'I've just had a long chat with Jane, and she say's that you've been behaving.' as though they were old friends, I was ten years old, and just around the corner. I rang Hilde, who was at *her* parent's house, and tried to speak about everyday things, the way people who are close do; but we were separated and it felt awkward. Yes she missed me, and she couldn't wait until I got home.

The Grandfather had pegged it during the year, his chair at the head of the table to be taken this year by George, the eldest of Jane's three

TWO MINUTE NOODLE

brothers. The brothers had been 'shockers' when younger, I was told. They'd played Ozzie rules football with the sole intention of fighting with any member of the other team. Failing this, they would 'blue' with anybody offering opinions on the touchline, or if the post match drinks failed to produce a scrap - would fight each other. It was in this atmosphere that the clan had gathered - to sort out the estate; four hours into Boxing Day the bell rang.

'Andrew (Calvo), you were born a ****, you grew up a ****, and you're still a ****' said the oldest brother. Only the referee - in the shape of Don's glare, Calvo's cool head and Jane's sobriety, stopped the bout before Christmas was on the ropes.

A few days later, nursing bad heads round the raging Aga, Jane entered her kingdom, and looking daggers at cousin Hugh, announced...
'I've got a bone to pick with you Hughie!'
'Ohhh!' groaned Hughie 'I didn't make Jack climb the water tower, we all did it, didn't we Howie?' We had; all eight of us - rolling and staggering, sliding round the top, shouting at the stars and the booming Peterborough surf and philosophising in the way only eight drunks on the top of a water tower can.
'You're digging y' self in Hugh.' said Jane.
'Ohhh! I'm sorry Jane, whatever I done... what did I do?'
'You were in my kitchen last night, when I came in with the girls from my bridge club... d' ya remember?'
'Nooo!'
'You were talking to the dog, eating all the ham...' 'Sorry Jane.'
'....naked!'
'Ohhh!'
'It's alright Hugh,' said Don, his eyes sparkling - cheeks bright red...
'They didn't see y' dick.'
'Well that's a relief Don... how come?'
'Y' had it hidden up the dog's arse!'

Calvo and I lived in the small house across the paddock, its walls stained by the wrath of the sun, the smoke from barbecues, and the russet bore water - flung out from the sprinklers when there was any to spare. It was roomy. The dining room was empty apart from the beer fridge, which hummed to itself in the corner. I called it the ballroom.
I slept in the old office, which shared a glass wall with the sofa-ridden lounge - feed-store calendars, land maps and flies decorating the remaining walls. The kitchen, with its endless supply of meat, nachos and small town gossip, led through to the bathroom with its brown-stained iron bath, useless through lack of water. Four toothpastes and

brushes sunbathed round the sink, and through the fly-screen was the dunny - where the flies hung out playing craps.

The two sheep shearers that shared the house were Azza and Johnny; Big Johnny. Johnny was almost as tall as a gum tree, and bending down under a corrugated tin roof, barbering stupid sheep all day, had put a great strain on his back. The heat and the boredom, borne stoically by previous generations, hung heavy on his frame; he also liked to party. This led to Johnny invariably lying supine on the sofa or his bed.
 When awake, he gave a good impression of being a big dumb ox, and before any reply to a question - would let out an 'Aaaaaauughh...'
 But I knew there was a lot of thinking going on in that big tired head, and my presence had stirred him up. He was a hugely friendly man, and I had all the time in the world for him. Though shy, he eventually spoke to me in spits and spurts, and I learned that he wasn't content to spend the next thirty years shearing until his back bent double. He wanted to travel, and listening to me from the fringes, had decided that maybe he could do it. I hoped so.

Azza; was as short as Johnny was tall. He was dark, with the front teeth of a cheeky rat - just as quick, and nuggety like a Welsh miner.
 Azza was a trot-jockey - a junior champion, who was now struggling hard against the big boys. On my second day at Hopkins Hill - Azza made his first appearance in a brake-sliding, dust cloud which overtook the now stationary car and barrelled through the fly-screen door into the lounge. Out of the dust-cloud which was now settling on every surface, popped Azza.
 'Hev y' seen a k'wala yet mate?' 'No - not outside of a zoo.' I replied.
 'Hop in the car then!' We slammed off down the drive, squealed onto the metalled road, and stopped a mere hundred yards away.
 'There's the bastard,' he said, pointing up the tree with his teeth. I'd seen koalas before, usually doing the same thing - nothing. This was a bull koala, standing on hind legs, hanging onto the trunk with one hand. He was bellowing, honking, barking - rasping like a camel.
 'What's he doing... is there something wrong with him?' I asked.
 'Naa mate, that's what horny k' walas do. He's looking for a scruff.'
 It shinned down the tree surprisingly fast - Azza scuttling backwards.
 'He's a big bastard... look at him go!' as the koala ran across the road bellowing - into the bush, scattering gum bark, tinder leaves and dust.
 'How's it going mate... y' must be the Pom!... d' ya like nachos?'

The working day started early at the house, the three of them up before six, pottering round the kitchen like old maids.

'Anyone seen m' fucken boots?' Azza would bellow, on each circuit round the house. We knew they were lying where he'd left them the night before - in the lounge, as he did every night. But every morning he did his circuits, late for work, doors banging.

'Anyone seen m' fucken boots?' On or about the third or fourth circuit, passing them each time, he'd spot them and put them on.

'Where's m' singlet?... Calv,.. hev y' seen m' singlet?'

'Azza y' dumb bastard, it's on the bed where you left it last night!'

'Well y' don't have to get dirty on me, I'm only trying t' get to work.'

'But y' do this every fucken morning, it's 'where's m' boots?' next.'

'What y' hanging shit on me for?' A blue was brewing.

'Y' want a blue with me Calvo?'

'I just want you to shut up every morning... *and* do some cooking.'

'I cooked last Tuesday... chops.'

'You always cook fucken chops, no - you burn chops!'

'That's how me mum cooks 'em, you liked 'em didn't you Howie?'

'*And* you cremated the fucken chook!'

'That was perfect that chook... ah bollocks to ya.'

'What y' getting shitty for - y' nuggety little runt?'

'Right...' Azza said, whiskers twitching, 'you want a shot at the title, come on - in the ballroom!' And they'd fight, bouncing round the room, slamming, heaving and cursing on the bare boards; then get up with floor burns, bruises and gouges – panting and sweating.

'Right... I'm off... hard day's yakker ahead - where's m' keys? Calv... hev y'seen m' keys?'

'Aaaaaaauughh fuck off Azza before *I* take a shot.' rumbled Johnny.

'What you getting shitty for Johnny....?'

On another sunny morning, I woke to the CD blasting out Sheryl Crow – '*All I wanna do, is have some fun*' ... pulling on my shorts and walking through the lounge, '*I've got a feeling - I'm not the only one*' barefoot ... through the corner of the ballroom, '*I love a good beer buzz, early in the morning...*' Entering the kitchen, I saw the three of them dancing, thumbs hooked in the waistbands of their moleskins, chins stuck out, bow-legged, shuffling round the table, making snag sandwiches for their lunch, swilling tea - and joining in together on the last line...'

'*Til the sun comes up, on the San...ner...mon...ica...boule...vard*'

'Catch y' later Howie!' The three pickups roared out of the yard.

Tuesday night was shopping night; the nearest proper supermarket an hour drive away. At such a distance, 'travellers' (several cans of VB) were required to help the journey pass, and then we'd stock up on VB,

Nachos and other groceries. As the shopping took the whole evening - food was essential. I'd managed to avoid eating the Australian national fayre - until now. 'Foreign food' had always been available up until now - which was right up my alley. Standing in the takeaway - looking at the menu, I said to Calv...'I don't recognise any of that, apart from meat pie, you'll have to translate for me.'

'Dippy Dogs - they're hotdogs on a stick coated with crap.'

'Chicko roll - that's some shit that tastes a bit like chicken, with carpet underlay wrapped round it.'

'Yeero - that's Kebab, you know them.'

'Dim Sim - they're soggy pancake rolls...'

'I think I'll stick to the meat pie then.' I said.

'You have to ask for a maggot-bag then.' he replied.

'There's a letter for you in the post box Howie!' shouted Jane from across the dusty yard.

It was from Chantal - long and glorious, painting pictures of places I wished I was sharing with her. It had been forwarded from England and with it - a note from my mum. 'Uncle Peter is in Melbourne on the 28th, Park Royal Hotel, if you want to go and see him.' Love Mum xx

My uncle and family were from Connecticut. Uncle Peter had left the family home at fifteen - unable to poke up with his father anymore.

Grandad Gwilym used to frighten me. A teacher and a disciplinarian - he took us to Bristol cathedral, and leaving my brother and me in the pews holding hands for bravery, re-appeared in the form of the church organ he was playing; blasting; trumpeting; echoing; We were terrified. I've hated organs since. There was no trace of Uncle Peter after he'd left. In the sixties, when we were living in Manly, someone sent my Mum a clipping from a rural Canadian newspaper.

A Peter Gwilym had been involved in a bar fight, where a man had been killed. There was no follow up to explain the outcome or if it had indeed been the right Peter Gwilym.

One day in 1984 the phone rang. My Mum - picking it up and asking 'Who is it?' heard - 'It's Peter, your brother - Hi Margaret.'

Many trips back and forth from England to America followed, and I became great friends with my new American family. They'd come to Australia now, to see another brother who had emigrated - Winford. He was the last sibling that Peter needed to be reunited with; hadn't seen him since taking off down the Rhonda Valley for the wide world - aged fifteen. It seemed stupid not to go and visit, so I did.

PARK ROYAL HOTEL, MELBOURNE

I walked into the foyer of the Park Royal Hotel, with my grubby backpack, shorts and boots; the inside of the heels rubbed shiny from rushing past each other to find the next thrill, laces hanging limp - the stitching suffering from a frayed temper. I looked up at the glass lift, glistening in the hanging gardens of the hotel's atrium.

'Can I help you Sir?' asked the uniformed concierge, who I guessed to be about eighteen years old.

'Uh... yes, can I have the keys to room 806 please... Gwilym.'

Even as I spoke it sounded like the stupidest question I'd ever asked. Why would they give a key to a scarecrow?

'Certainly Sir, we've been expecting you. Would you take this gentleman's bag to room 806 please?' he asked a bellhop.

'Oh that's okay...' I said, 'I've carried it quite a long way myself.'

The family were obviously out, so after dropping my backpack in a corner – I rode the shiny elevator down to the sparkling bar.

'Could I help you Sir?' asked the barman.

'Yes, I'd like a cold VB please.' Surprisingly, it wasn't much more expensive than anywhere else I'd been.

'Enjoy your drink Sir.' he said.

'Listen... you don't have to call me sir, I'm just a backpacker - you saw me come in earlier.'

'You may be a backpacker, but until you check out from this hotel - you are Sir.'

I was cosseted for days. We dined out on Malaysian, French and Italian food - excluded from paying by Peter's generosity. We cruised the botanical gardens with the whole Gwilym clan; a flock of uncles, aunties and cousins.

Hilmar - a cousin I hadn't seen since I was four, had strangely mirrored my work and personal career - on the other side of the world.

Morgan - Peter's son, had expressed an interest in backpacking and was asking the same questions I asked myself - 'How do you... ? what do you... ? where ...?'

To give him some idea of how things worked and show him the ropes, we strolled down to the Nunnery – a popular hostel near the centre.

'That's the reception where you check in, but only for one night - until you've figured whether it's any good. If it's not – you move on fast.

That's the notice board where everything you may need is sold, hired or shared. The kitchen - where you cook what you like, treat it with respect though. Dorm room - eight beds, fairly tidy...

'Hey didn't we meet in Sydney?' Television or reading room...

'Hi, this is Morgan - he's thinking of going backpacking... yeah that's what I told him.'
Patio - for evening socialising... Front door.' Then we were back outside; the tour took about eight minutes all told.

I decided to call Hilde in Belgium.
 'Hi Hilde, how are you? Do you miss me? No?' There was something wrong. She had a problem that she couldn't tell me about.
 She was really sorry – 'perhaps it would have been better if we hadn't...' I'd heard this one before and knew where it was going.
 'I'll ring you in a few days when I get back to the farm.'
 I slammed the phone down. Shit! shit! shit!
The room was very empty. I headed down to the bar.
 'A glass of cold beer Sir?... or shall I just bring a bucket?'

The bar was also empty, but I had some thinking to do. Three men came in - one of whom I thought I recognised, and sat behind me.
 'Shall I move the table over for you Mr Boon?' the barman asked, but it didn't click. Two more came in - younger, with caps back to front.
 'Hey - Boony! how's it goin' mate?'
 'Alright Warney - it's your shout, three of the same mate.'
 'Are these Australian cricketers?' I asked the barman quietly.
 'Yea, this is their Melbourne base; you Poms beat them today.'
By now I had become completely surrounded by the whole team.
 'Mr Boon... there's a Pommie backpacker here - wants to buy you a drink, he thinks you may need it after today.' I looked at him in horror.
 'It's alright...' he whispered, 'the hotel's buying.'
 'I was more worried about staying alive!' I said.
Contrary to expectations – they didn't 'sledge' or 'roast' me - they chatted to me; asked me about travelling; where had I been? what was it like? where was I going? and why was I in this hotel?

As we spoke, I noticed a group of midgets jumping up and down at the window to see their heroes, before coming in noisily. Seeing my puzzled expression, Boony explained...
 'They're doing the pantomime at the theatre - Snow White of course.'
 When I retired to bed, Peter was sitting, checking through the incredibly long bill.
 'Have a good time in the bar? - was it quiet?'
 'No... it was quite lively,' I said, 'I had a drink with the Australian cricket team and the Seven Dwarves.'
 Smiling – not quite sure if I was ribbing him or not, he reminded me...

'We're leaving pretty early in the morning - so don't get up. I've told reception you can leave when you like. They'll send me the bill.'
They had spent more money in ten days than I had on my whole trip so far; but each to their own – *and* they had a great reason for it. All I've got to say on the matter is... 'Good on yer Peter.'

I arrived back at the farm with what appeared to be good timing.
'Y' goin to a B & S Ball - Howie.' said Calvo.
'What's one of those?' I asked.
'It stands for Batchelor and Spinster Ball.' he replied.
'Stands for Beer and Sex ball more like!' Azza threw in...
'Sixty dollars for the whole weekend, free beer and food, band and music. They shout the Bundy, there'll be loads of Ute work, and if y' can still stand up, you'll get a scruff; Sunday's recovery day. We'll have to kit you out in battle dress.'

I had no idea what to expect – but as the weekend unfolded, it all became clear. After a trip to the bottle shop and the chemist, we set off on the several hour journey - breaking it at a little one-eyed town.
There was already a row of Utes parked in front of the milk bar, bullbars snarling, aerials stabbing ten feet into the air, tarpaulins stretched tight across the back - bracing themselves for the weekend. They belonged to Calvo's mates - Scotty Tucker, Johnno and Angus. While they tucked into Chicko Rolls, Dim-Sims and Dippy Dogs, they talked of 'four point five litre, fully-worked V8 engines and 'working' and 'yea - listen to the note on that engine!' Soon we were off in convoy and the heat from the sun through the windscreen had me dozing off, until a NASA space shuttle hammered past – gggrrraaaannnggg!
'Jesus wept!' I said, jumping - what was that Calv?'
'That was just Scotty overtaking mate, there, in the distance. You should see him work it.'
'What *is* 'working the Ute' Calv?' I asked.
'Well y' get your Ute on some sand or dust, put the fucken pedal to the floor, and spin it around on its front wheels.'

There could be up to four thousand people at a B & S - all farm owners, stock agents, shearers and Jackaroos. It was the closest thing they had to a village dance, but some had to travel hundreds of miles to get to it.
Arriving at the site, amongst hundreds of Utes, we donned the battle dress. Off came the moleskins and T shirts, but not the Blunstone boots, and on went evening wear; dress shirt, bow tie and black trousers. Girls threaded through the car park in posh frocks, little black numbers or long dresses. Each and every hand had a bottle, can or

glass, stuck or welded to it, and a girl with a broken arm had a stubby holder cast into her plaster.

Between the music tent and us, a dust cloud hung, that bulged at the edges and barrelled this way and that into the bar, and over the car park. A Ute, invisible inside the cloud, was spinning in manic circles, the scream of its engine muffled by the dust - a queue of others waiting their turn. Another raced in, and the crowd waited for the scream of twisted metal and broken glass. A madman, arms above his head, walked slowly into the nightmare, and it seemed forever before he emerged the other side, dust-brown, arms still aloft, unharmed - and the two Utes could be heard, still gunning round and around inside - oblivious of the other.

As the evening grew, people wrestled on the ground, sleeves torn off - the colour of mud. Bodies fell from high places, disappeared into the bushes, threw up theatrically to applause; danced like one-legged cats burying turds on ice.

'Bundy's on!! came the shout.

'What's going on Scotty?' I shouted, moving with the crowd.

'The Bundaberg rum's been opened - stay with me mate; just drink it 'til it's finished.' They were six deep at the bar but the Bundy came back over the heads in cups and glasses, cupped hands - even by mouth.

'You the Pom, that's staying at Calv's?' asked a girl. 'Yep.'

'D' ya wanna scruff?'

'No, not now - the Bundy's on!'

'Catch y' later then eh?'

'Didya get a root yet?' asked a bloke I didn't even know.

'No... they all look like sheep or blokes to me.'

'So what!' he replied, and poured his beer over my head. I repaid the compliment.

I retired to the back of the Ute just before dawn, people still dancing despite the fact the music had finished, and woke a few hours later in a hot sun. As I looked over the tailgate, I saw bodies scattered, in swags, almost in tents, in the road; some crawling along caked in mud.

'D' ya wanna beer Fliptop?' Calv asked - pissing in the hedge.

'Be madness not to.' I said. And he threw me one.

We raced across the country into South Australia - 'Indian Country.' said Calv. It was called Recovery Day. They had moved the whole shebang a hundred odd miles to the beach at Robe, and partied on. I saw no signs of recovery; I did see the drunkest man I've ever seen in my life and I wondered how he was still alive.

From over the top of the beer lorry came a dead sheep, landing amongst the crowd, where it danced and drank beer for a while. But when it was slam-danced even I was shocked. It was low, sick, and others seemed to think the same, as it was buried in the dunes after a confrontation with its owner. Wrestling with Calvo, I was hit from behind by two shearers.

'Sorry mate,' one said 'y' glasses are bent.' as I looked up from the ground spitting out sand.

'You the Pom that's sleeping on the office floor at Calvo's?'

'Yep.' I said to the man who lived over two hundred miles away.

'Hey Howie!' said Angus, helping me up, 'There's a girl over here wants to talk to you.'

There were two of them. I'd seen them walking along the beach earlier. They were from Melbourne University, taking a weekend at the beach, and were fascinated with the 'country' goings-on.

She looked French, with anthracite eyes - very attractive, despite the Gallic nose. She was nineteen, and also fascinated by my accent.

'Just say something!' she demanded. I worked my way round Scouse, Geordie, Cockney and Brummie - she repeating after me, like a lesson; but she particularly liked West Country.

Much later, after Calv had crashed a friend's Ute up the back of another, and flattened the occupant who objected - after the pub had been cleared - long after closing, we were standing on the roof of the Bank House, an historic building where Angus lived.

'I could listen to you all night.' she said.

'You could, if you slept here with me.'

'I would like that very much indeed young man.' she said, in a perfect Home Counties English accent.

As I banged the fly-screen door, heading for my sleeping bag on the floor of the office, Azza shouted from the kitchen...

'Did'ya get a root Howie?' It was his most important question.

'No Azza,' I said, and he started cackling, 'I got a scruff.'

I pulled the sleeping bag over my head, to shut out the Antipodean sun.

I carried on with painting the house until the end, which coincided with Jack going back to school; so, saying my goodbyes to Calvo and Don at the farm gate, I hitched a lift down to Melbourne with Jane, took the short walk across the city, and into the Nunnery.

Sitting in the stifling comfort of the reading room, I reflected on where I'd got to on my trip. I was finding it hard to see anything new or exotic; it was all too familiar. I longed to be back in Asia. Realising that the only way that could happen was to carry on round the world to England and start again, I left Oz the next day, resolving to make the most of New Zealand.

NEW ZEALAND

From the sky, New Zealand resembled a green baize snooker table that had been attacked from below by hammers of all sizes. Pressing my nose against the window, I watched the white specks grow into sheep as we descended, and they seemed to graze right into the heart of Auckland.

As usual, I took the first hostel bus offering a decent price, and found myself in a suburb on the fringes of the city. It wasn't a good hostel; full of bread-heads and time-wasters. Speaking to as many as I could, I found that they seemed to have no aim, which was the last thing I wanted at the moment - as my own aim was running cock-eyed.

I'd sat blank, on the flight from Australia - an automaton. I rang Brian Harding, who lived in Dargaville at the northern end of the island. Brian had lived and worked in Hambledon for a couple of years, and had probably fitted in the most out of all the travellers; loud, funny, messy; stories of him are still bandied around the area - even today.

'Hey Howie! good to hear from y' mate - hard case! No, go and stay at our family flat in Mount Eden. The key's under the pot by the backdoor - help y' self to anything; there should be some beers in the fridge - just leave ten dollars in the bread bin when you leave. I'll get my niece Melissa to pick you up when she finishes work on Friday; she'll bring you up here. Spot y' soon mate.'

I conned the hostel into taking me over in their bus, and let myself in to the flat with the key from under the pot of geraniums. It was just like the little bungalows that they give to old people in England, when they can't manage a whole house, or their partner has died. It was in a row of others exactly the same. It was a haven. I could lock the door - take a long bath. I had it to myself; the first piece of real isolation I'd had since leaving home. But it all felt wrong – like my old life. I phoned Hilde - Coronation Street whining away in the background on the telly.

No, I hadn't heard wrong back in Melbourne. Everything had been wonderful, but if I knew about her problem I would probably hate her.

'Try me.' I said. 'Sorry.... I can't.' she said. And that was that.

'That's alright Hilde...' I said, 'perhaps we can talk about it when I get home, I may be able to help. Take care, and keep in touch eh!'

I wandered back into the lounge and stared at the screen, the actors whining away, and suddenly I wanted to smash Mike Baldwin's face in, play baseball with Bet Lynch's head and set fire to the Rovers Return.

TWO MINUTE NOODLE

Mt Eden, Auckland

Dear Mum and Dad,

Hope you're all well? As you probably gather, I made it to NZ. The thing is, I write this letter very guiltily - but I can't help it. You see, when I left Oz, it was in the frame of mind of – 'New Zealand tomorrow, so what?' I should have arrived here buzzing; people at home dream of coming to NZ - I used to dream of it too. I'm sure you would have loved it yourselves; I know you always said Dad - if we'd emigrated to New Zealand instead of Oz, we'd probably still be there.

I think I'm just tired; stuffed to the gills like a child in a sweet factory. It's been ten months now and I'm grinding to a halt. The irony is that I'm only half way round the world. I stayed at the flat in Auckland, had a little break, a bit of a retreat, before going up to Brian's for Bank Holiday weekend. It was odd. Brian looked very different, and acted differently too. He was so distant the first evening I wondered if I'd got the right person. And he'd become so serious. But I figured it out. He isn't travelling – he's back home, and he's working hard on the crops - and of course they're his now and not someone else's.

It turned out a good weekend though, and Brian loosened up as time went on, in fact he got very loose. Anyway, his Kumara crop isn't ready for picking yet, so there was no point me hanging around there at the moment.

So.
 I'm back in Auckland, looking for a way to spend a week or two before the picking, (bearing in mind I don't have much money) Will write soon, I'm having a job writing anything for the book - stuck I suppose! Letters are about all I can stomach. Hope all is well and Bumble OK?

Cheers now.

Howie xx

It was the kind of morning where mushrooms jumped up with a booh! The air was aquamarine. Cresting a hill, I walked through a breeze that tasted of bread dough; it smelled sweet and warm and was falling out of the Tip-Top Bakery windows in bucketfuls.

Aeotorea - the land of the long white cloud. Looking up at the sky, it could be empty apart from an impish, cotton-wool cloud peeping over One Tree hill. Then looking down for a second, and up again, you'd find clouds dancing across hills, running over the sea, and not just one type; wisps, vapours, cauliflowers, blankets; white, grey, bruised purple; as though the weatherman had gone mad and thrown his box of symbols into the sky. Closing your eyes for a second, they all swapped places like naughty school children.

Auckland City was pocket-sized, and I soon found the hostels - on the same road as the strip clubs of course. These were the biggest I'd come across since Chungking Mansions, albeit a lot cleaner. They were seriously well-run hostels, they had to be; the turnover was frightening.

All nations were represented here in seemingly equal proportions, but these travellers had their packs stacked with money for thrill seeking. I spent an hour in the travel shop on the ground floor, trying to take in the huge selection of activities available in countless locations.
I looked through the comments in the visitors book, and tried to assimilate the opinions:
  'Go on the Kiwi Experience - not the West Coast Express.'
  'The Kiwi Experience drivers are tossers - West Coast is much better, unless you're a bloke who likes dressing up as a woman, and you want to spend a whole week pissed and not see New Zealand.'

I was looking for a fairly budget way to spend a couple of weeks, to stretch out the time until the kumaras (sweet potatoes) were ready for picking at Brian's, and I saw a comment that made me chuckle - it had me rolling on the floor. My old friends the Israelis, had sent their emissary to New Zealand, one of the most staggeringly beautiful countries in the world - where every adventure you could possibly imagine waited on a plate, and had commented...
  'New Zealand is okay, but I really miss the great adventures that we have back in my great country - Israel. We didn't really want to visit NZ, but we did, even though I would rather have been back home in the best place in the world.'
  It's funny, but any desire that I ever had to visit Israel had disappeared since travelling; strange, but true.

TWO MINUTE NOODLE

The Coromandel: a peninsula to the South East of Auckland, easy to reach, beautiful and quiet, also offered the distinct possibility of surfing. I took the Round-Coromandel bus pass, which was cheap, and allowed you to move on at will.

Stopping at Thames, Coromandel and Whitianga, I realised that although the hostels were more than pleasant, the travellers were all trampers - serious walkers; 'anoraks' we'd call them at home. None had been to Asia or had any desire to, other than to climb Everest, and I had little in common with them. At this stage I didn't actually have much in common with the rest of the world, or my own head for that matter. Nobody was going onto Whangamata; it was off the circuit and didn't have a walk that had to be done. I went to Whangamata.

Using my fingers and thumbs to form an oblong, I framed the scene in front of me. It had more things in it than is possible - apart from perhaps in a child's painting. The sky was still mid-day blue, but also had a sunset glowing, a moon hanging, a forest, an island, waves crashing, a sand beach - but with plants growing on it, a river estuary - boats at rest, surfers shredding waves, families collecting mussels, storm clouds, cotton bud clouds. You could even see the wind, as the spray from the sea and the swaying trees. I painted the scene, sitting in my shorts, the saltwater still clinging to the surfboard beside me – using a child's painting set from the toy shop.

Whanagamata,
N.Island,
New Zealand

Dear Martin,

Hey bro how's it going mate? Hope Ness and the kids are okay. Found it at last! Came into town on a bus(the only passenger) and gave the driver the address. He was sure it was still open. It looked like an 'ex-hostel' and it was - but when I found the owner on the third floor, he said I could stay. My room was a whole unit - normally for six. His mates were like something out of 'Surf Nazis must die', stoned as pebbles, and I spent the first night with a chair against the door. Was a little concerned, but when I went up in the morning to checkout, both the owner and the Maori with the half-face tatto, were really friendly. It takes a while to get used to the Maoris, they can seem scary at times. The sandbar was working, right in front of the hostel - about eight foot; a solid lefthander but messy. They were paddling out with the river, dodging between the fishing boats coming in, a long hard paddle that ended behind the line-up. I left it until the morning when it had cleaned up and was more like six feet, and asked where I could hire a board.

'Nah y' can use mine mate, I don't surf much now; it's on the balcony.' So I went out, shorts and Saigon T shirt, but through the break to the right. I hung in close picking off the ones that were missed by the pack, because believe me they still had a hundred metres to go when they got to me. A bloke paddling back out after a long ride shouted 'Yer too far in mate!'

'Yeh...' I shouted back – 'I'm a visitor, I'm trying to keep out the way of the pack'. 'Aaaghh fuck that mate come out and join us, you'll catch more waves'.

I think I held my own Martin, didn't make a twat of myself - but what an attitude ay! There were a lot of girls out too. A Japanese girl moved into the unit next door, a body-boarder who told me her name was Risa, so I had some company when I needed it. All I did though was surf, read, paint, eat and sleep. 'D' Bar – Whangamata; top place - hard case.

I've been here for ten days, but Brian's crop is still not ready for a couple of weeks, so I'm going back to Auckland, and then hope to do the South Island on the money I've got left. Write to y' soon.

By the way, I said goodbye to the Japanese girl. 'Risa, Risa,' she said 'my name is Risa!' and then it clicked. Her name was Lisa.
Twatty Englishman.

Catch y' later bro.

Howie.

❖

Standing in the queue at the food stall, for bratwurst with sauerkraut and mustard - $3 with a coffee, a schoolgirl asked where I'd come from.
'Ooorrggh Oz is choice ay?' Above us, a backpacker was rap-jumping down the front of the Novotel Hotel like spiderman.
Walking towards us - as though on a catwalk, came a six foot Maori, stunningly beautiful, ramrod back; her chin tattooed black like a goatee beard. Seeing my puzzled stare, the schoolgirl said...
'She's probably royalty.'

TWO MINUTE NOODLE

I decided to go to the cinema to see 'Once were Warriors', a new film about Maoris trying to come to terms with modern life. I thought it might shed a bit of light on the people I was starting to meet.

The cinema was an Art-Deco building, and entering the foyer, I could have been on a Cunard liner. Hidden lighting in red, blue and green, crept out of alcoves and smothered itself across pharaohs, frieze and chandelier, and was mopped up by the thick, swirling carpet. Sunk back into the studded leather chairs that shouted 'horsehair!' I imagined a Yank in crisp GI threads, swirling down the stairs with an Auckland girl, floral dress flapping round her North Island tan. There were enough curtains hanging in the auditorium to sail a velvet armada.

Holding on to the past seemed to be something the Kiwis were particularly good at; but they didn't let it bog them down. The whole of New Zealand was a museum to Art-Deco: the roads choked with the history of British motoring. Morris, Hillman, Austin and Ford had filled the roads with Corsairs, Snipes, Hunters, Gazelles, Oxfords and Cambridges - but the Kiwis balanced this with modern, eco-friendly Japanese motors. New buildings were built to fit in with old; to harmonise. At a nightclub, I knew all the seventies soul records they were playing, and thinking they were still locked in the past I asked...
 'Is this the sort of music you have to play?'
 'Yes mate. Rave and Techno is old-hat now - even Acid-Jazz is jaded. This is the latest - it's huge.' They were way up there with London.
 Driving through a small village... somewhere, I saw a cinema with a sign that snapped my head around.
 'This week's presentation is 'A Clockwork Orange - by Stanley Kubrick'. I'd wanted to see this film forever, but had never been allowed in prim and proper England, where it was still banned.
 Back in the Auckland cinema, two old biddies were watching the most violent film showing in New Zealand, and after being 'shusshhed!' by neighbours for chatting, fell to gasps of shock - 'tutt-tutting' at nasty bits. 'Do they have to say that all the time?!'
 I had a feeling that they'd come in around 1939, and never left the cinema - unaware that a world like that could exist. It was a shocker of a film, but I felt that you could substitute the Maoris with Scousers, Geordies or Glaswegians: it would be the same story.
 I went into the travel shop, bought a half price bus ticket to Wellington, and booked up for the West Coast Express - leaving out of Nelson. It would finish off my money, but at least I'd be able to see some of the South Island, even if I couldn't join in with all the activities. I was going along for the ride.

On the public bus down, after a short stop at smelly Rotorua, we pulled into a refreshment stop. The driver announced...
"You can get tea or coffee, a snack or a meal here: there are handicrafts for sale; if you'd like a jet-boat ride they're round the back, or if you'd prefer a flight round Mt Ruapahue, the airplane takes off over the road there - see them waiting? We'll pick you up about half an hour up the road."
As we slipped past Ruapahue on the main road I saw snow hiding in the folds of the mountain, whilst summer covered its eyes and counted to a hundred, and I smiled quietly at the possibility of being asked by a waitress...'Tea or coffee?' and answering ... 'No thank you, but a flight around a mountain might be quite pleasant.'

The bus was scheduled to arrive in Wellington at 6.40pm. It arrived at 6.40pm, and Wellington had its gum boots on.
The light glowed feebly from the art-deco windows of the News building as the rain lashed them like rice on a drum. Walking round the city, it felt like a Horlicks advert; people rushing here and there, the collars of their overcoats turned up to their hats against the rain - scurrying past the chip-shop, The Rialto, Woolworths and the coffee-bar. I steamed into the harsh glow of a take-away, and took a maggot-bag and coffee - 99 cents; ate it in a doorway of a closed shop, whilst the flames of Olympic style torches, outside the wine-bar opposite, hissed and spat - cowering from the rain.
The clothes and backpacks in the dorm room sat steaming on radiators, or dejected in corners. I tied my old sarong to the balcony outside the window for a spin in the Wellington washing machine, where it waved frantically at the heads of the buildings below.
It had gone without me in the morning I noticed, as I packed my bag and rolled down to the quay; I resolved not to use Chantal's for anything but sleeping.

The weather changed as soon as the ferry pulled itself away from Wellington. A childish yellow sun shone down - picking out the whites of the ropes, the deck, and people's smiles. As we crossed Cook Strait on a peaceful sea, the merest suggestion of white horses on the swell, I was staggered to see a long queue of people paying to go into the dark to watch a film.
Outside, a fledgling wind swept into our faces and gulls chased us into the Marlborough Sounds, where dolphins piloted us through the inlets and islands, past coves and bays full of secrets and surprises. Verdant canopies covered the heads of the islands and dipped into the water; land plant - then sea weed, as the sea rose up and down.

I hadn't bothered with a Lonely Planet for New Zealand, it seemed a bit unnecessary. It would have been a good idea. Unaware of what was at Picton - the ferry harbour, or the route to Nelson, I ambled off the boat after the rush had gone. I'd figured that as I had a whole day to waste on an 80k trip, I could enjoy it; and save precious dollars of course.

What I should have done was organise a ride on the boat, as most of the cars were gone by the time I got off. There was only one road out of Picton and all of the traffic came from the arriving ferries. The road ahead of me was a string of solitary hitchers. The bus that I could have caught, which cost only 5 dollars, stopped alongside, its doors opening.

'You sure you don't want to get on board?'

'No thanks,' I replied, thinking twice, 'I've got plenty of time.'

'Ah well... I'll be back for the next ferry in two hours, I'll keep my eye out for you.' I saw him stop at each person ahead.

Several cars stopped to tell me they couldn't pick me up, and that the rest of the traffic would be turning off left further ahead. I walked the first five kilometres until I got my first lift; a dung lorry. There was room for me in the cab - but not the backpack.

'Throw it in the back mate, it's clean shit!' the driver exclaimed.

He took me 10k until his turn-off. I sat on the roadside, thumb out for nearly an hour until, bored, and doubting the Kiwis famous hospitality to hitchers, walked on another 5k. The next ride got me a whole ten down the road until a right fork in the road.

'You need to go down that road.' she said, dropping me off.

Crossing over and dumping my pack, I watched the traffic sail on down the first road. Nobody came down mine except a rabid Plymouth with the family from hell inside. They came past three times, eyeing me up for dinner I thought, and kept my thumb in my pocket - praying they wouldn't stop. Armed with a can of Coke from the shop opposite, I settled down on the verge - getting up for each of the three cars that passed. The shop closed an hour later and the owner called me over.

'I'm going your way.' she said, and she did - all 3k of it, and dropped me off outside a closed winery; she lived in the house over the road. The road stretched as far as I could see in each direction, empty. A car came past so fast, it shifted the verge three inches towards Nelson. I was the only thing that what wasn't getting nearer Nelson.

And then, as the sun was thinking of calling it a day, a car stopped. It was occupied by three young Japanese, two boys and a girl, who didn't look old enough to drive a peddle-car. The boys in front admired their new mirrored sunglasses, lighting and relighting their Marlboro with brand new lighters, and driving round bends like old grannies. The girl in the back next to me, seemed overcome, and blushed - but pressed herself as close to me as she could get. She gave a running commentary as we drove... tree!... river!... lake!... sheep! We had to stop at each thing and take their photograph with it, on each of their three cameras. They explained that this was their big holiday after school before they started their careers; they had two weeks! Once working, they would get three days a year... if they were lucky.

They dropped me in Nelson, and after courteous handshakes, drove away in kangaroo hops - the girl waving out the back window. I rang the hostel from a very English looking public phone - Pete's Place.

'We were expecting you earlier,' Pete's missus said, 'I'll come down and pick you up.' By the time I'd arrived and sat down in their kitchen to sign in, a red-purple glow hung outside the window. It had taken seven hours. Two Japanese girls, here learning English, cookery and etiquette, placed freshly-baked scones, raspberry jam and fresh, sweet coffee in front of me. I tucked in.

'Would you like me to sign-in?' I asked Pete's missus.

'Ah, you already have love, you've eaten your scones.'

❖

THE WEST COAST EXPRESS

Pete gave us a lift across Nelson in the morning, to the YHA, which was where the West Coast Express departed.

And there it stood; a 1961 coach, charabanc, bus; dolphins dancing, whales wailing, trees swaying all over and around its body like The Illustrated Man. It would have been at home smoking down the A303 to Stonehenge or Glastonbury, a family of new age travellers pressing their studded noses to the windows.

The weasel-like Englishman, who'd also been at Pete's, and me, were the first on the bus. I watched, heart sinking, as our new companions trooped aboard. The bus filled with Anoraks, Young Christians, Hitler Youth, Librarians, Young Farmers, Mr Walking Tramping Trekker Scout, and two deaf Germans - they were all blokes. I had to spend a week with these people.

But, stopping at another hostel in the centre of town, the remaining places were filled by a generous portion of women, a tattooed Liverpudlian – 'Hi ya people, how's it goin' like? ... sound!' and an Englishman who appeared to be wearing my flip-flops, the ones that had disappeared from Captain Cook's washing line.

'Welcome to the West Coast Express,' said the bug-eyed, bushy-bearded driver,

'You'll have noticed your customised seats (they each had a sheep-skin cover), and of course there's air-conditioning if it gets a bit hot.'

'How does that work?' someone asked.

'Well, see the windows just above y' heads? ... y' open them.'

Then we were off, and managed nearly two hours driving before, on a steep climb and near the summit, the bus held its hands up in surrender. The driver, pronouncing it in a critical condition, flagged down a tractor that was heading for Nelson, shouting - 'I'll see you later.' And jumped on the back.

By the time he returned the passengers had started to gel, barriers breaking down, the bus fool already established, the deaf Germans still keeping to themselves and their own private and silent world.

He had brought us a new bus, a much newer model – 1962, only slightly more modestly decorated than the last, and we rolled down the West Coast – ticking off Westport, Greymouth and Blackball.

New-Zealand is like a child on Christmas morning, its little arms overflowing with presents which drop to the floor in the form of sun, rain, sights and sounds, and each time the bus came to a halt - we rushed out and scooped them up; blowholes, pancake rocks, mirror-lakes, gargantuan Kauri trees, basking seal colonies, pounding beaches. We climbed Fox Glacier with a guide, crampons and wide eyes. One of the only two advancing glaciers left on the planet, it glowed turquoise at us and barked, as it trundled forwards at a breathless four feet a day. We paddled canoes slowly up a crystal river, skimmed breakneck down another in a jet boat; Ian the Scouser hollering loud enough to be heard back in Liverpool. Gold was panned and beer was downed; the evenings spent sitting and talking.

We had a core group; Ian, John (the new owner of my flip-flops), Desiree - a Dutch girl who was growing on me, then Gunter and Holger. They were the first really funny Germans I'd ever met. They were two of the funniest *men* I have ever met, and the four of us were now 'signing' with them quite well.

'Why don't the other Germans on the bus talk to you?' I asked them.

'They are embarrassed by our handicap.' Gunter explained, miming their looks of distaste.

'They are the ones who are handicapped Gunter,' I said, 'they were born without humour.' His eyes shone, and he hugged me. Wherever we went, Maoris treated them like long-lost chieftains and took time out to sit and talk to them with eyes and hands, perhaps feeling an affinity they didn't share with the native white people.

I shared a room with them and John, and in an early morning half-light, Holger was up and packing. He was rustling his plastic super-market bags (the bane of dormitories) super loud, slamming in and out of the door to the toilet, and humming to himself. There was no chance of sleeping in the din, which went on and on. Gunter joined in; possibly noisier. Then, at last they went out, leaving a deafening silence. I was smiling now at their innocence, and hearing John below muttering... 'Nice one guys!' I burst out laughing.

The door opened, the light came on and they jumped back into the room, hooting with their peculiar deaf laugh... 'Hoy, hoy, hoy... hey hey hey!' They'd planned it the night before – to see how polite we would be.

The trip rolled to its finale at Queenstown. If New Zealand is Christmas, Queenstown is Santa Claus. It huddles in a crooked elbow of Lake Wakatipu, looking up at The Remarkables above - a mountain range whose colours change with the mood of the sun, earning them their title. Yes, it is a tourist trap, a ski resort, a summer resort, but unique and exciting - busy but peaceful; an amusement park.

TWO MINUTE NOODLE

From Queenstown, you can fly; in stunt planes, strapped to sky-divers, beneath silk canopies, glide under delta wings, buzz around in goggle-eyed helicopters or fall screaming for a hundred metres with a piece of elastic tied to your leg.

You can float, drift, plummet, ride or splash down rivers: on kayaks, boogie boards, rafts, jet boats; in the sun or the shade of vertical walled canyons and gorges: in the hidden streams and caves, with stalactites above in place of clouds.

Personally though, I had no pocket money to go on the rides, and had to watch my playmates enjoying themselves. We ripped it up for a couple of evenings until all but a few of the crew had moved on: just a group photograph left behind. And then there was just Desiree and me; and we were close.

She decided that she'd like to come up to Dargaville with me to pick Kumaras. I rang Brian, who said that we could start on Monday. If we could get up to Auckland for Friday evening, he'd meet us at the flat and we'd go out on the town for the night. We hitched a lift to Christchurch the first thing next morning.

Christchurch is a city of two halves. The hostels were of course, in the rough half of the city, contestants in an ugly building competition, milling around waiting for the start.

In contrast - walking into the centre, I could have been in England - as we walked down Worcester and Gloucester streets, along Cambridge Terrace, beside the river Avon. The nimble fingers of the willow trees dipped in the stream that ducked under stone bridges, dribbling round green-lawn bends. It chuckled on down to the old university buildings, all weathered stone and arches - now the arts centre, and we sat out for a decidedly English evening, drinking best bitter in a fresh breeze; specks of rain in the air.

I was as far away from England as it's possible to be, but in the most English place possible.

(I'm Slowing down now; so tired. I have seen so much; dozens of sunrises, hundreds of sunsets, a million trees. I've had to say goodbye to a hundred people. I've been Thomas Cook, Livingstone, Alan Whicker, Shirley friggin' Valentine. I need to go home now; enjoy some time at Brian's, earn some dollars to fund my way home. Curious, that I am resigning a complete continent to a stepping stone home. Perhaps the discontent I heard and saw in Vietnam is begging questions of my next destination - the USA. Or am I just missing Asia far too much to want bottomless coffee and cherry pie?)

DARGAVILLE

We'd booked a bus ticket up to Auckland - it was too short notice to guarantee hitching there in time, and stood waiting in the hostel lobby at 5.30am. A drunken rugby fan, still looking for a last drink before bed, buzzed us like a horsefly.
'Ah, sweet as! I've been t' Queenstown an all, yeh... once.'
'Ah, Dargaville, I know that, good as! Whatcha goin there for?'
'Kumara pickin?... hard case! Y' can't pick kumaras - only blacks do that, you'll stick out like a dog's nuts!'

We stopped overnight in Wellington, which was wearing a sou'wester this time, trying to keep out the storm that was barrelling through. It rattled and shook the timber hostel that perched up on the hill, the wind trying to fight through the weight of the rain pitching down.

It seemed only a matter of minutes later that we'd rocked up to Auckland, rolled around the bars for a night, and were bouncing up Brian's drive to the bungalow on the hill above the kumara fields; almost the length of New Zealand away from Queenstown.

We started picking on the Monday morning at an outrageous time. Work seemed such a long time ago - but it was fresh and cool... at first. It was a small team: Brian and Lance - the bosses, and eight pickers - a 'pick and mix' of ages, both white and Maori.

The tractors rucked up the earth along the rows, but the only way to extract all the kumaras was to grub into the ground with bare hands, knock off the clinging soil and twist then from their vines.

Straddling the row, there were only two positions with which to pick - bent from the waist down, or scrabbling along on the knees. By the end of the first row my back was aching; the backs of my legs pulling. I looked at the endless rows ahead of us - heart sinking, and then across at the other fields waiting their turn, bigger than this; we'd been warned. I bent over and started filling the next bucket.

So, to get through the tedium, repititon and pain, you started giving yourself targets.

'I can get to the end of this row.... only two more rows until smokoe, then I can straighten the back - have a drink.'

'If I pick the last twenty metres fast I can stand up straight for a minute before the others catch up and we start the next row.'

'I can keep going for another hour, and then we can knock it on the head until tomorrow.'

For Desiree and me it was a matter of principle; we wanted to keep up with the others who'd done it before, and we did get faster. I could keep up to a point – but Desiree was knocking us all into a cocked hat. I stood up in the middle of picking a row, bucket full, and saw Kim - a dreadlocked Maori ahead of me, watching Des pull away from him. He was shaking his head, and turning, he asked me...'How she do that!?'
'It's all the tulips she picks at home,' I shouted, 'ay Cloggie?!'

Between rows and breaks, we started to get to know our fellow pickers. New ones came along; two lads from Somerset, one baby-pink - a day out of England, the other on his second visit; Billy - an ageing and huge Maori with emphysema, whose breath wheezed and farted out like an old steam train, and who was expected to keel over at any time; an English girl - all prissy, who lagged behind and found every excuse not to keep up; we called her Dolly Daydream. A team of Maoris from another farm turned up on their day off. All young - they were rapid, and we called their leader Sam Speed; even Des trailed in his wake. At times it was like picking with LL Cool J, Cypress Hill and a gang of yardies from Trenchtown, but they had time for us and asked questions about our travels. Most hadn't even been to the South Island...
'Ah it's too cold down there brah!'
'I've heard of Holland...' they'd say 'that's Amsterdam isn't it... yeh I want to go there man... get some real good smoke.'
'So you pick tulips then Des?'
'No, I work at a ski-resort on Mount Edam.'... 'Choice!'
'I work on the chair-lifts in the winter... and for a summer job I am employed to stick my finger in dykes'... 'Hard case!'
Just one more row - and then it's the weekend.

The Harding family had been at Dargaville from its conception, and there was even a Harding Park - which wrapped itself around the base of a hill. This was topped by an ancient and sacred Maori 'pa' site, and the Dargaville Museum. In front of the museum sprung the masts of The Rainbow Warrior, which had been sunk by the French, and they cast their spindly shadows over the family cemetery.
The Hardings also had a beach house (batch) on Bayley's Beach, 10k to the north, tucked in the lee of a sandy, shrubby bowl - with a jumble of other batches. The beach was 110k long.

'It's the weekend guys – let's go to the beach!... come on Sam!'
Brian called in his dog - Sam. Still really a puppy, he was a pig-hunting dog, and could clear my head with a leap. Hunting wild-pigs is still a big thing in New Zealand. They are dangerous, and it takes two dogs to

pull one down. Sam was still learning to find them, so a domestic pig was allowed to roam the farm at will. Its name was Practice. At this stage Sam didn't know what to do when he found the pig; his parents would have show him that. (Brian wrote to me later... *"Sam got his first pig recently with the help of his father, and then he gave his dad a bloody good hiding!"*)

Driving there in the pick-up, Sam on the flatbed like a Pointer - ears flapping in the wind, I watched the countryside roll past, and it seemed very much like Sussex or Shropshire; apart from the houses. They weren't lichened stone or mellowed-brick - folding themselves into the ground, but stood up straight, in dazzling white ship-lap. They had two eyes and a tall mouth, like a child's painting, and over-fat cows and woolly-bully sheep were scattered around the yo-yo hills; their 'mooos' and 'baaahs' floating in speech bubbles above their heads.

Just like Fraser Island, the beach was also the road. We drove along it looking for signs of fish, or the brown patches of plankton that they'd be feeding on. But we could see the fish themselves cruising in the waves; mullet - like submarines in a cold-war scramble. It was fishing the way it should be done.

Each carrying a pole attached to a rolled 100 metre net, we pushed out into the waves - sometimes bobbing over them, sometimes below, then creeping behind the shoal, unfurled it to full length and pull-pull-pulled it into the beach, closing the net around them like an old lady's drawstring purse. The mullet shouted to their friends - 'Over here!' and they rushed over and jumped into the net. We pulled them out of the sea in sixes and sevens until, tying them up with dune-grass, we had a Huckleberry Finn string of fish. The scales were flicked off with a mussel shell, the firm stomachs opened - golden roe spilling onto the sand, then we washed them in the sea and took them up to the'batch.

Cooked fresh under the grill, we washed then down with cold beers and basked in the sun, watching the sea go about its business.

A whale cruised across in front, and spying only surfers, gave the signal for the rest of the school to cross. I borrowed a body board from another batch and joined the line-up; played like a fool in the waves.

I spent the rest of the afternoon drinking in sunshine, beer and friendship, and I knew that I wanted to finish my life on a beach; sit facing the sea - watching the sunrise and the sunset and every minute in between. And I'd know that if I dipped my toes in the sea, I'd be joined clear round the world by it - to Manly, Waimea, China, Croyde and Padangbai beaches. Looking behind, I'd want to see a familiar road that, turning the corner, becomes a strange road going nowhere; in case the urge to go walkabout came upon me.

Heading back, the dying sun turned the trees blue and purple, the sky green, and then - as my eyelids drooped with happy tiredness, the sunset gathered behind and gently pushed us back to Dargaville.

'Just a couple of more bucketfuls and I'll be at the end of the row.'

'One more row until smokoe and I can soak my arms in the water-trough to take the pain away.'

The constant pulling at soilk and twisting the kumaras from the vinesk had buggered my arms. From wrist to elbow they looked as though they'd been blown up with a bicycle pump. I had tendonitis and could hardly move my fingers. Soaking them in the cold water kept me going for short periods, but my days were numbered.
'Stop, or do some real damage.' said the doctor.
So, I had to sit up at the bungalow and watch them in the fields below, crawling up and down the rows, slowly turning green strips to brown. At the end of the day, Desiree would trudge up the hill - hot and tired and dirty, and try and make me feel better. But I was doing nothing; earning no money. We were still going out to the pubs, parties, cricket matches - family gatherings, and my finances were seriously low.
Then one day a letter arrived, brought over from the Harding's big house, and I was already confused. I opened it, as I watched Sam twitching in his sleep - dreaming of pigs. It was from Chantal, still chundering around India and Nepal. She took me trekking in the Himalayas, showed me things she'd seen, made me feel that I was there as well. And then she turned my world over ... yet again.

" in the meantime I'm back from the group trek and have spent seven days trekking on my own ... It's nice to stop and sit when and where you want ... I did a lot of thinking ... what I wrote to you before. I really want to see you again. To be honest I wish this moment was right now. I miss you so much. I'm going home at the end of March and will let you know when and where to find me ... if you want to of course!"

Take care.

Chantal x

She was already home. Things were conspiring against me. I wanted to go home. I felt guilty - as Desiree and I were very close, but we'd made no promises together, no plans, nor talk of the future.

It was another weekend. Brian, Des and I took a trip up to the far north of the island - to Cape Reinga. We left early, and with Sam and some bags of kumaras in the back, sped out of Dargaville up the western route. The mist still settled like an eiderdown on the nodding heads of village cottages; sheep wriggling around the fatback hills like maggots.

We stopped off after a few hours in a small town, at a tin shack brewery, and stocked up with a most excellent beer - which fuelled us into Waipoua Forest, the home of the mighty kauri tree.
 Brian stopped pulled over so that we could see Tanemahuta - the tallest kauri tree of all. Much of travelling seemed to be concerned with collecting or visiting these freaks of nature or man-made constructions; 'The oldest Banyan tree' ... 'the highest waterfall' ... 'largest temple'... 'oldest building'. I was getting a bit tired of this habitual contest.
 I took a visit to the Ancient Chinese House in Hoi An, and whilst being guided by a lovely, bashful girl, I asked – 'How old is it?'
 '200 years old!' she exclaimed.
 'Ah... it's quite new then.' I said – rudely.
 'No... ancient!' she exclaimed. Teasing, but being truthful, I told her...
 'That is quite new in England. We have houses 500 years old - and some older!' I didn't carry on with it, as she looked close to tears...
 'But they're not as beautiful as this.' Her smile returned.

Tanemahuta wasn't the oldest, just the biggest – or maybe it was the tallest? Far better for me, was the clump of smaller, ordinary kauris we saw ringing a crystal pool - where ferns fanned the ground, birds shot through the sunrays like exploding fireworks and moths spiralled down like snowflakes.
 We crept up switchback, un-metalled roads, and along stony tracks, which reminded me of Vietnam's roads. I was seeing bits and pieces of other countries everywhere in New Zealand, it was that sort of place.
 Stopping off in Opononi for a quick lunchtime drink, we were still there a half a day later. We'd been befriended by a gang of Maoris - and had started drinking and playing pool with them. They looked unnervingly like the ones I'd seen in Once Were Warriors, with full and half-face tattoos - some wearing white slaughterhouse boots flecked with dried blood.
 'You're on the table next brah... y'playing me.' one of them barked at me. It didn't seem a good idea to refuse or argue.
 'I know Holland - that's Amsterdam! I'm going there one day...' my new friend said. 'Good smoke there in your country brah.'
 'I'm not Dutch...' I said, 'I'm English.'
 'So what?' he replied.

Much later, an argument brewed. 'They're staying at my house!'
'Naah they're staying at mine!' We were being pulled unwillingly into the argument. I wasn't going to be staying at anyone's house!
Brian reappeared from outside and handed over a sack of kumaras to the landlord. They whispered together. Coming over, Brian hollered...
'Who am I playing next?' and as he passed me he whispered...
'We might have to get out through the toilet window.'
Nudging up to Des, I said...
'Go to the ladies Des, it's next to the exit door. When I knock, come out quick and head for the pickup – fast.'
'Right - rack 'em up guys. Howie and me are going to get some more kumaras in - if anyone wants some? and then we're gonna show you how to play pool properly.' said Brian.
We slipped out, collecting Des on the way, and ran like hell through the rain to the pickup - keeping watch on the bar door as the engine failed to start. Sam started barking at the dark shapes of people emerging from the door. Just as they were getting near, the engine spluttered into life and we shot off into the dark.

The rain was so heavy it was like being underwater, and there was no way the four of us (including the dog), could sleep in the cab. Brian knew of a cheap motel in the next town, but we didn't really have the money for it. They charged per person, so as Brian woke the owner and got her to unlock a room, Des and I hid in the van.
'Yeh, it's only me,' Brian said 'nobody else... just one.' She went back to bed. We crept into the room under cover of darkness and sat on the floor for a few more beers - a relieved celebration; we conked out.
It was impossible to leave without being seen in the morning, as the office door was directly opposite, so when Brian knocked up the owner to pay, we strolled over as well.
'I thought you said you were on yer own? You *were* bloody noisy!'
'Ah yeh... I must have been confused.'
'Confused? .. bloody drunk more like it.'
'I'll only charge for a couple...' she said, 'as one of you must have slept on the floor.' Brian gave her twenty five dollars.
'Here, get y'selves some breakfast.' she said, handing ten dollars back.
'Ah, thenks,' Brian said through his hangover, 'next time I come through I'll bring y'some kumaras.'
'Make sure y'bloody do!'

We carried on up to Cape Reinga, and walked the deserted beach - its sand blowing across in wisps, like net curtains. We stood on the very tip, looking at the point where the Tasman Sea meets the Pacific Ocean, and there was a straight line, where the two blues of the different seas met. It looked as though Moses had just disappeared into the distance.

After tripping down to the perfect little beach at the base, we were met on the way back up by a park ranger.

'I have to shoot your dog.' he said. 'Pardon?'... we said in unison.

'Didn't you see the sign - No Dogs Beyond the Fence?' We hadn't.

'That is a 'pa' site down there; you've desecrated it with the dog and by rights I must shoot it.' I saw Brian's hackles rising and the knuckles bunching. Playing the stupid and innocent tourist I quickly replied...

'Sorry officer we're tourists, we don't know the rules.'

'He should know – he's from Dargaville.' he countered.

But he let it go, which I was very pleased about, as I shudder to think where Brian would have put that shotgun if he *had* tried to shoot Sam.

It prompted me later to ask Brian about the Maori situation. A large number of Maori inhabitants of a town to the south, were occupying their own town square at the time - refusing right of entry to any white people. The Government were at a total loss as to what to do. It was a 'pa' site - sacred, and they were everywhere in New Zealand; so in the Maoris' eyes they owned everything.

'Brian - a lot of your friends are Maoris, but I've heard it from some of the more militant ones in town, that they'd be up here to take your land back - when the uprising comes.'

'That's probably true, but if they come up - me brothers and me will be there with our guns. It may have been theirs once, but we've been here for a hundred and fifty years and done something with it. Until it happens though, we'll be mates. Anyway Howie - why worry?... if dogs worry - we shoot them.'

I managed to pick a couple more fields when we got back, as my arms had rested, but my time was running out as fast as my money.

It had been raining steadily for a while - so picking kumaras was out of the question. There was, however, a crop of 'squash' on a nearby farm, that was already partly submerged but could be rescued for its young owner if we worked fast enough. It was his first crop.

We spent our last day tramping down the foliage, cutting the vines, and heaving squash into the trailer - until the tropical heat faded into a chill evening wind, and then darkness fell all around.

The squash were as soul-destroying and tiring to pick as the kumaras - and I was beat. Writing this, I realise that I almost ran out of Dargaville at a trot - to get away from that bastard picking.

Saying our good-byes and picking up our pay packets, Desiree's fatter than mine, we were given a lift down to Auckland by Brian's sister. We were back in the little flat in Mount Eden in no time; just the two of us.

I put my flight back so that I could spend another day with Des, and we enjoyed each other's company - quietly.

❖

Sitting alone on the veranda, on our last evening, Desiree soaking in the bath, I tipped philosophy from my beer bottle. It came as a hard knock - a real shock, but I knew in my heart it was true. It was over.

A trip has a length, starting before you leave - in planning and longing, and runs out before you come home. Oppositely - a trip can carry on long after you've stopped moving.

John Steinbeck wrote: *'A man in his middle years travelled to Honolulu and back, and that journey continued for the rest of his life. We would watch him in his rocking chair on his front porch, his eyes squinted, half-closed, endlessly travelling to Honolulu.'*

I knew now that I would ride along the Vietnam dirt track again, often stroll around Hanoi in my dreams, rock back and forth on a bristled jumbo head through wet hills - Chantal at my back.

My journey ended right there in Auckland - the city of sails; the wind blown out of the trip, leaving me becalmed, limp. I tried to puff it up - blow some life back into its lungs, but no, it was dead and gone. The irony was - I was only half-way round the world.

I heard Des tinkering in the kitchen, fresh from her bath, and I asked myself... what have I learned from this trip?

'Do you want a beer Howie?' Des shouted through the fly screen.

'Madness not to!' I replied, and thinking of her – realised what it was. The most important things I'd learned were to say hello and goodbye. I'd learned to approach new things and places and people, walk straight up to them - look them in the eye and ask - 'Hello... who are you? - dare them not to reply; otherwise you stay ignorant and alone.

And that there *are* no goodbyes. If I watch a boat disappear over the horizon, there will be people on the other side seeing it appear, and they will be saying hello. So, when Des plonked my beer on the table and put her arms round me, I smiled. I loved her... and Chantal... and Hilde... and even Harry, and I knew we'd be saying hello again... soon.

I flew out of the land of the long white cloud the next morning; there wasn't a cloud in the sky.

U.S.A

Hawaii, despite standing alone in the centre of the largest ocean on the planet, is the USA, and I'd had difficulties getting into the land of opportunity before.

The immigration official was moon-faced, with yellow parchment skin - eyes boring through my papers; bored.
'Do you have a visa?'
'No, I'm English... I don't need one.' His eyelids lifted.
'You've been travelling through Asia!'
'Yes.' They lifted some more.
'How much money do you have?'
'350 New Zealand dollars.'
'But you state here that you are staying for a month!' His boring little face was alight. He knew it wasn't enough.
'I'm not intending staying as long as that now.'
His eyelids dropped like a venetian blind with the cord cut, and his voice and head lowered with them.
'Where's your outward ticket from USA?' the top of his threadbare head said.
'It's here.' I said, childishly sticking my tongue out and crossing my eyes as I took it from my bag. I slapped it on the table and shrugged at the rest of the queue. They had to let me in now, I had an escape route.
'Your flight from New York to London was last Thursday.'
My eyes focused on the little square on the ticket, which said 5th April, not... May. My mind went screaming into a foxhole. Although my mind stuttered - my tongue didn't. Taking a leaf from Big Johnny's phrase-book, I let out a long 'aauuuuuugghhh ...' and then...
'I have to change that while I am here - it's a variable ticket.' A what!?
He flipped through my papers and tickets, occasionally looking at me with disdain. I affected the face of a jovial English vicar, albeit with sweat blinding my eyes and my mind registering quietly that I had 350 dollars and no ticket home.
His head sighed with scorn, and he dismissed me as a twat - with a hefty stamp in my passport. Like any good Englishman abroad I said 'Thank you.' and sauntered through customs undetained, with a kumara in my pack: a crime second only to smuggling cocaine, or strolling through JFK airport with John F's head in your hand luggage.
It was 3.00am, I was three sheets to the wind - and that was without a drink. I grabbed the first hostel-tout to the North Shore, and smoked four cigarettes while I waited for the minibus to fill; each one only heightening my awareness that I was up shit creek without a paddle. I

went over all the things I wished I'd said to the bastard immigration man - and some of them were incredibly cutting and clever; but you can never think of them at the time can you?
The billowing base of the heavy, low clouds glowed orange from lights of Waikiki - below.
'Thee that glow brah... over there path the airport,' the driver lisped, 'that's one of the biggeth tourith traps in the world, it'th chocker. You're thenthibly heading for the North Thore brah!'
'Choith!' I said.
Carried along by disbelief at my own stupidity and the hostel bus, I arrived at Plantation Village just as dawn got up and shook her tousled hair. Even the cockerels' chorus failed to keep me awake - though lord knows they tried hard enough. I woke mid-morning and groaned at my situation. I didn't have enough money to get across America as planned - unless I stopped and worked. I didn't want to work in America – I didn't want to stop in America at all now. I groaned again.

But there again, I was on North Shore - Oahu, and it would have been unthinkable to fly past the hallowed ground; my Mecca - the Holy Grail. Even as a piss-poor surfer I'd drooled over the photos, shivered over the horror stories of those brave or foolhardy enough to take on the giants that roll in to this shore.
Hawaii is like a fat green spider in the middle of its web. From anywhere on its spokes, a pressure system can develop like a thrashing fly - the shockwaves travelling into the centre. These arrive like charging bulls on Oahu - and the biggest, strongest and most frenzied - rage onto the North Shore every winter. 400 metres to my left was Waimea Bay; 800 metres to the right - Sunset Pipeline; the two most famous waves in the world. Peru has the longest rideable wave in the world, and at Jeffrey's Bay in South Africa, waves barrel in with the relentlessness of a Zulu army. Ten metre high waves thunder in at Waimea and wipeouts require lungs like hot water bottles, an allegiance with God - or a helicopter rescue; *if* the waves allow you to the surface. Pipeline, though not always as big, has the added attraction of pushing you into coral caves - never to come out.
Hawaiians measure their waves from the back, so a five feet wave could have an eight feet face; and to me that would have felt like ten.
'Waimea's flat brah - it needs a storm to crank it up.' they said.
'Sunset's flat... maybe one foot.' they said.
So I decided to go and sit and try to imagine what it looked like with big waves. There were quite a few surfers out, bobbing up and down on a tiny swell; I wondered why?

Rummaging through my pack for a book, I took my eyes off the surf for ten seconds, and looking up, a solid six foot wave was peeling left and right - a surfer on each shoulder. Behind it, the second of the set was still jacking up, two surfers wind-milling their arms to catch the pouting lip, the rest duck diving to escape to the back. I'd never seen waves appear from nowhere before, and now I understood the magic of Hawaii. Sunset could pull rabbits from a hat - and the rabbits had teeth. Late takeoffs were pitched over the falls - slammed into the sand. I was watching a feeble Pipeline; it was still impressive.

But I had to leave Hawaii. I know that, although I may not be too good at surfing - I *am* a surfer. However grungy we look, we are true romantics - looking for liquid perfection, eyes glazing over at the shape or colour of a wave. Surfers are tuned in to the feel of the water, the wind and the rush of the ride. Often - on the beach after a surf, in the pub, or in a silence round a fire, I would hear...

'Look at the stars... I love sitting in the ocean when the sun goes down... the feel of rain when I'm out there... being in the surf when dawn arrives... seals in the line up... the rush as you go down the wave'

It's difficult to get closer to life than to tie a board to your leg and throw yourself into the elements, where all your senses are coaxed and bullied at the same time. The tiredness felt after a good surf session comes in a box marked 'post-orgasmic'.

Heading down to the airport before dawn, we drove past Waimea Bay.

'It'th going to be huge brah!' said the driver, peering out into the darkness, picturing himself out there later in the day.

'I know.'

I could hear it pumping up. I tried to block the sound out. Missed it.

I was always missing the surf. If this had been a surf trip – it would have been the most unsuccessful in history.

❖

HOME

As the plane rolled along the tarmac to its parking space, I could see that I was in Los Angeles. The parked aircraft - in contrast to the sleek silver or white liveries of Europe, were dressed like gaudy circus performers. Here was one whose logo was a silhouette of Bob Marley, or an eskimo; there - a chocolate and orange design - a flying iced lolly, and Nevada Airways looked like the flier for a Rave Club.

The hostel tout was pretending to be one; they didn't have a bus. I was taken, way across the car-park, to her boyfriend's clapped out wreck of a car. She had to pay him to take me to the hostel.

It was really just a few rooms above a launderette, playing at being a hostel; the most crowded hostel since Chungking. I had seventeen bodies in my small room, stacked like a wine-rack; the solitary toilet groaned in the corner.

"'Right on world-famous Venice Beach" - the hostel flier had said. I took a walk along the beach, passing a film crew fawning over some beach-babes. They put their false smiles and tans on - over their false tits, some of them decidedly out of whack, and shivered with cold when the camera turned its beady eye away. Lines of wannabees took notes on the sidelines, their eyes flitting frequently to the Hollywood sign away on the hill behind.

Venice was a travesty; humans with false muscles, dogs dressed as humans, earthlings on another planet - all ignoring where they really were - because the sun was shining.

I went back the next day, a wet Sunday, and saw Venice in all of its glory. A few desperate stallholders had still turned out, in the hope that the sun and a few customers may show and that just left drug-addicts, pushers, tramps and me, on the strip. In whichever direction I looked, I could see a police patrol car crawling - four cops in each.

The escape from the hostel squalor was a visit to Hollywood or Paramount studios - where you could believe you were somewhere else, the shopping-malls - where rubbish was sold at a fairy-tale price, and a drive past the homes of the 'stars' - where you can believe there's no justice in the world. L.A. sucked; north to San Francisco or south to San Diego? I flipped the coin – heads. I jumped on the first bus I could get - down to San Diego.

I'd given up on the idea of doing a road trip across America long ago. It was time to call Uncle Peter and get the hell home. He offered to send enough money for an internal flight across to New York, (my ticket home had been renewed by the airline for a small fee) so I had a couple of days to spare in San Diego.

I headed for a beer festival in a big flashy downtown bar and spotted a man from my hostel, who I'd overheard earlier to be German; a German – beer festival – what better company could I wish for?

We introduced ourselves; he seemed just as pleased to have an Englishman to drink with, and we sampled a few featured beers. A jolly old afternoon seemed on the cards – until we called the waitress for our next choice.

'I think you've both had enough.' she said sternly.

'Enschuldigen-sie?' said my new friend.

'I think you two ought to leave.' she said crossly.

'But it's a beer festival, and the beer doesn't have much alcohol in it?' I remonstrated.

'Do you want me to call the cops?' she said angrily.

To our shame, we laughed at her, laughed our socks off, wet ourselves as we rolled out of the bar - clinging to each other through lack of breath.

'Can you believe we have been thrown out of a beer festival for drinking beer?' he asked, between sobs.

'Yes I can ... we are in America!' I replied caustically.

The hostel did a weekly trip into Mexico... just. It was a night-out in Tijuana which was basically a cheap piss-up, but I thought - one last party before I go home. They gave us all the warnings; stick together, keep your passport safe, if the police hit you say thank you; don't wander up side-streets.

'So, where is your passport?' asked the officer at the border.

'It was stolen from me in the Red Square Club.'

'You will have to stay in Mexico and go to your Consulate.'

Neither I, nor the Aussie with me, had much money, and now - no passports. He was cursing and stomping, holding his head in his hands; probably best as he was off his head on something.

'Great...' I thought 'I get to spend a few days in Mexico trying to arrange a new passport - with a demented bludger.'

We sat on the floor and tried to work our way through it; I didn't have the clearest of heads myself. I went back to the desk - explained again; gave him my passport number which I knew off-by-heart by now.

'I couldn't let my mother in without papers,' he said 'you are here to stay; go and find a hotel.'

'We don't have enough money - we'll have to sleep here on the floor.'

He shrugged.
We slept against the wall for a while - fitfully, and each time I woke up I tried the guard again. And then, as the faint light of an American dawn crept into the lobby, I noticed that there was a new guard on duty. I explained again.
'You are English and he is Australian?'... 'Yes.'
He didn't look very happy. He looked down at his papers, and pointing at a small alleyway leading to a door, mumbled...
'Go through there.' I hesitated...
'GO!' he shouted, and I grabbed the Aussie.
'Where we going man?' he asked, as we climbed over a barrier.
'I don't know.' I replied, looking over to the guard.
'NOW!!' he screamed.
I pushed the door open, and looked out into the open air... of America.
'Move man!' I said 'we're out... in.'

'You had your passport stolen in Tijuana Mr Cobb?' asked the lady at the British Embassy in London.
'Yes.' and I could hear her thinking, wearily - not another one!
In my hand was the group photo of us all in the Red Star Club, shouting at the camera - one of the waiters, his arm round my shoulders, his hand just above my buttoned pocket with the passport in.
'So where are you now?'... 'San Diego.'
'No, where are you right now?... 'San Diego.'
'You can't be in America if you lost your passport in Mexico.'
'They let us in.'
'They don't let anybody in without a passport.'
'They did!'
'They don't!!... oh just apply for an emergency one when you get to New York. Stop bothering me.'
So I went out with a bang; but at least it wasn't the banging of prison doors. I hopped over to New York for a pleasant week with Uncle Peter, skipped across the Atlantic to England, which from the air looked exactly like England should - and jumped from the last of the aeroplane steps to the tarmac. Home... Shit yeh!

❖

THIS IS NOW - THE EPILOGUE

THE HOMECOMING

A voice called up from the yard to my first floor flat above the garage.
'Is anyone up there?' it asked. I looked down the stairs.
It was a friend, and with her - a very attractive girl. It was the girl I'd been waiting for all my life, the one I wanted to spend every day of my life with - and every night in between.
'Come on up' I replied.
And we were married a year later.

❖

I'd been back home almost a year. On my return I had headed straight for Hambledon House to find accommodation, the same place I had met all of the travelling Ozzies and Kiwis years earlier. Fortunately there was a room – a whole apartment, which seemed a luxury to me after all of the shared rooms and dormitories I'd slept in during the last year, and on top of that - I was back amongst my previous friends; back to my own local pub; which was when the first surprise came. Naively I'd expected some chat, some interrogation. I'd sent many postcards and letters to friends – had very few replies, which was sad, as letters are very precious when travelling. As I walked through the familiar heavy doors (that I'd often stumbled out of) and headed for the bar, a few familiar faces turned and smiled.

'Hi 'H' good trip?' Well I couldn't answer that in a short sentence, so I answered briefly and ironically... 'Yeh - not bad.'

I sat on the sticky vinyl stool, took a long cold drink from my beer and prepared for the questions; they didn't come. The talk had gone back to the building site, concrete pouring, yesterday's Formula 1 race.

Double-checking that I was actually still there and visible, I listened in politely to their chat, to see if it was a joke – but no. Discombobulated, I ordered a second pint and watched other old friends and colleagues arrive. The pattern continued, a brief but friendly 'hello' and muted, disinterested enquiries as to how my trip had gone.

It left me in a troubled state – floating and ungrounded, and kept me to my own devices for the evening. The next day, having retrieved Bumble from his sitters, we took off together across the hills and fields

– reveling in a pleasantly sunny, English spring day. I'd often dreamt of this in more desperate times, whilst baking under a burning sun and breathing arid dust.

The fresh sweet air laden with pollen, the scent of primrose, and the sound of trees rustling their new leaves, blew the cobwebs and confusion away. I could see where my lukewarm reception had come from and why; understood immediately.

When someone goes travelling, the lives of the ones left behind are untouched – unaffected; life goes on the same as always. Letters from abroad just tell you what you are missing. There is no excitement in a 'hello' at home, it's a well trodden path, and the same conversations are addressed to the same people, day in day out..

I was wrong to expect people to be excited to see me, to ask for all the details of this and that – to be anything other than be pleased to see me again. So when I went back to the pub that night, I bought my beer, sat on a stool, and asked the lads next to me if they'd seen the Liverpool match last night. I heard an almost audible sigh of relief pass down the bar and back – relief that I wasn't going to regale them with tales of my travels. I would have to do that in my own way, and in my own time.

❖

Knowing that (according to her last letter) she should be home, I'd written to Chantal several times during those first few months; received nothing in return. I only had a postal address, so my options were limited. I was enjoying singleton freedom, earning some money and having my own space, and time was slipping past like a gentle float down a placid river - but my thoughts kept wondering where Chantal had got to and why she hadn't bothered to contact me.

Don, the landlady's pot-bellied toady shouted…'letter for you Howie' across the yard, as I got out of my campervan. It didn't have the familiar red and blue border I was used to with letters from abroad, but it did have a stamp on it from Belgium. I rushed up the stairs, kicked off my work boots and flipping open a can of cold beer, settled on my balcony for a read.

The first thing that came from the envelope was a small card – it looked like an invitation. The wording was in Flemish, so I couldn't understand it, but *there* was a picture of Chantal smiling, and underneath - a date and time. 'She's getting married' I thought, *and* had the bloody cheek to invite me to the wedding! COW! BITCH!

I threw it off the side of the balcony, looked daggers at the sky, took a hard pull on the beer bottle, and unfolded the letter that had accompanied the card. It was from Chantal's parents. They had heard of me from her letters, and what we had meant to each other, and they were sorry it had taken so long to write... but they hadn't had the strength. Her plane had crashed just before it reached home, her family waiting at the airport to welcome their beloved daughter. They had sent me the funeral card. My light went out and darkness crowded round.

A few days later, I gathered the courage to sit and write through the tears. They had shown great kindness by including me, albeit in their tragic situation, and I needed to give them... something.
  I found one of the last letters she had sent, and in case they hadn't known I passed on what she had written to me. It told of wonderful things she was seeing, experiences and feelings – showed that she had been having the time of her life and would have had no regrets.
  It wasn't enough by far, but it was all I had.

❖

Each night on returning from work, I would look at my travel journal sitting neglected on the table, the photos I'd taken pinned to the walls, the sarong on my bed - and ask myself... when I was going to try to write that damn book I'd been telling everyone about. It was time.
  So, after a trip to PC World, and a quick lesson on how to use a 'mouse' and a 'program' from a friend, I tapped in the words...
'Two Minute Noodle' and watched them appear on the screen; a cursor blinking at the end, begging me to carry on.

Life back in England settled into a routine. I carried on my building career as a labourer; running up and down roofs all summer, carrying tiles and cement, being paid to bodybuild and get a tan. Then at night and on weekends, I would slowly tap a few more pages into one more chapter - alternately liking, being uncertain, or hating what I'd written.

One Sunday evening on my balcony, watching a sunset catch alight behind the sentinel beech trees, I stumbled upon some childish, but wise words from Mark Twain - one of my favourite writers...
  'Don't get it right... get it writ.' It was as though he had been watching me struggle, and this was just the fuel I needed to carry on to the end. I resolved not to try and get it perfect – I just needed to get the sights and sounds, the experiences and my thoughts down onto paper, so that I could draw a line under 'that trip'. Perhaps this was also

necessary to initiate the next trip as, weary of everyday England, I had been starting to feel the urge to move my feet again. I had been taking my passport out of the kitchen drawer every now and then to look at the pages full of customs and border stamps – all bearing tales of arrival and departure, and the happenings in between.

The book was finished. It travelled to Guildford on a floppy disc, and then when printed, hitched a lift in a van to London to my distributor. It was a decidedly low-key launch, as I had little or no expectations of success, or fame and fortune – merely the contentment of a job finished; but it stirred the flutter of a butterfly's wings, which spread the word, which magnified; and then one day...

A voice called up from the yard to my first floor flat above a garage. 'Is anyone up there?' it asked. I looked down the stairs – and there was Paula.

A new and fantastic journey began.

❖

TRAVELLING – BACKPACKING

Our wedding list was far from usual. In place of the toaster, cutlery set, vacuum, coffee machine, were... vaccinations, malaria pills, diahorrea pills, walking socks and boots, train tickets from Hanoi to Ho Chi Minh, white-water rafting trip, trekking gear.

Paula was just as keen to make travelling part of our lives together, as I was; she had even spent time on a kibbutz when younger. So we decided to get started right away – on our honeymoon; six weeks in Nepal, Thailand and Vietnam would be a great first trip.

So, as well as the usual heights reached on a honeymoon, we also scaled Machupuchare in the Nepalese Himalayas, camping in Alpine pastures, creeping upwards through stone villages - bashful children waving, being overtaken by small people carrying huge burdens, and being spoilt rotten by an eleven-man team of porters.
   Then from Pokhara we rafted down the Trisuli River – camping on river beaches, floating quietly or thrashing through manic rapids, and straight on to the Chitwan National Park to trek through the bush, and

flee from a charging rhinoceros up a tree; and all without TV screens, Hollywood blockbusters, discos or mobile phones. It was just like the travelling I'd enjoyed five years earlier; the uncomplicated, quiet contemplation of life in an unfamiliar place; eating, drinking and talking – meeting new people who were doing the same. And then it was down to Bangkok I fear.

Bangkok.. mad, bad and sad. The Khao San Road had filled. There were more bars with glass fronts – the same films to be seen, but now there were adverts for Full Moon parties everywhere. The body count was much higher and definitely younger. The travelers who had previously dressed themselves as hippies were now kitted out as 'new age travelers' and 'ravers' - but they had traded in their ancient vans on the A303 for British Airways jumbo jets, and Ibiza for Ko Samui.

We were staying in the same back alley as Rhanee's, which was still there - 50 yards away. As we sat, eating and enjoying life in general, it was hard not to notice the large group of Scandinavian teenagers; incredibly young and steadily getting more and more drunk. 'Nothing wrong with that' I hear you say – and I totally agree, but there was a new thing that I hadn't seen before, a public computer. Between songs and shouting matches, they were taking turns on the computer – emailing. We'd never seen email before and didn't know what they were doing; they spent the whole evening emailing.

Again, I hear you say – 'Nothing wrong with that' but to me it seemed wrong. It made me think about my travels and what had appealed to me – still does; and it was…escape. Travel should be about getting away from your usual habitat, not doing the things you would normally do; it's about leaving 'stuff' behind – in many different ways. Travelling with your usual friends, doing the same things that you do at home, is not going to have much effect on your life.

It hadn't occurred before, but aside from a Sony Walkman and a camera, my fellow backpackers had moved around with no access to gadgets. We could only correspond by writing and receiving letters, which might sit waiting in a Poste Restante whole countries away for weeks or months before you could pick them up. Phone calls home were incredibly difficult and expensive, and only used for emergencies. We had no mobiles to call or text friends just round the corner, nor game consoles to eat up our time.

Backpacking was changing. Did that bother me? No. I just felt very sad for the new generation that would be missing that intrepid, exciting and sometimes scary experience.

❖

Two things worth keeping as a mantra, if you are thinking of going travelling (it doesn't matter at what age) are talking and tipping.

Talk to as many people face-to-face as you can. The local people will benefit from your speaking to them in English, you will benefit from them by gaining knowledge, and the travellers you talk to along the way will become new friends.

If you are visiting Asia - put a contingency sum in your budget for tipping and buying things you don't really need; twenty dollars a week - the equivalent of four pints of beer. If you spread that amount around twenty people, each will have a special day - much better than it would have been otherwise.

Even as I write, Burma has opened its doors to tourists after years of a closed border policy. If I had the opportunity to go travelling right now – I'd have been knocking on the Burmese Embassy's door months ago, clamoring for a piece of paper to allow me to roam its countryside and talk to its people.

So Paula and I did what we could with Thailand; took the pre-arranged trip to Kho Samui, avoided the resorts and full-moon parties and found a small horseshoe-shaped bay with white sand, canopied by high, palm-covered slopes, and a small bungalow of our own with its toes in the sea. There was no TV, no video, no party. Bliss; it *could* still be found.

❖

VIETNAM

It's a very awkward situation – introducing your new wife to your mistress; you really hope that they get on, but you don't expect them to be enamored straight away.

It's fair to say that Paula 'hated' Hanoi at first, which of course disappointed me, but I was already seeing things in a different light than I had when alone. It *was* a hard and unforgiving place to be at times, and the Vietnamese people could frustrate and annoy at the drop of a hat. But I knew that Vietnam was something that seeped into you by osmosis – gradually, and with nonchalant ease, so I let her do her job in her own way.

We retraced my earlier steps to Halong Bay, which this time meant an air-con minibus on a smart tarmac dual-carriageway; the sheer volume of visitors testifying to the tourism explosion that had happened in the preceding few years. By the time we'd worked our way down to Hue and its Imperial Palace, roamed the Emperor's tombs and floated up the Perfume River to the iconic Thien Mu Pagoda – Paula had mellowed under Vietnam's embrace.

At a café one evening we were charmed by a trio of street kids, one only five years old called Li. We asked if they were a family; the answer - no. One came from Hanoi, one from Saigon – one from inland somewhere. They had all come here to earn money and lived on a houseboat on the river with 'Uncle' – the general term for an older male. We asked ourselves why life was so hard for some children. We asked ourselves what we would do if our attempts to start a family in England faltered. We decided right there what we would do.

Hoi An captured our hearts and still holds them today. Saigon – the Paris of the East, was still pretty rough at the edges, more 'special of the day' than 'a la carte', but the sparkle was starting to show through; the people shaking off their grudges and putting on a happy face - a truly happy face.

We flew home to England replete, Vietnam having filled us with the sights and sounds we'd hoped for and dreamt of, but it had also thrown up a fresh new dream for us which before could only have been a fairy story. It had also filled my head with questions, to which I demanded answers; of myself, and of the rich and powerful of this world. I was determined to find out much more about this amazing country.

Little did I know that the next time we went to Vietnam it would be as a couple, but we would return to England – a family of three.

❖

I sat under our ancient oak beams, the fire glowing, Autumn blowing hard and mean outside with a nippy north wind, a glass of warming red wine beside me, and looked back to my first Vietnam trip.

I remembered that game of late night football in Hang Chai in Hanoi, with Harry and the street kids...

Choosing Diep's brother as my first team-mate, I said to him...
'We'll be England!'
'No,' he said 'USA number one! always number one.'
Confident – I said...'England - number two then'
'No, Sweden number two.'
'Why?' I asked.
'Sweden help us in the war.' he replied.

This confused me, as in truth I knew little about 'The American War', but even with the little I *did* know I failed to see how that trauma and horror could be treated so lightly.

So one morning, sitting by Hoan Kiem lake on an art-nouveau bench, chatting in schoolboy French to one of the Beret-topped elderly men, his wispy white beard waving in the breeze – I asked...

'What do you think *now* about the Americans... and the war?'

'It was a very small war.' he replied without irony.

Incredulous I asked... 'How can you say that?'

'We fought the Chinese for thousands of years, then the Cambodians, the French for a hundred, then the Japanese. The American war was very small.' It was time for me to fill in the gaps in my education.

I researched and read all I could from different angles; read books by Americans, Vietnamese, French and British. I searched out writings on Presidents Johnson and Nixon, the lead up to the war, its terrible build up and the inevitable defeat of the US. Two pieces in particular stood out and spoke to me. Stanley Karnow's 'Vietnam A History' is truly illuminating. As a Time Magazine war correspondent, and initially a supporter of the war, he ended it as a very unpopular figure and in opposition – much to the chagrin of the US Government.

'The Sorrow of War' *by Bao Ninh* was translated and published in English for the first time - the year that I first visited Vietnam, and paints a harrowing picture of the real life as a North Vietnamese soldier. It *is* raw and uncompromising but an invaluable window into the past, and of course - the sorrow of war.

I have no desire to vilify America as a nation, merely to try and gain some understanding as to where the Vietnamese people obtain their strength, but I do hold the US Government in contempt for its attitude towards its own people as well as those it seeks to dominate. This is not a political study of the 'American War' – merely an opportunity to point out a few things that *I* never knew and that the majority of English people still do not know today; this mainly due to careful screening by the British media. Here then are some observations and occurrences, some of which fuel my distaste, and others that reinforce the esteem in which I hold Vietnam and its people.

After ridding themselves of the French after a hundred years of colonial occupation, a long hard military campaign and the remarkable victory at Dien Bien Phu, the North Vietnamese – led by General Vo Nguyen Giap and Ho Chi Minh, had every right to feel that they would at last reunite Vietnam and regain independence. The Geneva Conference however, saw fit to divide Vietnam into North and South – the North led by Ho Chi Minh, the South under a weak Prime Minister supported by the USA and China.

This left Ho Chi Minh, desperate to reunite the country, with only one course of action – to fight; at first against the South Vietnamese, and then of course the rapidly growing number of American troops who were being sent in to support them.

❖

When the US Government 'advised' the North Vietnamese that they would not tolerate their advance into South Vietnam and would oppose it militarily, Ho Chi Minh replied…

"You can kill ten of our men for every one we kill of yours. But even at those odds, you will lose and we will win."

❖

The number of Vietnamese military personnel and civilians killed during, and as a result of the war, is approximated at 3,000,000.

The number of American servicemen killed throughout the course of the war was 58,000.

Ho Chi Minh had been wrong; he had lost 50 of his countrymen for each US soldier in order to win.

❖

The allied forces fighting Vietnam comprised America, Australia, New Zealand, South Korea, Thailand and China.

❖

During the Vietnam War, between 1962 and 1971, the US military sprayed nearly 20,000,000 gallons of material containing chemical herbicides and defoliants such as Agent Orange in Vietnam, eastern Laos and parts of Cambodia. Estimates are that 400,000 people were killed or maimed, and 500,000 children born with birth defects as a result of its use. Today – the United States refuses to acknowledge its use, or to discuss any form of compensation.

❖

In the Paris Peace Accords, the United States had agreed to provide $3.3 billion over five years to help rebuild the shattered infrastructure of Vietnam. Rather than meeting its obligations, the United States extended to all of Vietnam the trade embargo set against communist North Vietnam, that had been ratified under the 'Trading with the

Enemy Act'- passed during the early years of the conflict.

The United States further marginalized Vietnam by halting credits and loans from monetary institutions such as the World Bank and the International Monetary Fund. Seeking acceptance in the international arena, Vietnam attempted several times to join the United Nations, only to be halted by American vetoes. This had the effect of making Vietnam the fifth poorest country in the world.

❖

Whilst in this poverty stricken state, the Cambodians – supported by the USA, China and Britain, harassed the Vietnamese from across the border, escalating into all-out war from 1975 to 1979. The Vietnamese invaded Cambodia in 1979, overwhelming the Kampuchean Army.

The Khmer Rouge regime had been systematically killing its own population throughout this time, whilst exhorting its own people to participate. The Vietnamese invasion put a stop to the horrors that were being perpetrated but, almost without rest, the Vietnamese army turned around and sped to the North - as the Chinese had invaded in retaliation for the Cambodian defeat. Despite leaving a path of destruction behind themselves, the Chinese were routed once again.

❖

After fourteen years of waging war against poverty and economic crises, the Vietnamese Government opened its doors to tourists. I was there a year later, blundering about the country on a worn out Russian motorbike; Vietnam would continue to be locked out of the world's trading markets for another year.

When I reached Saigon, at the end of my trip, I was less than gracious about the city, its war museum and its inhabitants. I have learned much about the terrible times endured by Saigon and Vietnam since and have returned many times to soak up the beauty, the drama and the fun. So I sincerely apologise to you Saigon, and to you Vietnam – my second home.

"It was patriotism, not communism, that inspired me." Ho Chi Minh.

❖

VAN HAI

Sister Hai walked into the room cradling an infant, his great limpid eyes staring across the room at us. She reached out and handed him to Paula. 'That's him...' we said 'there he is!'

For eighteen long months we sat on a waiting list to begin our adoption, attending parenting courses. Unlike birth parents, we were tested on our ability to look after a child, asked our thoughts on religion and education; probed for long explanations of our family past. As well as that we had to pay a social worker to come to our house over a long period of time to carry out a home study, and then be judged by a panel as to our suitability.

We had been introduced to a family who had adopted a boy from a Saigon children's home a year previously - Maxine and Andy; Maxine was to become our guardian angel.

After meeting them and their adorable boy, we were determined that we should carry through with the dream we had conjured up in Hue, on our honeymoon. Like Maxine, we decided to take the straightforward approach rather than use an agency, to ensure that our adoption was ethical. She talked us through the mountain of paperwork and the maze of the system – and seeing the doubts growing in our faces reassured us… 'You *can* do this you know.' Thank God we had her to help.

With our home study finally started, we began to amass the necessary paperwork, but an obstacle arose – Surrey County Council; we had innocently informed them that we might move to Devon at some point during the process.

'If you do that you'll have to go back to the start and do a home study down there.' they said.

After a stressful weekend, Paula suggested that I ring the appropriate department in Devon to test the water. I rang them and talked to a soft-spoken lady with a lovely Devon burr, explaining what had happened.

'Oh that's a nonsense m'love...you just get yourselves down 'ere quick mind, we'll look after you.' They did, and in a very short and trouble-free time our papers were authorised by the Foreign and Commonwealth Office in London and sent to the British Consulate in Ho Chi Minh City; where we would join them very soon.

Again it was Maxine who guided us through the legal process and departments that we had to negotiate in Ho Chi Minh City; and then it was time. We presented ourselves and our papers in person to the Director of the children's home. Sister Hai was a Catholic nun, the height of a child - with a moon face, and was round like a dumpling. She was omnipotent in her realm and scared us both at first, appearing in the background silently, or walking past the open windows and doors of offices where we sat – often wondering what the hell was going on.

On a tour around the home, we were struck by the numbers of babies lying swaddled in the infants' room, rows of metal cots from wall to wall. More shocking was the silence in the rooms of the toddlers and younger children; the same rows of cots, with straw matting as beds, and silent staring children - just the odd one or two responding to smiles and our chatter.

We had presented our papers weeks ago, and had become increasingly frustrated, whilst waiting impatiently at our hotel for the phone call. We returned to the children's home once again. Sister Hai invited us into her office where we sat in the shadows and sunrays from the shuttered window. Mr Nanh - the gatekeeper, translating for us, spoke quietly to her; the talk went back and forth for the longest time. We sat quiet and anxious. Sister Hai left the room, motioning for us to stay put.

'Please wait...' Mr Nanh said 'Sister Hai has a boy – he was small but he is a big boy now.'

'How old is he?' we asked. 'I don't know.' he replied.

I don't know how long we were waiting, but in that endless quiet, when neither of us dared to talk, I know we were both wondering whether a teenager might come strolling through the door. Sister Hai walked softly into the room, cradling an infant - his great limpid eyes staring across the room at us. She reached out and handed him to Paula.

'That's him.' we said together.

'You take him to the reception, play with him, feed him,' said Binh 'then come again and see him tomorrow, and at the end of the week you tell us whether you want him. His name is Hai.'

'No – we *do* want him, he is ours, that's him!'

Mr Nanh smiled and left; Sister Hai smiled a happy smile.

On a steamy day, with thunderhead clouds hovering above, we scampered downtown to collect Hai's papers from our translator. He appeared fascinated as he handed them over and asked where Hai would be going to live. We stopped for a coffee on the way back to the hotel, happy as kids at Christmas. I leafed through the medical records, shocked at some of the information within them, and then a date jumped from the page - 24th August 1999, his date of birth.

We had been given Ethan on his first birthday.

QUOC BAO

'This baby will die if he stays here' our doctor said, '...but I don't think they will let him go.'

Hai was now three years old, and leaving him safe with his doting grandparents, we were carrying another set of hard-won documents to Vietnam - to enable us to search for a brother or sister for him, and another precious child for ourselves. We had heard that Sister Hai had retired as Director, but still confidently strolled into Tam Binh with our mountain of legalised paperwork.

After looking round the children's home full of babies and children, we sat down to our interview with the rather stern new Director.

'Yes, we already have a son from Tam Binh – he is three.' we said.

'We have no children for adoption right now.' said the new Director. Disappointed and bewildered, we visited the other large children's home in Ho Chi Minh City. The answer there was also a 'no.'

But we were told of a home where there *were* children needing adopting. We found it on the map, way down at the far tip of the Mekong Delta, almost on the Cambodian border; a six hour drive away.

❖

Rach Gia is a border town and fishing port and at that time had almost no passing tourists. Consequently we soon came to realize how hard life can be when you can only converse in sign language. The driver dropped us at the children's home outside of the town, and weary from his long drive, headed straight back to Ho Chi Minh City - wheels kicking up dust in the ramshackle driveway.

The Director was Mr. Nam, and we met him the following day. He was short, enigmatic, very handsome, and spoke no English. He was quite obviously amused by our naivety, smiling when talking about us to his staff, but with a local English teacher helping translate, Mr. Nam promised that he had children available for adoption. We should file our papers at The Ministry of Justice and then return to Ho Chi Minh City until called.

On returning to Ho Chi Minh City, we realised that the weeks we had assigned for completing the adoption had been eaten up, and that Hai would be missing us at home. I also had a business to run and needed to get back to it. We decided it would be sensible for Paula to stay in Vietnam until we were given a referral, and then I would head back and journey down with her to deal with the paperwork.

TWO MINUTE NOODLE

'I've just got back from Rach Gia and I'm in the Bi-Saigon Hotel. You need to get out here quick.' Paula said, on the surprisingly clear phone line. 'We have a referral and I've lodged our papers with the Ministry of Justice. It's a boy, he's three months old and he's gorgeous – a bit of a cough, but otherwise healthy.'
I looked out of my window at the cold English wind plucking smoke from the chimneys opposite, and thought about the warm blanket of heat in Vietnam; I rang Thai Airlines.

'This is him... his name is Bao' said Paula, spiriting a small black & white photograph from under the table at Vietnam House Restaurant on Dong Khoi. I looked closely at the picture, the first sight of my new son. 'Yes it is.' I said through tears.

It was early morning when the Doctor lifted Bao's thin vest and moved the stethoscope over his tiny chest; we could see the desperate drawing in of his lungs, sucking for precious air.
 The doctor turned to me...'This baby will die if he stays here in Rach Gia' he said, 'he has bronchial pneumonia...but I don't think they will let him leave.'
 'Can we get permission to take him to Ho Chi Minh City' I asked.
 'I will try.' he promised.

And then came the longest day – of phone calls between Rach Gia and Ho Chi Minh City, between our doctor, Mr. Nam and the hospital in HCMC, while Paula held Bao, trying to keep his temperature down with cold flannels and Paracetamol; lungs slowly failing. Then at last, as evening drew in and bats spun around the gloom, we were allowed to take him; but only if we took a chaperone in case we tried to abduct him. We waited impatiently for the chaperone to come from the town. She was a young girl called Kim, tall – giant by Vietnamese standards, and spoke no English. We were soon to discover that she was our new guardian angel. We raced up to Ho Chi Minh City in the mini-bus.

Bao had a bed in a shared room at the children's hospital in HCMC. We took turns with Kim – she stayed overnight, sleeping on the bed with him, nursing him, and we arrived in the mornings so that she could wash, go out to eat and visit people that she knew in the city, and so we could spend precious time with Bao. We couldn't converse vocally with Kim, but we soon understood each other enough to work in harmony and often had hilarious conversations using the phrasebook as a go-between. We became very fond of her.

The families of the other sick children also shared their beds, bringing in food for them, nursing them, and sometimes administering the only medicine they could afford – a perfume in a green bottle, which they dabbed on the temples. I was soon to find out why they stayed with their children and did their own nursing.

Before plunging a massive needle into Bao's tiny bottom, producing a heart-rending scream, and telling us to go to the long queue for the oxygen mask, the Doctor scribbled a note and instructed me to take it to the pharmacy.

It was outside in the hospital gardens, and there was a mass of people gathered around the counter, some three-deep at the front, squawking and shouting at the nurses dispensing medicines and taking money; some just milling around. It suddenly clicked into place; this was the dispensary and I needed to pay for Bao's medicines and treatment. I handed over the note from the Doctor and received an assortment of boxes in return, as well as a computer printed bill.

I looked at the total amount - $75, thinking how expensive it was; but he needed it and *of course* I should pay the 'foreigner' rate. The people who had been milling around had come close now and were waving their bills at me pleadingly; others in the front seemed to be telling them off. I asked the smiling man next to me if I could see his bill. It was for more than a hundred dollars. I remembered then that Vietnam had no free health service, so everything had to be paid for – or simply not had; which is why the parents were nursing their own children with perfumed water and bringing in their own food. I wished I could pay all of their bills, but I couldn't and it would have caused chaos to try to pay just some. I sloped away; and though I knew I had to do the best for Bao, I felt ashamed of my wealth.

When Bao was well enough to leave the hospital we decamped to our guesthouse in Pham Ngu Lao, and our curious but happy family arrangement continued – Kim acting as chaperone at one end of the room, whilst Paula and me were Mum and Dad at the other. It seemed we waited an age for our adoption hearing, but it finally came and we travelled down to Rach Gia to complete our adoption officially. And then we had our permission for Bao to leave with us - to travel to his new home and family waiting in England.

'And that..' Bao told me recently, 'was when I discovered that I hate mushrooms.'

MY LOVE

The baby's arm was brown
Nut brown, burnt umber
Toast on a winter's fire
And it rested on her arm
Brown honey with a glimpse of maple
In an autumn glade
Full with love and need.

His fingernails were dewdrops on her skin
They echoed the tears in the foothills of her cornflower eyes
His eyes were black
As night
With stars sparkling
Shooting novas in their tiny galaxies
Curtained by gossamer butterflies
Fluttering in the slight breeze of sleep.

His slumber was full
Her attention complete and divine
They rode the waves of his rhythm of life
He - asleep in love
She - alert in love
He was she
She was he
She is
My love.

Howie Cobb, Saigon 19/8/2000